CRIME AND PUBLIC POLICY

CRIME
AND
PUBLIC
POLICY

JAMES Q. WILSON

Editor

ICS PRESS

Institute for Contemporary Studies
San Francisco, California

 Distributed by Transaction Books, New Brunswick (U.S.A.) and London (U.K.)

Inquiries, book orders, and catalog requests should be addressed to ICS Press, Suite 811, 260 California Street, San Francisco, California 94111—415–398–3010.

Library of Congress Cataloging in Publication Data
Main entry under title:

Crime and public policy.

    Includes bibliographical references and index.
    1. Crime prevention—Government Policy—United States
—Addresses, essays, lectures. I. Wilson, James Q.
HV7431.C7 1983   364.4'04561'0973   83–8465
ISBN 0–917616–52–9
ISBN 0–917616–51–0 (pbk.)

CONTENTS

V
Conclusion

PREFACE

In the past two decades, the United States has experienced a rapid and alarming increase in crime. Today crime is a pervasive problem that leaves few Americans untouched.

Our present situation can be understood as the product of two kindred developments. Along with the rapid rise in crime rates during the 1960s and 1970s came another important occurrence: the breakdown of the consensus that hitherto had guided public policy in coping with crime. By the late 1970s, experience as well as systematic research had cast serious doubt on a number of key concepts that had shaped policymakers' decisions concerning patrol, arrest, prosecution, sentencing, incarceration, and release of offenders. Most notably, researchers had been able to find no real evidence for the effectiveness of programs aimed at rehabilitation—a concept at the very center of our approach to criminal justice. Other elements of our crime-fighting strategy were also called into question, including the effectiveness of police patrol methods, the adequacy of prosecution and sentencing choices, and the potential of broader social reforms for reducing crime.

Two lessons emerged from the experiences of the decade: first, that crime was a far more intractable problem than we had earlier been led to believe; and second, that there was clear room for improvement in our deployment of resources to control crime.

The failures of the era defined a new agenda for research and policy reform. New concepts evolved, many of which are explained and developed in the chapters of this book. Among the most promising are the ideas of the "career criminal" and "selective incapacitation"—which together suggest that prosecutors, working with police, might be able systematically to identify, prosecute, and incarcerate those few criminals responsible for disproportionate amounts of crime.

In 1982, the Institute for Contemporary Studies asked James Q. Wilson to gather together leading experts on all aspects of the crime problem for a comprehensive review of the issues. The aim of the present volume is to help lay the groundwork for new policies to prevent and control crime, based on the latest research in the field. The authors discuss a range of key concepts, including the "career criminal" notion, and explode a number of unhelpful myths. Topics treated include the relationship of crime to unemployment, the effect of the exclusionary rule on criminal justice, and the impact of family life on crime, to mention only a few. Like the Institute's studies in such areas as government regulation and the federal budget, CRIME AND PUBLIC POLICY is designed not merely to summarize research but also to point the way to practical policy reforms.

This thorough analysis of the crime problem should provide a solid foundation for rethinking an issue of grave social concern.

Glenn Dumke
President
Institute for Contemporary Studies

I

Introduction

1

JAMES Q. WILSON

Introduction

The essays in this book were written in order to show how social science might inform the effort to control crime. I use the word "inform" advisedly. Social science is not and cannot be an unambiguous guide to policy: though a useful source of knowledge, that knowledge is neither sufficiently comprehensive nor adequately tested to constitute a wholly dependable guide. And even if it were comprehensive and well-tested, it would consist chiefly of statements about the relationships that generally obtain among two or more phenomena (such as, for example, the relationship between heroin use and criminality, or between the frequency of police patrols and the number of reported offenses). Policymakers ought to be interested in these relationships, but they cannot be guided solely by what is generally true. They must also make judgments about what is true in individual cases, taking into account the particular circumstances of time, place, personality, and condition. Moreover, while social science can suggest what trade-offs exist between two possible policies (for example, how much more crime will be committed by existing heroin users as a result of efforts made to reduce the recruitment of new heroin users), the policy-maker must decide what the trade-off ultimately ought to be. This is not the same as saying that scholars offer "value-free" information while policymakers alone make value choices; as will be evident, every essay in this book reveals, explicitly or implicitly, the values of its author. But it is to say that policymakers must carefully examine the preferences of the authors to see if the conclusions of the latter depend on those preferences and, if so, whether those preferences should be accepted.

By saying all this, I run the risk of leading some readers to conclude that scholars have little or nothing to contribute to the making of policy regarding crime. Having spent twenty years studying crime and law enforcement and, on occasion, offering advice to members of the criminal justice system, I am acutely aware of the skepticism that exists within that world—and perhaps in the world at large—toward academic pronouncements on crime and its control. When police officers or prosecutors refer to you as a "sociologist," they are not so much describing your profession as repudiating your views. Many scholars have returned the favor by investing the word "cop" with roughly the same connotation as "storm trooper."

However, relations between scholars and practitioners in the field of law enforcement are much better today than was once the case. The two groups no longer view each other in quite such stereotypical terms as "fuzzy-headed" academics versus "heavy-handed" cops. In large measure this has happened because of many collaborative ventures that have, over the past decade or so, brought scholars and law enforcement personnel into close working relationships. The Rand Corporation in Santa Monica has worked with prison officials, the Police Foundation in Washington, D.C., has carried out experiments in which police departments were full partners, and INSLAW (the Institute for Law and Social Research, also in Washington, D.C.) has helped prosecutors design and implement new information systems. There are many other examples. To a great degree this collaboration has occurred because the federal government, together with a few private foundations, has spent money in ways that made it possible. Whatever the high costs, oft-noted mistakes, and uneven record of accomplishment of the federal effort to reduce crime, that effort has increased our knowledge of crime and its control (often as a result of trial and error) and, just as importantly, has brought people together in ways that have led researchers and practitioners to form a new and sounder understanding of what each can contribute to a common objective.

It would have been difficult, if not impossible, to produce this book fifteen years ago. Not only were scholars and practitioners in an adversarial relationship, but there were precious few scholars who had much interest in systematically examining the consequences of current public policies and trying to design and test better approaches. Some of the authors of this volume were thinking about crime two decades ago because they were then, as now, professional criminologists. But most of them came to the study of crime from outside the field of criminology—Jan Chaiken, Peter Greenwood, and Alfred Blumstein have backgrounds in engineering, operations research, and mathematics; Richard Herrnstein is an experimental psychologist; Richard Freeman is an economist and Mark Moore a student of political economy; Steven Schlesinger, Charles Murray, and I are (or have been) political scientists. These people have been drawn into the study of crime because of interest, accident, and opportunity with the result that, in my view, the study of how policies affect crime is today a far richer and more exciting field than ever before. Federal financial support of research and experimentation has been important in creating and sustaining this more analytical approach to crime policy.

The topics included in this book were selected according to several criteria. First, I wanted to summarize for the reader the latest and best information about "what works" with respect to the principal institutions of the criminal justice system—the police (Lawrence Sherman), prosecutors (Brian Forst), and correctional officials (Daniel Glaser)—and with respect to one institution, the labor market, that is often thought to have a dramatic influence on crime (Richard Freeman). As the reader will quickly discover, we know a good deal more about what doesn't work than about what does. Some will take this to mean that scholars are merely critics who have nothing "positive" to offer. That view, at least in this instance, is mistaken, for it ignores how the scholarly enterprise customarily proceeds. Knowledge about human affairs rarely advances because someone thinks up a clever new idea and then makes it work; rather, it advances as investigators slowly and carefully reexamine common beliefs about how the world already works. For example, most new ideas about how best to manage police patrol or to supervise offenders while on probation were invented by nonscholars, usually by practitioners. The difficulty confronting anyone seeking to change accepted practices is such that those few persons with the imagination, zeal, and perseverance necessary to accomplish the reform are usually persons who, because of that zeal, are not inclined to take a detached and objective view of whether their idea really achieves its objective. Social scientists are best at evaluating changes that have already been made. This implies that knowledge advances most rapidly when two things happen—a change is made and an objective evaluation occurs. In short, our soundest knowledge usually comes from experiments.

Second, experiments are not always possible and therefore we must depend, at least initially and sometimes indefinitely, on a careful analysis of how people already behave. I have tried to include in this book examples of the most sophisticated analyses of what *might* happen *if* a change were made. These analyses are principally to be found in Jackson Toby on schooling, Moore on "criminogenic" substances (alcohol, guns, and heroin), Schlesinger on the rules governing criminal trials, Greenwood on sentencing, and Blumstein on prison population. The data and techniques necessary to perform some of these analyses literally did not exist in the field of criminal justice a decade ago.

Third, I have included essays on some of the causes of crime— the human personality, the family, the neighborhood—in order to give a complete picture of the nature of the crime problem, to indicate how limited are the possibilities of making major changes in the crime rate, at least given the constraints we usually accept about the proper limits of public intervention, and to suggest the extent to which dealing with crime requires private and individual action. The essays by Herrnstein, Murray, and Travis Hirschi are reminders that an understanding of crime requires an understanding of some of the most fundamental and intimate features of the human condition.

Finally, Jan and Marcia Chaiken not only introduce us to our subject by analyzing what we know about those factors that cause crime rates to rise, but they also give us some modest hope for the future by noting how these factors (in particular, the age structure of the population) may lead to crime reductions over the next decade.

This book is addressed both to laymen and to those persons officially concerned with crime. Most members of the latter group are to be found in state and local government, not in the federal government. Advising public officials on how best to cope with crime would be easier in countries where the relevant policymakers were all gathered at one level of government. In the United States, however, we must speak to a numerous, diverse, and dispersed collection of officials located in 50 states, 3,000 counties, and countless cities and towns. Many scholars find this frustrating and even deplorable—there is nothing the academic policy analyst likes better than to have but a single, receptive ear into which he can whisper. Many politicians, on the other hand, find this state of affairs exhilarating. Every elected official can, if he wishes, run for office pledging to "do something" about crime and then, when in office, shift the burden of doing that something to another level of government.

Because the management of the criminal justice system is almost entirely a state and local responsibility, we are commending this book chiefly to officials in those jurisdictions. But there is a federal role in criminal justice, though it is often badly defined. Speaking for myself (and, I think, for several of my colleagues as well), a federal role exists when one or more of the following criteria are met:

- A particular criminal activity requires the creation and exercise of federal jurisdiction because it:

    1. materially affects interstate commerce,

    2. occurs on a federal reservation or in the District of Columbia,

    3. involves large criminal organizations or conspiracies that can be presumed to operate across state lines, or

    4. is directed at a federal official (such as an attempt to assassinate the president).

- There is a need to discover, test, and disseminate strategies for coping with crime and disorder. (No city or state should be expected to pay the costs of research and experimentation when the benefits of such efforts will redound to the advantage of citizens everywhere.)

- Provisions of the federal Constitution or federal law are interpreted by the courts as setting procedural requirements for state and local law enforcement agencies.

- Local law enforcement agencies face acute burdens because of federal programs and policies (as when large numbers of immigrants come to particular localities as a result of federal actions).[1]

In this book, we say something about four of the matters that implicate the federal government—large criminal conspiracies (Moore on heroin), interstate commerce (Moore on guns and alcohol), federal rules that constrain local law enforcement (Schlesinger on the exclusionary rule), and the need for a vigorous federal program of research and experimentation (everybody on almost everything).

A final point: whenever we speak about crime, we mean, unless we say otherwise, common predatory street crime—muggings, assaults, robberies, burglaries, thefts, and the like. We do not discuss organized or "white-collar" crime, though these are important matters. We emphasize predatory crime because it is of greater concern to the general public. Moreover, we have written largely, though not exclusively, about stranger-to-stranger (rather than familial) crime because that is the more fearsome kind and because it is the kind with which most parts of the criminal justice system are chiefly concerned. We recognize, however, that much needs to be said and done about such matters as spouse assaults and child abuse.

In the concluding chapter I attempt to summarize the main arguments of the authors. Not every author may agree with how I have treated his or her views and I do not touch on the disagreements that may exist among the authors themselves. In inviting scholars to participate in this enterprise, I have sought to obtain the best possible authorities—not necessarily the ones who have the most views in common.

II

Crime Rates and Criminals

2

JAN M. CHAIKEN

MARCIA R. CHAIKEN

Crime Rates and the Active Criminal

Contrary to the impression of increasing crime conveyed by much public discussion, most data sources suggest that crime rates have recently remained fairly stable in the United States. Moreover, forecasts of crime rates based on projected changes in demographic composition of the population, drug use patterns, and other factors lead one to believe that crime will decrease slightly in the near future. Nonetheless, the statistical tracking of crime is not a simple matter, and projections are never certain.[1] Critical to the interpretation of crime rate statistics is an understanding of the impact that individual offenders have on the crime rate as a whole—and it turns out that a very few criminals are actually responsible for prodigious amounts of crime.

The views in this chapter are the author's own, and are not necessarily shared by the Rand Corporation or its research sponsors.

Defining Crime Rates

Much confusion over patterns of crime arises from varying usage of the term "crime rates" and from conflicting trends in different sources of information about crime.[2] The term "crime rates" may refer to jurisdictions, such as cities or counties, or to individuals. When referring to jurisdictions, rates are typically expressed as the number of crimes per population or per potential target (for which an example is business establishments). However, trends are often reported for the total number (or *volume)* of crimes in a jurisdiction, leading to possible confusion.

In 1981, for example, the *Uniform Crime Reports*[3] (UCR) showed that the total number of reported violent crimes[4] in the United States was 1,321,900—an increase of 1 percent over the 1980 figure (1,308,900). But the estimated U.S. population increased 4 percent over the year, yielding a decrease in the violent crime *rate* (number of violent crimes per 100,000 population) from 580.8 to 576.9. Thus crime went up but the crime rate went down.

In contrast, when referring to individuals, crime rates are typically expressed as crimes per unit time (say, per year)—more specifically, to the number of crimes divided by the amount of time the person was free (unincarcerated) to commit crimes.

Typically, one would expect that if a city's criminals have high crime rates, the city has high crime rates too. But it can happen that one city has higher crime rates than another, even though its criminals have lower crime rates. A jurisdiction's crime rate (for any particular type of crime) is related to its criminals' crime rates in the following way:[5] it is a product of two factors, the fraction of the population engaged in committing that crime,[6] and the average number of crimes per year committed by each of those people who commits the crime. The number of crimes an offender commits in a year is influenced both by his annualized crime rate and by the amount of time he spends incarcerated. For example, if a city has 3,000 burglars per 100,000 population, and on the average each committed two burglaries a year, the city's burglary rate would be 6,000 burglaries per 100,000 population, a very high rate. Alternatively, if the city has 300 burglars per 100,000 population, each committing on the average twenty burglaries per year, the burglary rate would also be 6,000 per 100,000 population.

When crime rates increase, one or more of three things are happening:

- More people are committing crime.
- Offenders have higher crime rates.
- Offenders are spending less time "locked up."

Often it is difficult, even in retrospect, to sort out these three influences and draw clear deductions about the underlying circumstances of a change in crime rates.

Sources of Information about Crime

In the United States, the FBI's *Uniform Crime Reports* has been a standard source of national crime statistics since 1932. The UCR data presently provide the only fairly consistent data for measuring changes in crime rates over time, even though the reports have been heavily criticized and are likely to undergo change in the near future. The main failing of the UCR information arises from differences in recording practices among the police departments that originally provide the data. An increase in the UCR count of forcible rapes, for example, can reflect an actual increase in rapes, an increase in the proportion of rapes reported to the police, an increase in the proportion of reported rapes recorded as rapes (rather than some other crime) by police, or any combination of these.

Block and Block,[7] in a study of noncommercial robbery incidents in Chicago during 1974–75, estimated that 50 percent of them were reported to the police, 73 percent of these (or 36.5 percent of the total) were initially recorded as robberies by the police, and 79 percent of these (29 percent of the total) were classified by the police as actual crimes and included as robberies in the Uniform Crime Reporting statistics. Thus changes in citizen and police reporting practices could, in the extreme, bring about an apparent 3.5-fold increase in the robbery rate in Chicago.

In 1973 the National Crime Survey was instituted,[8] partly to overcome such difficulties. During each six-month period, approximately 132,000 members of 66,000 households are interviewed to determine the crimes of which they have been victims. (From 1973 to 1976, robberies and burglaries of business establishments were also measured by the survey method.[9]) The survey demonstrated that a change in UCR crime rates due to changes in reporting practices not only was possible in principle but also seemed to be a primary phenomenon underlying crime trends. Eck and Riccio[10] analyzed the relationship between UCR and victimization survey data and concluded that the UCR is a much more volatile index of crime than the survey. Comparatively small changes in reporting and recording behavior have high leverage, yielding apparently large shifts in reported crime rates.

A large number of seemingly minor distinctions between the UCR and the victimization survey prevent direct comparisons between the two. For example:

- The survey counts crimes against people and their residences, while the UCR includes crimes against businesses and other organizations.

- The survey counts crimes against the *residents* of a jurisdiction (wherever they occur), while the UCR counts crimes that *occur in* a jurisdiction.

- The survey (until recently) omitted series victimizations (those that the victim could not recollect as discrete events), while the UCR included them or not, the same as other crimes.

Yet the casual observer of crime statistics expects to find that major trends in crime rates would be reflected similarly in both sources. Such, however, is not the case, as the next section shows.

Past Trends

First, let us consider homicide, a crime for which definitions and reporting practices are stable over time and across societies. Data for the United States suggest that homicide rates declined fairly steadily since the 1860s, with dramatic interruptions for increases that lasted about a decade.[11] The homicide rates in 1960 were estimated to be about one-fifth to one-seventh of their 1860 levels. When the President's Crime Commission[12] examined data through 1965, the willful homicide rate appeared to show an unremitting decline since the late 1940s and was not a matter of great national concern.

The following decade saw a dramatic increase in homicide rates. At its high point in 1974, the UCR homicide rate for cities (11 per 100,000 population) was more than twice its low point at the end of the 1950s. The next seven years showed a slight decrease and increase. At this writing (1981 statistics available), the U.S. homicide rate is near its high level of 1974.

What has happened since the 1960s? Nothing peculiar to the United States, it seems. In London, the increase started earlier but was just as dramatic. Murders (including attempts) in London increased by a factor of three from 1955 to 1974, from 0.6 to 1.8 per 100,000 population. As one researcher put it,

The most remarkable postwar phenomenon is the near universality of rising crime in Western societies during the 1960s and early 1970s. The British and North American experience is in no way unique. The late 1940s and early 1950s marked the low ebb of common crime in virtually every English-speaking country. Thereafter the trends were consistently upward.[13]

The patterns were similar in Scandinavia: in Stockholm from 1950 to 1970 the murder rate (also including attempts) rose 600 percent. Another study[14] shows a similar pattern for the homicide rates of seven cities: Amsterdam, Belfast, Colombo, Dublin, Glasgow, Helsinki, and Tokyo. In short, many cities around the world experienced a postwar homicide boom.

For crimes other than homicide, the data are murkier but the patterns similar. All evidence suggests that during the 1960s and early 1970s the United States was experiencing a rapid increase in crimes of all types. Beginning in 1973, crime has been generally steady, with some data sources showing small declines and others slight increases. For example, for the period from 1974 to 1978, the National Crime Survey's victimization rate for aggravated assault declined 6.7 percent, while the UCR showed an increase of 13.5 percent.[15] The survey's victimization rate for forcible rape declined 1 percent (not statistically significant) over the same period, while the UCR rate increased 11 percent. Some other crimes showed generally consistent declines in the two sources. For example, the rates of both motor vehicle theft and burglary decreased from 1974 to 1978 in both data sources.

Table 1 shows the victimization survey trends from 1973 to 1980. They appear to show that the least serious types of crime measured in the survey have been increasing, while the serious crimes show steady or declining victimization rates. How different a picture they give from the "crime epidemic" that some claim to see in the UCR statistics!

If we're not quite sure what have been the trends in crime rates in the recent past, it seems folly to predict what will happen to them in the future. Perhaps a useful perspective on "crime forecasting" is that the figures for crime rates published in the *Uniform Crime Reports,* reflecting as they do a combination of actual crime and the reporting practices of the public and police, must be related, in some empirically discernible way, to the characteristics of the population and police departments. To the extent that those characteristics can be forecast, then future levels of UCR crime rates can in principle be anticipated.

A myriad of research studies have quantified the correlations between characteristics of a geographical area and its crime rates. Some of these studies have been longitudinal, e.g., within a single

Table 1

Trends in Victimization Rates in the United States, 1973–1980

Sector and type of crime	Average annual percent change	Significance*
Personal sector		
Crimes of violence	0.26	n.s.
Rape	−0.16	n.s.
Robbery	−0.43	n.s.
Assault	0.44	n.s.
Aggravated	−1.26	.10
Simple	1.52	.05
Crimes of theft	−1.35	.05
Household sector		
Burglary	−1.21	.05
Larceny	2.43	.05
Motor vehicle theft	−1.86	.05

*Shows whether the change between 1973 and 1980 was significantly different from zero.

Source: Calculated from table 3 in Adolfo Paez and Richard W. Dodge, "Criminal Victimization in the U.S.," *Bureau of Justice Statistical Technical Report SD–NCS–N–21* (Washington, D.C.: U.S. Govt. Printing Office, 1982).

city over a period of many decades. Others have been cross-sectional, comparing crime rates among census tracts, communities, cities, counties, or states at a single point in time. Since later chapters of this book explore in detail various influences on crime rates that are subject to policy control, we focus here on influences that move primarily with broad demographic and social changes:

• urbanization,

• age structure of the population,

• racial composition of the population, and

• crime opportunities and control in the community.

Urbanization

Big cities have substantially higher crime rates than smaller cities and suburbs. The UCR index of crimes has always shown a monotonic relationship between crime rates and the size of the reporting jurisdiction. (The figures for 1980 are in table 2). The pattern is strongest for property crimes and is essentially the same for all crime types except homicide.[16] (For homicide, rural counties have higher rates than small cities.[17])

A natural conclusion from these cross-sectional data is that as cities grow, their crime rates must increase. However, international longitudinal analysis (at least for the crime of homicide)

Table 2

Variation in Crime Rates with Urbanization

Population group	Index crime rate per 100,000 pop.
Cities over 250,000	9,356
Cities 100–250,000	8,671
Cities 50–100,000	7,112
Cities 25– 50,000	6,457
Cities 10– 25,000	5,346
Cities under 10,000	4,688
Suburban counties	4,447
Rural counties	2,284

Source: *Uniform Crime Reports,* 1980. Calculated from table 10.

reveals a paradox: as cities become larger, their homicide rates may either increase or decrease—there is no predominant pattern. "The key to interpreting this paradox," according to Archer and Gartner, is "that the rates of major cities have consistently exceeded their national rates. The determinant of a city's homicide rates, therefore, is not the absolute size of a city, but its size relative to its contemporary society."[18]

Yet even if increasing urbanization of a country's population does not "cause" increasing crime rates in the cities to which people move, it does cause higher average crime rates in the nation as a whole. As the proportion of the population that experiences big-city crime rates increases, the national average crime rate increases in response to that proportion. Conversely, as people move out of cities, the national average crime rate tends to decline.

As Wesley Skogan has pointed out,[19] this perspective lends importance to one of the major demographic changes in the U.S. during the 1970s: the depopulation of large central cities and declining population growth in the metropolitan areas around those cities. Recent trends have shown accelerated growth in smaller metropolitan areas and in nonmetropolitan (including rural) areas.

One Rand Corporation study asks, "Will this deconcentration continue? No one really knows, but, on balance the evidence suggests that it will. The preference for smaller communities seems to be both widespread and deepseated."[20] If this is correct, a clear implication is that—all other things kept constant—the national crime rate will tend to decline in the coming years.

Age Structure of the Population

Since the bulk of crimes are committed by young people, the "baby boom" of the late 1940s and the 1950s has been widely credited with the sharp increase in reported crime during the 1960s. However, in 1967 the President's Crime Commission[21] puzzled over the fact that the increase in reported crimes was substantially larger than the increase in the crime-prone age groups of the population. Working with arrest data (because for many crimes the age of the perpetrator is not known), the Commission showed that only about 46 percent of the increase in the volume of arrests then apparent could be attributed to changes in the total population, its urbanization, and its age composition. For example, if the same proportion of teenagers had been arrested in 1965 as were arrested in 1960, the total number of arrests for teenagers in 1965 would have been 536,000, compared to the actual figure of 646,000, which is 21 percent higher.

It seems apparent from comparisons of this type—rough as they are—that changes in national crime rates cannot be explained simply by demographic shifts. Nonetheless, more complicated mathematical models that rely primarily on demographic information have proved fairly accurate in predicting crime rates. (An example is discussed in the next section.) Such models—if moderately accurate—are useful, since fairly reliable methods exist for estimating demographic data. More accurate models for projecting crime rates, relying on variables such as expenditures on the criminal justice system, unemployment rates, and annual rainfall, are less suitable for making forecasts.

Racial Composition of the Population

Marvin Wolfgang and Bernard Cohen have spoken of the need to "determine the extent of overlap between two poorly conceived terms—namely 'race' and 'crime.'"[22] Wolfgang and Cohen note:

An examination of many studies in many cities throughout the country over time spans and by specific offenses, by age, sex, and race, shows consistently that black adult crime and juvenile delinquency rates, measured by arrests, are higher than white rates.[23]

More recently, Wesley Skogan noted that

victimization surveys and victims' descriptions to police of those who 'got away' paint a similar picture. At the neighborhood level the volume of crime is strongly correlated with the size of the black population. Thus, trends and conditions in the black community exercise a disproportionate impact on the overall crime rate.[24]

The relationship between demographic descriptors of the black population and overall crime rates is so strong that James Alan Fox was able to construct an accurate econometric model of crime rates using only these exogenous variables:

- percentage of the population that is nonwhite and aged 14–17,

- percentage of the population that is nonwhite and aged 18–21, and

- consumer price index.[25]

Fox also designed a somewhat weaker model by using two variables for the proportion of the *total* population in the ranges 14–17 and 18–21, and a third variable for the proportion of the population nonwhite (together with the consumer price index as the final variable). In short, the age-race combination proved more relevant for predicting crime rates than the age distribution and racial composition separately.

Fox's model is quite complex, incorporating current and lagged endogenous variables for violent and property crime rates, clearance rates for both types of crimes, expenditures on police forces, and the size of police forces. Yet for purposes of forecasts the only data supplied to the model are the annual values for the three exogenous variables listed above.

Fox's model has been criticized, especially for the central role played by the consumer price index,[26] but it has proved quite accurate. Using two different sets of demographic assumptions, Fox predicted that the increase in the UCR violent crime rate for cities for 1972 to 1978 would be between 36.7 and 39.7 percent; the actual figure was 38.5 percent. His model predicted a 1980 violent crime rate in cities between 735.9 and 752.4 crimes per 100,000 population; the actual figure was 745.9. His forecasts for property crime rates were not quite as good, yet he forecast the 1980 property crime rate to be between 6,566 and 6,632 (compared to 4,535 in 1972) and the actual 1980 rate was 6,492.

What does Fox's model foretell for the future? (He had the courage to display numerical predictions through the year 2000). Beginning in 1981, according to Fox, the UCR violent crime rate will decline gradually to a low in 1992 that is about 19 percent below its current value. For property crimes, the forecast is that the rate will level off until 1985, before resuming its increase at about 14 percent per year. Alfred Blumstein, Jacqueline Cohen, and Harold Miller predict decreases for both violent and property crime rates, lasting even later into the 1990s.[27]

These conclusions of a near-term decline are the direct consequence of the so-called "baby bust," a precipitous decline in fertility from the postwar peak of 3.8 children per woman in the late 1950s to fewer than 1.8 children per woman in 1976, the lowest level in American history. In the absence of catastrophes or very large shifts in migration, the relative numbers of teenagers to older people in this country can readily be predicted: they will decline until at least the 1990s. Consequently, any prediction of crime rates that depends primarily on the age distribution of the population shows a leveling or a decrease in crime for the near future. The 1981 UCR figures[28] seem to support the forecasts: both violent and property crime rates declined slightly from the 1980 levels.

Crime Opportunities and Control in the Community

One condition that portends possible future increases in crime, despite the demographic trends to the contrary, is an increased opportunity for committing crimes. Lawrence Cohen[29] has suggested two major factors contributing to this condition: the increase in production of lightweight durable goods since World War II has effectively increased the number of suitable targets for crime; and the change in pattern of routine activities, with more people away from home for greater lengths of time, has resulted in an increase in criminals' accessibility to these targets.

Cohen's study suggests that continued upswings in the economy will lead to increased purchases of lightweight socially desirable goods, draw more women into the job market, and allow more families to leave home for vacation—all of which will produce greater opportunities for crime and further increases in property crime rates. From this perspective the changing economic status of women could contribute to higher crime rates in four distinct ways: each family's control over its own children is reduced; control over neighborhood children is reduced when women are not at home during the day; empty homes are targets for crime; and the women themselves are exposed to new opportunities to commit crimes in the workplace.

In addition to the increase in opportunities for committing crime, there has also been a change in social conditions that traditionally have brought about socially conforming rather than criminal behavior. Throughout history the period between physical maturity (the onset of puberty) and social maturity (the age for assuming adult roles and responsibilities) has been recognized as a troublesome interval. In tribal societies the arduous rituals and ceremonies that youngsters must fulfill, and in industrial societies the rigors of training on the athletic fields of schools and colleges, all function as means for socially occupying and physically exhausting potential troublemakers until the demands of marriage, family, and occupation produce the same results in adults. Societies that have failed to develop methods for channeling adolescent behavior have characteristically had high rates of deviance among their unmarried and marginally employed young males.[30]

In the past few decades, improved nutrition and health among children have contributed to sexual maturation at relatively young ages. During the 1970s the normal age of onset of puberty among American boys was found to be as early as 9.7 years.[31] During the same period, children have been required to stay in school for more years, thus delaying entrance into the labor market. Consequently, people are staying in their criminogenic adolescent period for nearly twice as long as in the past.

The early onset of adolescence may well explain why offenders appear to be committing crimes at relatively young ages.[32] And the increase in the duration of adolescence is linked to the seriousness of crimes committed by juveniles, since criminal careers are often progressive in terms of seriousness.[33] We must expect these trends to continue unless new or revitalized institutions begin asserting control over potentially criminal behavior of adolescents.

A gradual breakdown in social control over criminal activity may help explain how the increase in the proportion of youth in the population created by the baby boom could have brought about a more than proportional increase in the amount of crime. The increase in the population of teenagers may have initiated a self-perpetuating spiral: the flagrant types of crimes committed by groups of teenagers lead to a fear of crime.[34] Fear of crime produces community disintegration and the loss of local institutions' capacity for social control.[35] Loss of social control leads to greater opportunity for criminal behavior, which results in greater amounts of crime. This spiral of crime and fear in some neighborhoods cannot be alleviated simply by a reduction in the proportion of teenagers.

Varieties of Offenders

Gibbons[36] has pointed out that the study of the causes of crime has two main analytically distinct parts—examination of the social structure, and discovery of the processes through which individuals become criminals. The factors we have discussed above are directed primarily at structural explanations. Now we turn to social-psychological factors that appear to increase either the probability of individuals' committing specific types of offenses or the rates at which they commit offenses.

Daniel Glaser[37] has suggested that "the first step in trying to understand complex phenomena is to describe them and thereby to classify their variations." Many attempts have been made to classify offenders according to theoretically derived categories or differences in empirical measures such as personality tests, arrest records, or self-reports of criminal activity. The major problems in using most typologies for practical purposes have been the overlapping nature of their categories and the often imprecise and subjective nature of the criteria used for categorization.[38]

Researchers who try to devise typologies are aware of these problems. For example, using interviews with California inmates and parolees, John Irwin[39] classified offenders according to the major types of behavioral "systems" with which they had contact before entering prison. Two of his eight types of offenders are:

- *Disorganized criminals.* They pursue a life of variegated criminal activity. Major themes are a devil-may-care attitude toward doing wrong or acting irresponsibly, constant availability for criminal activity, especially small "scores," and an uncohesive world view.

- *State-raised youth.* They develop their world view from repeated incarcerations in state juvenile facilities and are characterized by "toughness" and violence, clique-forming propensities, prison homosexuality, and a view of "the streets" as where one plays out wild episodes during short releases from prison.

Irwin cautions that "these systems are all nebulous to a degree. Their membership fluctuates and many individuals are ambivalent in their identity relative to the system." Still, he says, "these systems exist and tend to maintain some degree of cohesiveness and consistency."[40]

The validity of his last assertion is supported by the similarity of the categories that have been independently discovered using a vast range of techniques and theoretical underpinnings.[41] The existence of categories of offenders who commit different mixes of crimes for different reasons alerts us to avoid oversimplification in asserting what causes higher crime rates among individuals.

Relationship between Categories and Crime Rates

Using self-report and official record data for nearly 2,200 inmates in California, Texas, and Michigan, we categorized the offenders into "varieties of behavior" according to the combinations of crimes they committed during one- to two-year periods. The categories were ordered in a way that roughly reflects public perception of the seriousness of various crimes. The most serious offenders, called for our purposes "violent predators," were those who had committed three crimes: robbery, assault, and drug dealing. We found that violent predators typically also committed burglary, theft, and other property crimes.

More important, violent predators were also the most troublesome criminals as measured by the annualized rates at which they committed crimes. Ten percent of violent predators committed over 135 robberies per year, more than two times the 90th percentile rate[42] for robbers in other categories. Similarly, other 90th percentile rates of violent predators were 18 assaults per year, five times more than the equivalent rate for mere assaulters; 516 burglaries per year, three times the equivalent rate for the burglars; and 4,088 drug deals per year, a rate higher than for those who "specialized" in that crime. The great diversity and intensity of crimes committed by violent predators were independent of whether they were found in prison or in jail, in California or Michigan or Texas.

These findings suggest that any factors that increase or decrease the numbers of violent predators on the street will influence crime rates just as much or more than factors that increase or decrease the total number of offenders.

Moreover, violent predators are significantly different from other types of offenders in several ways. Considering their effect on crime rates—especially for serious crimes—violent predators are extremely young. In the survey, they averaged less than twenty-three years of age when coming into jail or prison. Yet they also averaged considerably more total arrests than any other respondents, including those substantially older, and they had been committing the more serious crimes for at least six years.

The length of their criminal activity is implicit in their juvenile history. The predators typically begin committing crimes, especially violent crimes, well before age 16. They are likely to commit both violent and property crimes frequently before they are 18. They are more likely than other types of criminals to have received parole and had it revoked and to have spent considerable time in state juvenile facilities. Yet some of those who report the highest juvenile crime rates have no official records of juvenile criminal behavior.

Violent predators are also more socially unstable than other types of criminals. Few of them are married or have any other kind of family obligation. They are employed less regularly and have more trouble holding jobs. The more they are unemployed, the more crime they tend to commit. (This correlation between unemployment and higher crime rates holds true for other categories of offenders as well. However, employment problems are more chronic for the violent predators.)

They also have characteristic histories of drug use. Most of them begin using several types of "hard" drugs, and using them heavily, as juveniles. Indeed, their use of drugs and their criminal careers usually begin at about the same time. In addition to dealing drugs, 83 percent of the violent predators in the survey also used drugs during the measurement period. While heroin addiction has long been seen as part of the criminal subculture, often as the economic cause of crime, this survey revealed that certain types of drug use are even more characteristic of the violent predators than heroin addiction. Although they are more likely than other offenders to have high-quantity, high-cost heroin addictions, their more distinctive characteristic is multiple drug use: heroin with barbiturates, heroin with amphetamines, barbiturates with alcohol, barbiturates with amphetamines, amphetamines with alcohol, or multiple combinations of these.

When their drug use is costly and intense, violent predators are more likely to commit most kinds of crimes and at much higher rates. However, the nature of the drug use seems related to the kind of crime that the user will commit. Addictive use of heroin is more associated with robbery and property crimes than with assault, and there is some indication that cost, rather than the drug's physiological effect, provides the impetus here. As a matter of fact, heavy but relatively inexpensive heroin use is not associated with high crime rates. If the user has a cheap source of supply or can trade other services for his drugs, the heroin habit apparently has no effect on his rate of criminal activity.

In contrast, multiple drug use, especially use of barbiturates and intermittent, "recreational" use of heroin, is associated with assault; and extremely heavy use of nonopiate psychotropic drugs is strongly related to high rates for all crimes except the nonviolent crimes of burglary and auto theft. This association helps explain an otherwise puzzling finding of the survey, that white respondents committed assault at much higher rates than black respondents did. The whites used barbiturates more commonly.

In addition to shedding light on the relationship between heavy drug use and high crime rates, the survey also clarified some other aspects of serious criminals and their backgrounds:

- Juvenile drug use is strongly associated with rates of robbery and assault in this study, but there is *no* association between crime rates and juvenile use of marijuana or *experimentation* with hard drugs.

- Among people who wind up in jail or in prison, there are very few full-time criminals. Not even more violent predators use crime as their sole source of income. Their employment is less stable than other offenders', but the inverse relationship between level of employment and crime rates indicates that they use crime, at least in part, to supplement their "straight" incomes.

We do not know whether the violent predator is a new type of criminal. However, the extreme involvement with drugs that is characteristic of this variety of criminal suggests that even if he is not new, the numbers of this type of offender have increased. Not until the early 1960s was the demand for heroin adequate to force high prices,[43] nor was the recreational use of amphetamines and barbiturates very common. It thus seems possible that a part of the rapid increase in crime rates in the 1960s can be attributed to the emergence of these highly active and dangerous offenders.

Problems in Identifying the Violent Predator

Unfortunately, although violent predators appear to be distinctly different from other offenders, our study showed that it is very difficult to identify them reliably from their official records. An immediate problem is their youth: because most of them are so young, their adult criminal records do not usually reveal extensive prior criminal activity. And juvenile records offer little more enlightenment. Many of the violent predators' self-reports describe such heavy juvenile drug use and frequent violent criminal activity that they must have been highly visible to teachers, neighbors, and schoolmates. Yet some appear to have no official juvenile criminal records. (This lack of records is confirmed by their self-reports of having no contacts with police or incarcerations as juveniles.) Even when the violent predators have juvenile records, they rarely indicate the rate or seriousness of their criminal activities. Indeed, where self-reports and juvenile records disagree, the self-reports usually report more arrests and incarcerations than the records do.

When violent predators do have prior adult records, those records do not readily distinguish them from other (lesser) offenders. It might seem that checking an inmate's prior record to see whether he had ever been convicted of the defining crimes — robbery, assault, and drug-dealing—would provide an easy method of identifying violent predators. However, this method does not work: some offenders with convictions for these three crimes in their records are not committing them concurrently at the present time and consequently do not match the definition of violent predator. For example, in the sample of California prisoners, 5 percent of inmates who were not violent predators had been convicted of these three crimes at some time in the past. More important, the vast majority of those who did commit all these crimes had not been convicted of them. For example, in the California sample, 91 percent of violent predators did not have conviction records—juvenile or adult—for all three crimes: robbery, assault, and drug-dealing.

Sometimes official records show that a criminal has been arrested or convicted of robbery and assault and also has a history of drug use or addiction (usually an indication that he also deals drugs). But this information is not pragmatically useful for identifying the violent predator. Although violent predators are significantly more likely than other inmates to have this kind of history, we found a large number of "false positives"—inmates who use drugs but are not drug dealers. In the California sample, 35 percent of violent predators had official records of drug use and convictions for robbery and assault, but so did 18 percent of the inmates who were not violent predators.

Various other potential definitions of violent predators derived from their official records were tested. To sum up, there is no simple, straightforward way to identify robber-assaulter-dealers from the data in their official records—as those data are currently collected. A number of factors explain the records' limitations: plea bargaining, imprecise definition of drug use, and the fact that some offenders successfully evade arrest and conviction for crimes they commit frequently.

Future Outlook for Prevalence of Violent Predators

Trends in recent research suggest that the heyday of the violent predator may be coming to an end. These offenders characteristically engage in serious violent crime at young ages, yet McDermott and Hindelang[44] demonstrated that the rate of personal crimes attributable to juveniles remained stable from 1973 to 1977. Juveniles committing theft-oriented crimes were more likely to choose crimes that required stealth than force or the threat of force,[45] and the proportion of victims injured during crimes committed by juveniles did not increase.[46]

Use of most hard drugs seems also to have stabilized among juveniles. Between 1975 and 1981, use of heroin and barbiturates did not increase among high school students, and the intensity and duration of use of both amphetamines and barbiturates appear to have declined.[47]

Stability or decrease in the rates of juvenile violence and the rates of frequent use of hard drugs (both highly characteristic of violent predators), combined with a smaller population of juveniles, give reason to anticipate that fewer violent predators may be developing. Additional evidence is based on the finding that although there was a 12.3 percent increase between 1975 and 1977 in rates of juveniles referred to courts for property crimes, there was a 7.6 percent decrease in rates of juveniles referred for crimes against people.

Perhaps ironically, a possible counterinfluence is the incarceration of these lesser juvenile offenders. Not only are a greater proportion of less serious juvenile delinquents being processed formally in the courts, but a greater proportion are also being committed to institutions such as reform schools.[48] As is discussed by Daniel Glaser elsewhere in this volume, incarceration may reduce crimes committed by serious offenders but prove also to be criminogenic for less serious types, resulting in more offenses.

For the most part, crime rates respond to broad demographic and cultural trends that are not under the control of policymakers. But because a small number of violent predators are responsible for a large volume of crime, the processes that initiate, interrupt, or terminate their careers are central to the future course of crime.

3

RICHARD J. HERRNSTEIN

Some Criminogenic Traits of Offenders

Who commits crime? Depending on how broad the brush, the picture we develop of the typical offender may or may not reveal patterns of traits that predispose certain people to break the law. With too fine a brush, only the accidents of single lifetimes become salient; with too broad, it is only general sociological forces that emerge. Between these two pictures—the one too specific, the other too general to be very useful—lies evidence showing offenders, on the average, to be something other than a random sampling of the population at large. This evidence, reviewed here, also makes clear that the distinguishing traits of criminals cannot be fully explained as the result of society's treatment of them at home, in school, or in the workplace. Nor can they be entirely explained by the operation of the criminal justice system. The average offender is psychologically atypical in various respects, not necessarily to a pathological degree, but enough that the normal prohibitions against crime are in some measure ineffective. In

31

designing public policy, it is helpful to understand that a society that successfully deters crime in 80 to 90 percent of its citizens may find it hard to deter it in the remaining 10 to 20 percent for reasons that have more to do with individual differences than with defects in policy.

Individual traits that, under given circumstances, predispose certain people to less internalization of standards of conduct, to greater resentment for inequity, to shorter time horizons, to frustration in the competition for good jobs or satisfying companionship, or to diminished sensitivity to criminal penalties are traits that may be called *criminogenic*. The evidence, although not complete in any sense, points toward a variety of criminogenic traits, which are reviewed in the remainder of this chapter.

Sheldon and Eleanor T. Glueck, husband and wife, conducted what was, and has remained, the most detailed and comprehensive longitudinal and cross-sectional study of male delinquency.[1] Starting in the late 1930s, they gathered data on a sample of 500 delinquent boys incarcerated for serious offenses and compared them with a sample of 500 nondelinquent Boston boys of about the same age, ethnic background, and IQ, and from neighborhoods equivalent in general quality and delinquency rates. Then they surveyed a large number of variables describing the boys themselves, as well as their homes, parents, and grandparents.

Note, to begin with, that any variable used for matching delinquent and nondelinquent samples is thereby ruled out of consideration as a correlate of delinquency in this study. For example, both groups came mostly from English, Italian, and Irish family backgrounds, and from slum neighborhoods. The lack of an ethnic or neighborhood difference between the samples reflects only the way the study was designed, not an absence of ethnic or neighborhood correlates of delinquency in the population at large. Similarly, the delinquents had an average IQ of 92 and the nondelinquents, 94—an insignificant difference, showing that this study succeeded in excluding IQ as a variable that might be correlated with delinquency.

For numerous other variables, the two groups differed significantly. Although both groups lived in comparably poor neighborhoods with matching delinquency rates, and although their families paid about the same rental per room, the delinquents' homes were more crowded, less clean, and less well provided with sanitary facilities. Similarly, although both groups were drawn from about the same (generally low) occupational levels, the delinquents' families had lower average earnings, in terms of both per capita income and number of breadwinners. In short, the two groups differed in general social and economic conditions, even after the deliberate effort to match them. This was further reflected in the educational backgrounds of the two samples, which were poorer for the delinquents' parents and grandparents. The delinquents' parents came from poorer homes than the nondelinquents' parents, and their families had a history of more public welfare support. They also had a history of more serious physical illness, mental retardation, emotional disturbance, alcoholism, crime, and marital discord between parents.

Individual Traits

These differences suggest that even within a relatively narrow and underprivileged sector of the population, still finer environmental gradations, at the level of the individual home itself, play a part in predisposing certain individuals toward crime. But beyond even those finer gradations, the Gluecks found differences among the boys themselves. They were about the same height and weight and were judged to be approximately equally healthy, but they had different physiques.[2] According to W. H. Sheldon's three-dimensional system of body-typing,[3] the delinquent boys were markedly more mesomorphic (muscular, squarish) on the average than the nondelinquent boys, and markedly less ectomorphic (fragile, linear). On the third dimension of body type, endomorphy (soft, round), the groups were about equal. The superiority in mesomorphic development was "expressed especially in the shoulders, chest, waist, and upper extremities, and outlining the picture of the masculine physical type with tapering torso, heavy arms, small face, strong neck, and wide shoulders."[4] Not only were they more mesomorphic (and stronger in handgrip) on the average, but the delinquent boys as a group were more homogeneous in body build than the nondelinquents, who represented a more typical mixture of physiques.

The difference in build, as well as other individual differences to be described, characterized not every delinquent but only the group average. Twice as many of the delinquents as nondelinquents were primarily mesomorphic (60 percent versus 30 percent), and more than twice as many of the nondelinquents were primarily ectomorphic (40 percent versus 14 percent). The percentages imply a fair number of nonmuscular delinquents and muscular nondelinquents, yet they leave no doubt that the delinquents did not represent a random sample of the ethnic or socioeconomic population of their origin. Other studies, including Sheldon's own,[5] have confirmed the association between physique and criminality, both juvenile and adult.[6] Although methodological flaws mar Sheldon's study on this point, the evidence overall cannot be denied. Exactly what psychological links may obtain between the static fact of physique and the dynamic facts about criminal behavior will be discussed below.

Although the two groups in the Glueck sample were almost equal in average IQ, their pattern of abilities differed. The delinquents were relatively weaker in verbal ability than the nondelinquents, even though the nondelinquents were verbally weak compared to the population as a whole. The delinquents did worse in school than the nondelinquents by any measure—academic, attitudinal, or motivational. When nondelinquents were asked to give reasons for disliking school, they tended to blame feelings of inadequacy as students. In contrast, the delinquents were more likely to express resentment toward the school routine or a sheer lack of interest. Delinquents' vocational ambitions included more frequent references to adventurous occupations, like aviation and going to sea. The delinquents misbehaved in school earlier, more often, and more seriously than the nondelinquents. Almost 90 percent of the delinquents had misbehaved prior to the age of 11, several years before adolescent male delinquent gangs tend to form.

Using the Rorschach inkblot test, an effort was made to characterize the boys' personalities. This projective test no longer enjoys the popularity it had in the 1940s, having been largely supplanted by more objective psychological inventories, but it distinguished the two samples in this instance. The written Rorschach protocols were interpreted "blind," that is to say, by experts who had no information about the boys other than their responses to the ink blots. Table 1 presents the breakdown of traits, paraphrasing only slightly and for convenience the experts' own characterizations. The first two columns list descriptions that significantly more often applied to delinquents and nondelinquents, respectively. In the third column are descriptions that did not differ significantly for the two groups.

Table 1 conjures up an impression of two distinct personalities for the two groups. The delinquents were assertive, unafraid, aggressive, unconventional, extroverted, and poorly assimilated into the social milieu. The nondelinquents were self-controlled, concerned about their relations with others, willing to be guided by social standards, and rich in such feelings as insecurity, helplessness, love (or its lack), and anxiety. Psychiatric interviews conducted independently confirmed the major distinctions between the two samples.

The Gluecks were able to follow most of the two samples into adulthood and later published a second account of them.[7] The differences in academic and socioeconomic success and in personality endured into young adulthood, and so did the differences in criminal behavior. Of the 442 nondelinquents who were located in adulthood, 62 were convicted for crimes by the age of 31. The crimes were, on the whole, minor, involving mostly drunkenness, violations of license laws, and offenses within the family, plus a few serious offenses—an armed robbery, an assault with a dangerous weapon, and a case of child abuse, to cite some examples. In contrast, the delinquent group proved prolifically criminal. By the age of 31, they had committed 15 homicides, hundreds of burglaries, hundreds of larcenies (greater than petty), hundreds of arrests for drunkenness, over 150 robberies, dozens of sex offenses, and so on. Four hundred thirty-eight of the original 500 in the delinquent sample were located, of whom 354 were arrested between the ages of 17 and 25. Between the ages of 25 and 31, only 263 were arrested, perhaps showing the characteristic decline of crime with age, or perhaps only the shrinking numbers not in prison. One hundred forty-seven men from the delinquent sample spent five or more years in jails or prisons during the eight years from ages 17 to 25, and 45 did so during the six years from ages 25 to 31. Despite spending thousands of man-years in correctional institutions, the delinquent sample had ample time outside for hundreds of arrests.

Table 1
Personality Traits in the Glueck Sample

Delinquents exceed nondelinquents	Nondelinquents exceed delinquents	No significant difference
Self-assertive	Submissiveness	Feeling not being taken care of
Social assertion	General anxiety	
Defiance	Enhanced insecurity	Feeling not being taken seriously
Ambivalence toward authority	Feeling unloved	Resignation
	Feeling helpless	Depression
Feeling unappreciated	Fear of failure	Kindliness
Feeling resentment	Adequate contact with others	Competitiveness
Difficulty in contact with others		Isolation
	Cooperativeness	
Hostility	Dependence on others	Suggestibility
Suspicion	Concerns about others' expectations	Spontaneity
Destructiveness		Feeling able to cope
Narcissim	Conventionality	Introversion
Feeling others will take care of one	Masochism	
	Self-control	
Sadism	Compulsiveness	
Impulsiveness		
Extroversion		
Mental pathology		

Source: Author's summary of data presented in Sheldon and Eleanor Glueck, *Unraveling Juvenile Delinquency* (New York: Commonwealth Fund, 1950).

Although the Glueck study was internationally cited, it was also criticized intensely, particularly by American sociologists.[8] In modern criminological texts, it usually earns short shrift. Nonetheless, most if not all of the distinguishing traits of the Gluecks' delinquent boys have been repeatedly confirmed in other samples. In retrospect, the methodological criticisms appear less decisive than they seemed to a criminological community whose theories often ignored the individualistic variables considered by the Gluecks, such as personality traits and physique. Moreover, to criticisms about the comparability of the delinquent and nondelinquent samples and about the objectivity of the measures of physique and personality, Sheldon Glueck offered what now seem adequate answers.[9] Less adequate was his defense of his attempt with his wife to construct an index for predicting criminality on the basis of individual characteristics; but that issue, although timely and interesting, is beyond the scope of this chapter. For our purposes, the only relevant point is that other workers have substantiated the existence of a special psychology of delinquents and criminals.

Corroborating Studies

There is, for example, a sizeable literature on delinquency in relation to performance on the Porteus maze tests. Developed as a supplement to conventional IQ, these tests consist of a graded series of pencil and paper mazes progressing from very simple to exceedingly hard.[10] Two measures of performance are usually taken. One is based on the highest level of difficulty attained and on the amount of practice needed to learn successive mazes; the other (the "Q" score) measures the quality of execution of the mazes—for example, the number of times the pencil is lifted, a line crossed, or a corner cut, all against the examiner's instructions. Both measures correlate at least slightly with conventional IQ scores, the first more so than the Q score. However, the Q score correlates better with delinquency in minors and crime in adults. Over a dozen controlled studies in Hawaii, the continental United States, and Great Britain have demonstrated significant deficits in Q scores for the criminal population as a whole, and especially large deficits for criminal recidivists and troublesome prisoners.

The deficits in the other score among criminals are marginal at most.[11]

What is there about delinquents that the Q score captures? The question cannot be answered with certainty, but Porteus's own account seems plausible:

Delinquents and criminals are not markedly inferior to nondelinquents in planning capacity as reflected in Maze test quantitative scores (the first measure); but in regard to quality of performance (Q scores), they had decided tendencies towards careless, haphazard, and impulsive reactions. Overconfidence in action was characteristic of many, but on the other hand, others were easily "rattled" or "nervous." Many also are unable to keep in mind specific instructions. They have good intentions but their tendency to impulsive reactions nullifies their planning. . . . Those who have not succeeded in setting up for themselves standards of self-accomplishment exhibit their disorganization by slipshod or hasty execution of the task on hand.[12]

Porteus pursued his hypothesis by asking school teachers to identify students who displayed "carelessness, hasty and impulsive reactions, and unsatisfactory disciplinary attitudes," but to "disregard intelligence as far as possible."[13] Compared to an unselected sample of schoolmates, the selected students had significantly poorer Q scores. He also noted, though without presenting substantiating data, that the selected group later showed high delinquency rates. Later work by others found that subjects who delay gratification poorly—for example, by taking an immediate and small reward rather than waiting for a delayed, larger one—also earn deficient Q scores.[14]

Eysenck and his associates have written extensively on the individual traits associated with criminal behavior.[15] From his findings with standardized questionnaires and rating scales, Eysenck has proposed an analysis of personality into three dimensions, which he calls "neuroticism," "extroversion," and "psychoticism." Each person's answers on a questionnaire define relative values along each dimension, in effect locating a point in a three-dimensional space. The extroversion dimension has outgoing, sociable, impulsive, adventuresome types at one end and introverts at the other, where the traits include reflectiveness, quietness, social reserve, and diffidence. The neuroticism dimension has excitability or emotionality or changeability at one end and emotional steadiness at the other. At the high end of the psychoticism scale people are characterized by cruelty, aggressiveness, atypical tastes and appetites, and deficiencies in social sensitivity. The three dimensions are said to vary more or less independently in the population as a whole.

The data gathered by Eysenck and his associates generally show criminals not to be a random sampling from the three-dimensional space defined by his measurement of personality. Offenders tend to be unusually high on at least one dimension and often on two or all three. High values for all three are particularly diagnostic of criminal behavior.[16] Excitable (i.e., "neurotic"), socially insensitive, or atypically motivated extroverts account for the highest rates of criminally deviant behavior. Moreover, it is the impulsive, not the sociable, side of extroversion that correlates with crime.[17]

Complementary results have been found by Megargee and his associates.[18] All of the male offenders incarcerated over a two-year period in a federal prison were given the Minnesota Multiphasic Personality Inventory (MMPI), a questionnaire comprising 556 true-false items for which there is a large body of standardizing data, including evidence of an association with delinquency.[19] A respondent's pattern of answers permits, first of all, a check on the questionnaire's internal validity and consistency. Secondly, it provides a relative position on each of ten clinical scales that have been developed on the basis of responses from groups of people known to exemplify the traits named by the scales (see below). A high score on, say, the schizophrenia scale (8) does not mean that a person is clinically schizophrenic; it means that schizophrenics as a group also earn high scores on the scale. The following descriptions are excerpted from Megargee and Bohn:

1. Hypochondriasis: "abnormal concern over bodily functions and preoccupation with physical complaints."

2. Depression: "feelings of hopelessness and self depreciation."

3. Hysteria: "tendency to use physical or mental symptoms to avoid stressful conflicts . . . unwillingness to accept adult responsibilities."

4. Psychopathic deviate: "tendency toward conflicts with au-

thority figures, disregard of social conventions and laws, inability to learn from experience, and shallowness in personal attachments."

5. Masculinity-femininity: "masculine or feminine interests, attitudes, and forms of self-expression" (high scores often correlate with homosexuality).

6. Paranoia: "abnormal suspiciousness and sensitivity."

7. Psychasthenia: "tendency towards obsessive ruminations, guilty feelings, anxiety, indecision and worrying."

8. Schizophrenia: "bizarre or unusual thinking and behavior, interpersonal withdrawal and alienation, inappropriate affect."

9. Hypomania: "high activity level often without productivity."

10. Social introversion: "shyness, social withdrawal and insecurity."[20]

Based on the patterns of questionnaire answers, more than 95 percent of the sample of 1,214 prisoners fell into one of ten characteristic profiles. Our interest here is not in the practical benefits of the resulting classificatory system—which may be substantial—but in patterns of personality traits. Figure 1 shows the overall profile of prisoners, the most deviant of the ten profile types (13.3 percent of classified prisoners), and the least deviant type of profile (19.3 percent of classified prisoners). On each clinical scale, almost 70 percent of the general population lies between 40 and 60, and averages 50. In contrast, the sample of prisoners (as well as other samples)[21] is conspicuous for higher values for psychopathic deviate (4), schizophrenia (8), and hypomania (9). The most nearly normal scale for prisoners was social introversion (10). Differences among the ten profiles were associated with differences in offenses, institutional behavior and adjustment, recidivism, and various other characteristics.

The most deviant profile defined a group of prisoners who had the highest probability of reincarceration and who comprised the highest fraction in trouble during imprisonment, whose work in prison earned the lowest ratings, whose siblings were most deviant, and who also had relatively severe problems of adjustment outside of prison, in school and on the job. In contrast, the least de-

Figure 1
MMPI Profiles of Prisoners

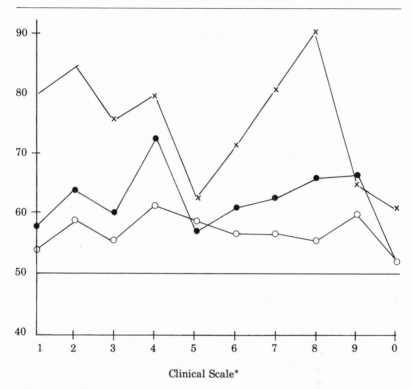

Clinical Scale*

● General profile
○ Least deviant profile
x Most deviant profile

*For each scale, the general population has a mean of 50 and a standard deviation of 10.

Source: Adapted from E. I. Megargee and M. J. Bohn, Jr. (with J. Meyer, Jr., and F. Sink), *Classifying Criminal Offenders* (Beverly Hills, Calif.: Sage, 1979).

viant profile belonged to a group of prisoners who had good prison adjustment, a history of relatively minor crimes (e.g., draft offenses, drug and liquor law violations, and a variety of property offenses), relatively few problems in school, and high ratings for dependability at prison jobs. They had the second lowest rate of recidivism, with the lowest rate earned by another profile group with a low level of personality deviance.

Although each of the ten types in the Megargee-Bohn classification differs somewhat, certain generalizations can be made. As a whole, prisoners deviated from the population at large in showing deficient attachments to others and to social norms, bizarre thinking, and hyperactivity—traits associated with high scores on the psychopathy, schizophrenia, and hypomania scales of the MMPI. Moreover, the more deviant groups of prisoners as measured on the MMPI typically had more serious behavioral problems, more serious crimes in their past, poorer prognoses for future contact with the law, and more trouble while in prison.

Effects of Institutionalization

The data reviewed so far came mainly from institutionalized subjects. Not surprisingly, this has been a point of contention for critics of the search for individual differences. It is not unreasonable to wonder whether institutionalization itself, or the biases in the criminal justice system, account for the distinctive personalities of offenders, rather than anything having to do with susceptibility to crime. The evidence, however, suggests otherwise. We cannot review all of it here, but it can be represented by a carefully executed prospective study conducted by West and Farrington on a sample of 400 boys drawn from a working-class district in London.[22] Gathèred over a fourteen-year period, self-report questionnaires, school and family protocols, and self-reports and official records of offenses enabled the authors to examine "the extent to which young adult delinquents differ from their social peers in personal circumstances, attitudes, and behavior."[23] The latest comprehensive report uses interviews at the ages of 18–19, but the official records carry them to the age of 21 or thereabouts.

About 30 percent of the sample had some sort of official record of delinquency by then—a figure about twice the national average, but close to that for comparable urban districts in England at the time. From the 22 percent of the sample that had been rated prior to the age of 11 as "troublesome" by teachers and peers, came about 60 percent of the recidivists by the age of 18. A scale to measure "antisocial" tendencies was based on various measures of attitude and such activities as smoking, loitering, getting tattooed, heavy drinking and gambling, involvement in such anti-establishment groups as gangs, and promiscuous sex. Of the 110 young men who scored the highest (i.e., the most antisocial), over 60 percent were delinquents; of the 72 who scored the lowest, 4 percent were delinquents. According to the authors, "One could hardly imagine a clearer demonstration of the close connection between officially recorded delinquency and particular attributes of character and lifestyle—the delinquent way of life."[24] Thi. study was concerned with criminogenic traits that surfaced well before a boy's activities intersected the arm of the law, so institutionalization could not have fostered them. Yet the offenders' characteristics were at least as distinctive as in Glueck's or Eysenck's or other samples of prisoners. From this, and from other corroborating studies, we must conclude that offenders in general, not just institutionalized offenders, show a constellation of personality characteristics.[25]

The evidence does not say that criminals are necessarily, or even usually, clinically abnormal, although some of them are. Most criminals are within normal ranges of variation for objective measures of personality such as the MMPI, but they do not constitute a merely random sample of the population at large. Different taxonomic schemes, different populations of offenders defined by different criteria of criminality, different points in a criminal career from childhood to mature adulthood, and different vocabularies mask an underlying uniformity in the predisposing traits for comparable samples. Summarizing the delinquents and adult offenders in their sample, West and Farrington described in clear language the traits they found. They could have been writing about many other samples of young adults with criminal records:

Virtually every comparison suggested that the convicted delinquents were more deviant. They were less socially restrained, more hedonistic, more impulsive, more reckless and distinctly more aggressive and prone to physical violence than their nondelinquent peers. They smoked more, drank more and gambled more. They had a faster lifestyle, they went out more, they visited bars, discotheques and parties more often, they had more contacts with girls, they were more sexually precocious and sexually promiscuous, they avoided educational pursuits, evening classes, or reading books, they earned more from highly paid unskilled jobs with poor future prospects, but they spent more, saved less and were more frequently out of work and in debt. On an attitude questionnaire the delinquents frequently endorsed anti-establishment opinions, such as "School did me very little good" and "The police are always roughing people up" and agreed with statements favoring violent behavior such as "I enjoy a punch up." Reports of conflicts with parents, and an expressed preference for living away from the parental home, were common among the delinquents. But perhaps the most striking characteristic of all was their high level of self-admitted aggressiveness.[26]

By some accounts, the distinguishing characteristics of criminal populations reflect the same sociocultural forces that produce the crime itself. Thus if criminals are, on the average, more impulsive than noncriminals, it is not because a static personality trait—impulsiveness—predisposes people to crime, but because society favors both impulsiveness and criminality in certain disadvantaged groups. The same is said to hold true if they are more aggressive or more unfeeling or more antisocial, and so on through the list of distinguishing traits. In effect, this approach assumes that every person is equally susceptible to the forces that promote or inhibit criminal behavior, and to the accompanying individual traits. Perhaps no one subscribes to this approach completely (for then it would be necessary to account in sociocultural terms not only for correlations with personality, but also for the differences in offending between, say, 7-year-olds and 25-year-olds), but the criminological community has long been drawn to it, as any survey of criminological textbooks would show. The evidence against the assumption of equal criminal potentiality is that crime correlates with nonsociological traits, by which is meant traits that are not accounted for by society.

Physiological Factors

An example of such an individual trait is physique. One may believe that society produces criminality, but hardly that it produces mesomorphy; yet populations of offenders have often been found to be disproportionately mesomorphic and nonectomorphic.

The correlation probably arises through physique's connection with personality. Even in populations of nonoffenders, mesomorphs tend to be adventurous, hyperactive, argumentative, and outgoing, while ectomorphs tend to be self-controlled, cautious, sensitive, shy, and reflective.[27] The traits of mesomorphy unleavened with those of ectomorphy yield a configuration that unmistakably resembles that found in populations of offenders.

We do not know whether the correlation between physique and personality is itself sociological—whether, in other words, society could make mesomorphs meek and ectomorphs outgoing. Nor do we know whether the constellation of typical personality traits among criminals—asociality, impulsiveness, high psychological energy, etc.—is a sociological necessity, or whether a society could recruit its criminals from the introspective, the conscientious, and the empathetic. But even without knowing what may or may not be possible in hypothetical societies, we can assert with confidence that in our society physique illustrates a constitutional, individual factor linked to the propensity to commit crime.

Other lines of evidence further undermine the assumption of equal criminal potentiality among all persons. Personality traits themselves, as measured by objective inventories, are significantly heritable.[28] While it may be premature to quantify heritability of these traits, it is already clear that the heritability is not negligible. If the predisposing traits are heritable, it follows that the tendency to commit crime should itself run in families for genetic reasons; and the accumulating evidence suggests that it does.[29]

In numerous laboratory studies, both institutionalized and non-institutionalized "psychopaths" (often called "sociopaths") have shown diminished physiological reactivity to certain kinds of stimuli.[30] Although definitions of psychopathy or sociopathy vary from study to study, the condition approximately corresponds to elevated scores on the psychopathic deviate scale of the MMPI, sometimes also including an elevation of the hypomania scale. Experimental techniques and results also vary, but in most cases psychopaths have been found to have trouble learning anticipatory responses, especially to imminent painful stimuli (such as a brief electric shock), to discount time unusually steeply in such procedures, and to have a weaker than average reflexive change in the electrical conductivity of the skin to sudden or stressful stimuli—which is known to be associated with the autonomic nervous system and hence provides a measure of emotional arousal.

Eysenck, who early recognized the bearing of findings like these on the analysis of criminal behavior, suggested that psychopaths and other potential offenders often have low levels of arousal of the cerebral cortex, and are consequently in a continual state of hunger for stimulation, expressed as a restless appetite for new and intense experience. According to Eysenck's theory, since the cerebral cortex is known to be at least as much an inhibitor as an excitor of behavior, deficient cortical arousal would suggest a lowered threshold for ordinarily inhibited activities, such as crime. Somewhat closer to the data is Hare's characterization of the population in these studies:

> The psychopath's apparent disregard for the future consequences of his behavior may therefore be seen as reflecting the failure of cues (visual, kinesthetic, verbal, symbolic, etc.) associated with punishment to elicit sufficient anticipatory fear for the instigation and subsequent reinforcement of avoidance behavior. Moreover, it appears that the psychopath's relative inability to experience anticipatory fear may be especially marked when the expected punishment is temporally remote, a reflection, perhaps, of an unusually steep temporal gradient of fear arousal.[31]

The Role of Intelligence

One significant dimension of human variation remains to be considered: intelligence as measured by standardized tests like the IQ. The understanding of intelligence as a correlate of crime may be completing a full swing of the pendulum. In the early days of testing, it was taken as proven that it was the major individual correlate of crime. By early estimates, the proportion of mentally retarded in American prisons was as high as 50 percent.[32] But the earliest estimates of retardation among criminals were the highest. As the tests themselves, the criteria of mental retardation, and the population sampled met increasingly rigorous and reasonable standards, the proportion rapidly shrank. Observing this change, many criminologists extrapolated it to the vanishing point, arguing that by the time research methods became genuinely valid, the intelligence of criminals would be seen to be no different from that of the population at large. The leading spokes-man for this view was Sutherland, whose fifty-year-old paper on the subject is still cited by those few textbooks on criminology in which intelligence is mentioned at all.[33] American criminologists seemed, judging from secondary sources, to have concluded that intelligence was not a differentiating characteristic of the crimi-nal population.

In fact, since the mid-1930s, the best estimates have converged on an average IQ deficit of about 10 points for the criminal popula-tion in at least the United States and the United Kingdom.[34] For recidivists, the IQ deficit may be even larger.[35] If the population at large averages an IQ of 100, and the criminal population accounts for 15 percent of the total, then a 10-point deficit implies an average IQ for offenders of 91.5—which closely approximates the more representative samplings in the literature. Not much is known about the precise shape of the IQ distribution for offenders, but it is likely to be truncated at the low end because even the most slapdash crimes usually require some mental competence. The high end probably lacks comparable truncation, although an average of 91.5 implies that the criminal population lies mainly in the so-called low normal and borderline region between 65 and 100.

It seems clear that IQ, independent of race and class, con-tributes to the risk of criminal behavior; indeed, IQ probably con-tributes more to the risk than either race or class. Judging from indirect evidence and a small amount of direct measurement, the intellectual level of the average prisoner represents that of crimi-nals at large reasonably accurately, although a small number of very bright offenders may well be eluding imprisonment.[36] The bright ones fascinate us, and fill both the fiction and much of the human-interest journalism about crime, but they are few enough to have only a negligible impact on the overall average.

Not all samples of criminals show the average deficit. In Megargee and Bohn's MMPI study, for example, the prisoners ap-parently had average intelligence. Their presence in a federal prison may be a clue to their higher scores, for an early study found different averages for different criminal categories. Pris-oners convicted for conspiracy, for violations of "blue sky" or securities laws, or for forgery had significantly higher scores than

48 RICHARD J. HERRNSTEIN

those convicted for homicide, rape, weapons offenses, and
assaults.[37] Evidence suggests that low scores are correlated with
the more impulsive criminal acts.[38] The offenses that lead to a
medium-security federal prison, such as the one used in the
Megargee-Bohn study, are probably heavily weighted toward
those correlated with higher scores.

The connection between intelligence and criminality has been
interpreted in two ways, both of which may be right to a degree.
Low test scores often mean failure and frustration in school. In
combination with certain personality traits and particular social
circumstances, the resulting alienation may start youngsters on
the road to crime. This view, expressed by Hirschi and Hindelang,
depicts low IQ as leading to crime when the legitimate paths to
success, which start at school, are closed. Gordon stresses a
different connection. Inasmuch as society's rules must be learned,
a low IQ impairs mastering the legal norms of conduct much as it
does the rules of spelling or long division. Purely on the basis of
the learning deficiency, according to this theory, the average offender probably learns social prohibitions less rapidly or fully than
the average nonoffender and hence is more likely to break the
law. Personality traits that favor acting out frustrations or that
retard learning about delayed consequences magnify the risk of
criminal behavior associated with low intelligence, by either of
these theories. Even more surely than personality, intelligence
has a heritable component.[39] It must, therefore, also count as a
predisposing individual characteristic, at least in the modern industrial societies where the data have been gathered.

Predisposition for Criminality

From obvious differences in body build, through personality and
intelligence, to subtle differences in time discounting, the people
most at risk for criminal behavior constitute an atypical population. In light of these findings the medical analogy is irresistible.
Just as sickness afflicts some people more than others, so also
does the social pathology called crime. This is not to deny the importance of social and economic conditions, any more than it
denies the importance of precipitating agents for disease; it is,
rather, to pay due regard to individual differences.

It is not hard to see why the predisposing traits for crime are what they appear to be. The rewards that crime can offer are enhanced by traits that minimize internalized prohibitions, inhibit learning social conventions, are associated with unconventional or extremely intense drives of various sorts, and cause deficient empathetic response to others. Traits that block legitimate success further strengthen the attractions of crime. The deterrent effects of legal sanctions are minimized by steep time-discounting, by an insensitivity to punishment, and by traits that reduce the opportunity costs of imprisonment, such as the low earning ability associated with low intelligence.[40] In each case, some populations of criminals have displayed the predisposing traits and, in most cases, the traits are abundantly present.

Some of these traits are heritable. Even so, neither the data nor any theory built around them justifies the Lombrosian conception of the born criminal, if that means an inevitable descent into a life of crime. Individuals are not simply criminals or noncriminals. Everyone acts according to laws of behavior that can equally well produce crime as noncrime, depending upon circumstances and predispositions. Poor law enforcement, long delays in the criminal justice system, inadequate teaching of society's standards of conduct, school systems that fail to educate the less gifted, and socioeconomic inequities that exacerbate feelings of alienation and resentment are among the factors that incubate crime—particularly among those with special susceptibilities. Instead of a typology of wicked people, modern psychology deals with the sources of criminal behavior, acting through our individual differences on all of us.

III

The Social Milieu of
Crime

4

TRAVIS HIRSCHI

Crime and the Family

For many years the Oregon Social Learning Center has treated families with problem children—children who bite, kick, scratch, whine, lie, cheat, and steal. As might be expected nowadays, this group started with the assumption that the proper way to train children is to reward their good deeds and ignore their bad ones. The idea was, of course, that eventually the children would be so wrapped up in doing good that they would no longer consider doing evil. After much struggling with such families and (one supposes) their own training, these scholarly practitioners came to the conclusion that children must be *punished* for their misdeeds if they are to learn to live without them.[1]

This conclusion may come as no surprise to those millions of parents who have spent years talking firmly to their children, yelling and screaming at them, spanking them, grounding them, cutting off their allowances, and in general doing whatever they could think of to try to get the little bastards to behave; but it is exceedingly rare among social scientists, especially those who deal with crime and delinquency. Criminologists become interested in people only after they are capable of criminal acts. By then, people (especially delinquents) tend to be pretty much free of their parents and too big for spanking. Not only is it too late to do anything about the family situation; it is too late to learn much about what the family situation was like during the "child-rearing" years. As a result, we have many explanations of crime that ignore the family, and those of us who consider it important in crime causation cannot say much in detail about specific deficiencies in child-rearing practices that are associated with an increased likelihood of criminality.

But I am being too generous. The major reason for the neglect of the family is that explanations of crime that focus on the family are directly contrary to the metaphysic of our age. "Modern" theories of crime accept this metaphysic. They assume that the individual would be noncriminal were it not for the operation of unjust and misguided institutions.[2] "Outdated" theories of crime assume that decent behavior is not part of our native equipment, but is somehow built in through socialization and maintained by the threat of sanctions. It is hard to imagine a family-based explanation of crime that would not take the latter position.

Thus the members of the Oregon group are swimming against the intellectual currents of our time, and are doing what few students of crime have had the time or inclination to do. They are actually going into the homes of families with potentially delinquent children and watching them in operation. And they are coming up with terms and ideas in many ways superior to those traditionally used to describe the situation one finds there.

For example, the traditional research literature reports that discipline, supervision, and affection tend to be missing in the homes of delinquents; that the behavior of the parents is often "poor"; that indeed the parents of delinquents are unusually likely to have criminal records themselves. This information is all well and good, and is enough to make us suspicious of those many explanations of crime that ignore the family, but it does not represent much of an advance over the firm belief of the general public (and those who deal with offenders in the criminal justice system) that "defective upbringing" or "neglect" in the home is the primary cause of crime.

Another large literature deals with the subtleties of child-rearing—what might be called the "fine-tuning" side of socialization. This information, too, is valuable. It is good to know, for example, that one should not rage and storm around the house, but should in all cases provide the child with a model of reasoned self-control. And I suspect most parents would be more than happy to follow such advice if their children were not so exasperating. But in talking about delinquency, we are not really talking about the difference between good and better behavior, but the difference between tolerable and intolerable behavior, and at this level there is not much we can take for granted.

In fact, the Oregon group starts pretty much from scratch. They tell us that in order for the parent to teach the child not to use force and fraud, the parent must (1) monitor the child's behavior; (2) recognize deviant behavior when it occurs; and (3) punish such behavior. This seems simple and obvious enough. All that is required to activate the system is affection for *or* investment in the child. The parent who cares for the child will watch his behavior, see him doing things he should not do, and correct him. Presto! A socialized, decent human being.

Where might this simple system go wrong? Obviously, it can go wrong at any one of four places. The parents may not care for the child (in which case none of the other conditions would be met); the parents, even if they care, may not have the time or energy to monitor the child's behavior; the parents, even if they care *and* monitor, may not see anything wrong with the child's behavior; finally, even if everything else is in place, the parents may not have the inclination or the means to punish the child. So, what may appear at first glance to be nonproblematic turns out to be quite problematic indeed. Many things can go wrong. According to the Oregon group, in the homes of problem children many things have gone wrong: "Parents of stealers do not track: ([they] do not interpret stealing . . . as 'deviant'); they do not punish; and they do not care."[3]

I am impressed by the simplicity, beauty, and power of this approach. I believe that it organizes most of what we know about the families of delinquents, and that it provides a framework for addressing many of the complicated questions about the place of the family in crime causation. I also believe that when we consider the potential effects of any governmental action on crime and delinquency, we should specifically consider its impact on the ability of parents to monitor, recognize, and punish the misbehavior of their children. When we conclude that the action would have an adverse impact on the family, we should be extremely reluctant to endorse it *as a crime prevention measure.* When we conclude that the program would have no impact on the family, we should at least hesitate to endorse it: in fact, we should immediately entertain the suspicion that the policy in question may have unintended adverse consequences on the crime problem.

The Independent Adolescent

The classic example is of course employment policy. If one asks professors of criminology why the crime rate is so high, or if one asks students in criminology courses why a particular group has an unusually high rate of crime, they will almost invariably mention unemployment or underemployment first. If one points out that homicide, rape, and assault do not typically produce much in the way of income, undergraduates as well as professors can quickly figure out how to get to these crimes from joblessness by way of something like frustration or rage.

The appeal of such explanations of crime is phenomenal. Year after year they are favored by students. Year after year criminologists produce dreadful warnings of what is going to happen if kids are not able to find jobs.

The source of the appeal of these explanations has already been mentioned. They suggest that people would not "turn to crime" if something better were available. This clearly implies that "faulty training" or other family defects have nothing to do with crime. In point of fact, such explanations often suggest in a not too subtle way that the families of "criminals" have done a better job of socializing their children than other families in the same circumstances. After all, isn't it normal for parents to teach their children to want to better themselves, to aspire to the good things of life?

So we ignore family considerations and, as best we can, concentrate on providing kids with good jobs. What do we expect to happen? Employment of the adolescent would presumably not much affect the parents' ability to monitor his behavior. Adolescents are outside the home a good deal anyway, and the employer would to some extent act as a surrogate monitor. The parents' affection for the child might, if anything, be improved by the child's willingness to reduce the financial burden on the family, and work certainly would not affect the parents' ability to recognize deviant behavior. The only element we have left in our model of child-rearing is *punishment*. How, if at all, does the employment of the youth affect the family's ability to punish his deviant behavior?

The power of the family in this situation will depend on the resources available to it relative to the resources available to the child. It will also depend on the child's aspirations. If the child wants to go to college at the parents' expense, continues to drive the family Buick on weekends, and is really only picking up pocket money on the job, the damage to parental control is presumably minimal. (Although even here it may not be negligible. Drugs cost money, and their purchase is facilitated by money that does not have to be accounted for.)[4] If the child does not want to go to college, his family does not own a car, and the money he earns provides him a level of living equal or superior to that of his family, he is by definition no longer dependent on them. His parents no longer have the material means to punish him, and the entire system of family control is vulnerable to collapse. Henceforth the adolescent is free to come and go as he pleases. Affection and monitoring had better have done the job already, because the "child-rearing" days are over. It is time to hope for the best.

This conclusion about the possible consequences of adolescent employment is more than a deduction from theory. It is also a finding from research. According to historians of the family and criminologists interested in comparing crime rates across developing societies, a major feature of recent times is the increasing independence of adolescents from the family made possible by expansion and differentiation of the labor market. This independence from the family results in increasing dependence of the adolescent on other adolescents. But adolescents cannot take the place of parents as socializing agents because they have little or no investment in the outcome, are less likely to recognize deviant behavior, and, most important, do not possess the authority necessary to inflict punishment.[5]

More to the point, research that looks directly at delinquents offers no support for the notion that they are economically deprived when compared to other adolescents in their immediate area. On the contrary, it finds that they are more likely to be employed, more likely to be well paid for the work they do, and more likely to enjoy the fruits of independence: sex, drugs, gambling, drinking, and job-quitting.[6]

By looking directly at the family we are thus able to resolve one of the minor paradoxes of our time, the fact that crime is caused by affluence *and* by poverty. General affluence to some extent weakens the control of all families. It especially weakens the control of those families in which the adolescent is able to realize a disposable income equal to that of his family almost from the day he finds a job. Unfortunately, life does not freeze at this point. Since the earnings from such jobs often do not keep up with the demands on them, our suddenly free adolescent can look forward to the not-too-distant day when his own son or daughter will, for a brief and not-too-shining moment, likewise have things "better" than he. He would do well to consider the consequences.

To make this point about affluence and against deprivation theories of crime, I have had to exaggerate the importance of economic factors. It helps the parents if they have money and the child doesn't, but poverty of the parents is not a large factor in crime causation,[7] and the eventual poverty of the offender seems to be explained by the same factors that explain his criminality: people untrained to get along with others, to delay the pursuit of pleasure, or to avoid force and fraud simply do not do very well in the labor market. For this reason, delinquency predicts socioeconomic status better than socioeconomic status predicts delinquency.[8]

Parents with Criminal Records

There is good reason to expect, and the data confirm, that these delinquents do not do very well as parents either. In fact, a recent well-designed and careful study reports that "the fact that delinquency is transmitted from one generation to the next is indisputable."[9] The extent of this transmission is revealed by the fact that in this same study fewer than 5 percent of the families accounted for almost half of the criminal convictions in the entire sample. (In my view, this finding is potentially much more important for the theory of crime, and for public policy, than the considerably better known finding of Wolfgang and his colleagues that something like 6 percent of *individual* offenders account for about half of all criminal acts.)[10] In order to achieve such concentration of crime in a small number of families, it is necessary that *the parents and the brothers and sisters* of offenders also be unusually likely to commit criminal acts.

Why should the children of offenders be unusually vulnerable to crime? If we had the complete answer to this question, we would be much further down the road to understanding crime than we are. But if we don't know for sure, we do have important clues. Recall that our affection-monitor-recognize-punish model assumes that criminal behavior is not something the parents have to work to produce; it is something they have to work to avoid. Such behavior is part of the child's native equipment, and will remain unless something is done about it. Consistent with this view, parents with criminal records do *not* encourage criminality in their children and are in fact as "censorious" toward their criminality as are parents with no record of criminal involvement.[11] Of course, not "wanting" criminal behavior in one's children, and being "upset" when it occurs, do not necessarily imply that great effort has been expended to prevent it. And if criminal behavior is oriented toward short-term payoffs—which it is—and if child-rearing is oriented to long-term payoffs—which it is—there is little reason to expect the parents in question to be particularly interested in child-rearing.

And indeed "supervision" of the child in such families is "lax" or "inadequate" or "poor." Punishment tends to be "cheap," i.e., short-term—yelling and screaming, slapping and hitting—with little or no follow-up. These factors do not, however, completely account for the concentration of criminality in a small portion of families. (Part of the reason, presumably, is that such factors are very difficult to measure adequately.) I suspect the reason is that the most subtle of the elements of child-rearing is not included in these analyses. This is the element of "recognition" of deviant behavior. According to the Oregon Social Learning Center research, many parents do not even recognize *criminal* behavior in their children. For example, when the child steals outside the home, the parent discounts reports that he has done so on the grounds that they are unproved and cannot therefore be used to justify punishment.

Given that recognition is necessary to the entire child-rearing model, it is unfortunate that so little systematic thought and research have gone into the question of what parents should and should not recognize as deviant behavior if they are to prevent criminality. Part of the reason for this neglect may be traced to "policy" concerns. The libertarian streak in all of us understands that by denying connections between forms of deviant behavior we can undercut efforts to reduce more serious forms (e.g., crime) by attacking less serious forms (e.g., drugs, alcohol abuse, delinquency). We therefore deny such connections and dismiss out of hand research and theory that attempt to establish their existence.

Parents concerned about their children cannot afford this luxury. In fact, parents successful in crime prevention seem inclined to err in the direction of over-control, to see seeds of trouble in laziness, unreliability, disrespect for adults, and lack of concern for property. (A thorough catalog of parental concerns among those successful in rearing their children as nondelinquents would probably read like "The Protestant Ethic" or "Middle-Class Values"—which tells us a great deal about why academics tend to be embarrassed by the entire subject of crime and the family.) Unsuccessful parents, in contrast, are considerably more tolerant, being inclined to see little if anything wrong with their children's behavior until it is too late. As a consequence, it may be true that "people in prison are more willing to accept the idiosyncracies of others."[12] It may also be true that, when they are not in prison, they are more willing to accept the "idiosyncracies" of their own children. If this kind of tolerance in parents tends to go with intolerable behavior in children, it may be exactly what is meant by those concerned with "moral decay." Little wonder those concerned with "moral decay" tend to feel embattled when they see the thrust of social policy moving in the direction of decriminalization and diversion on the one side, and the defense of "diversity" of life-styles and values on the other.

Children in Large Families

One of the most consistent findings of delinquency research is that the larger the number of children in the family, the greater the likelihood that each of them will be delinquent. This finding is perfectly explicable from our child-rearing model. Affection for the individual child may be unaffected by numbers, and parents with large families may be as able as anyone else to recognize deviant behavior, but monitoring and punishment are another matter. The greater the number of children in the family, the greater the strain on parental resources of time and energy. For this reason, the child in the large family is likely to spend more time with other children and less time with adults. Like the peers discussed earlier, other children are not as likely as adults to be effective trainers. They have less investment in the outcome, are more likely to be tolerant of deviant behavior, and do not have the power to enforce their edicts. One often sees a child demanding that parents punish a brother or sister. The brother or sister quickly learns to shift attention to the behavior of the accuser. Whatever the outcome of these particular contests, the parent is clearly dependent on the reports of surrogate monitors. If many parents are unwilling to act on deviant behavior they directly observe, fewer still will act on the testimony of children, especially when the behavior reported occurred some time earlier and has thus earned the forgiveness that comes with (even brief periods of) time.

If the analysis of these three confirmed correlates of criminality (adolescent employment, criminality of parents, and size of family) is sufficient to establish the plausibility of child-rearing explanations, we can now attempt to apply it to some of the more problematic issues in the connection between the family and crime.

The Single-Parent Family

Such family measures as the percentage of the population divorced, the percentage of households headed by women, and the percentage of unattached individuals in the community are among the most powerful predictors of crime rates. Consistent

with these findings, in most (but not all) studies that directly compare children living with both biological parents with children living in "broken" or reconstituted homes, the children from intact
homes have lower rates of crime. These differences amply justify
concern about current trends in divorce and illegitimacy rates.
The likelihood that the biological parents of a particular child will
marry and stay together throughout the period of child-rearing is
lower today than at any time in the past.

If the fact of a difference between single- and two-parent
families is reasonably well established, the mechanisms by which
it is produced are not adequately understood. It was once common
in the delinquency literature to distinguish between homes
broken by divorce and those broken by death. This distinction
recognized the difficulty of separating the effects of the people involved in divorce from the effects of divorce itself. Indeed, it is
common to find that involuntarily broken homes are less conducive to delinquency than homes in which the parent was a party
to the decision to separate.

With the continued popularity of marriage, a possible complica-
tion enters the picture. The missing biological parent (in the over-
whelming majority of cases, the father) is often replaced at some
point by a stepparent. Is the child better or worse off as a result of
the presence of an "unrelated" adult in the house?

The model we are using suggests that, *all else equal,* one parent
is sufficient. We could substitute "mother" or "father" for
"parents" without any obvious loss in child-rearing ability. Husbands and wives tend to be sufficiently alike on such things as
values, attitudes, and skills that for many purposes they may be
treated as a unit. For that matter, our scheme does not even require that the adult involved in training the child be his or her
guardian, let alone a biological parent. Proper training can be accomplished outside the confines of the two-parent home.

But all else is rarely equal. The single parent (usually a woman)
must devote a good deal to support and maintenance activities
that are at least to some extent shared in the two-parent family.
Further, she must do so in the absence of psychological or social
support. As a result, she is less able to devote time to monitoring
and punishment, and is more likely to be involved in negative,
abusive contacts with her children.

Remarriage is by no means a complete solution to these problems. Stepparents are often decent people, but they are not superhuman: many report that they have no "parental feelings" toward their stepchildren, and they are unusually likely to be involved in cases of child abuse.[13] The other side of the coin is the affection of the child for the parent. Such affection is conducive to nondelinquency in its own right, and clearly eases the task of child-rearing. It is for obvious reasons less likely to be felt toward the new parent in a reconstituted family than toward a biological parent who has been there from the beginning.

The Working Mother

The tremendous increase in the number of women in the labor force has several implications for the crime rate. Most analysts agree that this change has greatly contributed to the instability of marriage, a fact whose consequences for crime we have just discussed. Traditionally, however, the major concern with the working mother has been with the direct effect on child-rearing. An early study of this topic showed that the children of women who work, especially the children of those who work "occasionally" or "sporadically," were more likely to be delinquent.[14] This same study also showed that the effect on delinquency of the mother's working was *completely* accounted for by the quality of supervision provided by the mother. (Such complete explanations of one "factor" by another are extremely rare in social science.) When the mother was able to provide (arrange?) supervision for the child, her employment had no effect on the likelihood of delinquency. In fact, in this particular study, the children of regularly employed women were least likely to be delinquent when supervision was taken into account. This does not mean, however, that the employment of the mother had no effect. It did have an effect, at least among those in relatively deprived circumstances: the children of employed women were more likely to be delinquent.

More recent research reports that a mother's employment has a small effect, which it is unable to explain. The advantage of the housewife over the employed mother in child-rearing remains when supervision and other characteristics of the mother, the family, and the child are taken into account.[15] One possible im-

plication of this explanatory failure is that the effects of employment influence children in ways not measurable except through
their delinquency. This conclusion is at odds with the conclusion
we just reached (where "supervision" accounts for all of the
effects of employment). It reminds us that our scheme does not
allow us to separate the enduring effects of child "rearing" from
the temporary effects of child "control," something we should be
able to do if we are to devise effective programs for delinquency
prevention.

Another consequence of women's working is that it contributes
to the "destruction of the nest," where no one is home for large
portions of the day. The unoccupied house *may be* less attractive to
adolescent members of the family; it *is* more attractive to
strangers interested only in its contents. Research shows that the
absence of guardians in the home is a good predictor of residential
burglary.[16]

Child Abuse and Delinquency

As far as I can determine, the gross correlates of child abuse are
identical to the gross correlates of delinquency. Reports to the
effect that large portions of delinquents have been abused as
children are also common. The first fact suggests that child abuse
and criminality have common causes; the second, that abuse
causes criminality. These hypotheses are not necessarily mutually
exclusive, and it seems reasonable to suppose that there is a large
grain of truth in both of them. However, since "abuse" and
"punishment" have elements in common, it is important that we
take seriously the distinction between them. Otherwise, it will appear that punishment is conducive to delinquency. If so, our argument would be in serious trouble, to say the least.

One way to reconcile the abuse/delinquency results is to recognize that abuse does not occur in a vacuum. It is more likely the
less the parent cares for the child and the fewer the resources the
parent is able to devote to child-rearing. Recall that delinquency
is also more likely under these circumstances. But before delinquency is possible, there exists the potentially delinquent child.
This child has not yet been introduced properly. He or she is more
likely to be "demanding, stubborn, negativistic,"[17] "aggressive,"

and "troublesome."[18] When the uncaring or overburdened parent faces such behavior, he is unlikely to see it as his own creation. But if our analysis is correct, it is—at least to some extent. If so, the abuse that follows should not be confused with "correction."

The Family in Secular Society

Privately promoting conservative, tribal values through child-rearing is seen by most parents as simply one of the tasks of life, made easy or difficult by the luck of the draw in the nursery, by the devotion of others in the community to the same task, and by their ability to shield the child from contrary messages. With regard to the latter, there can be no doubt that the message of the media is often contrary, celebrating the very behavior parents attempt to teach their children to avoid. Gwynn Nettler has pointed out that "no moral community doubts [the] effectiveness" of the mass media in fostering corrosive attitudes among its members, and as a result, "censorship is a normal feature of . . . attempts to maintain moral difference."[19] By this test, few families qualify as moral communities, since few restrict their children's access to television, movies, books, or magazines in any systematic way. (According to some reports *everybody* watches television.)

This inconsistency between the values and the behavior of parents may stem from their feeling that they are simply no match for the media. It may also stem from the view that behavior is not much affected by images, whether good or evil. Our child-rearing scheme is consistent with the latter view (see notes 2 and 4). It suggests that the media's portrayal of a broad range of human experience is more likely to have a direct effect on the comfort and morale of parents than on the behavior of their children. But this leads to the possibility that the long-term effects of the media are to demoralize those whose task is to limit the range of experience of others. (Good, broadly informed people, it is often noted, are not necessarily effective parents.)

In any event, the impact of the media is very hard to assess. It seems reasonable to guess that children whose parents restrict access to the media are unlikely to be delinquent. I suspect, however, that it would be difficult to show that this particular restriction was responsible for the difference. Almost by definition, such families are already unusually sensitive to the moral implications of behavior. They are therefore already likely to have trained their children to be morally distinct from children in danger of delinquency. (Again, we must distinguish between the delicate issues that apply to basically socialized children and the crude issues that apply to children at the border between law-abiding behavior and crime. Parents concerned about the finer aspects of child-rearing are unlikely to have to visit their children in institutions.)

Improving Child-Rearing

The decline of the family, routinely reported by college students home to pick up money, clean clothes, and cheap advice from their parents, is real enough. The extended family that was so effective in controlling everyone's behavior remains only in vestigial form, and the nuclear family that replaced it does not have the stability and continuity it once had.[20] One response is merely to ascribe these facts to global processes of evolution over which government has no control. Another is to celebrate or bemoan the decline of the family on the grounds that it is essential to the perpetuation of current social and economic arrangements. From the perspective of crime policy, celebration does not seem to be in order. What, then, can be done to help the family?

Our analysis divides this question into two parts: Can parents or potential parents be better trained in the technology of child-rearing? Can they be induced to apply what they know?

In principle, education in *minimal* child-rearing does not pose particularly difficult problems. The techniques cannot be that complex: they are, after all, reasonably well applied by most parents. In principle, the best time to teach such techniques is when we have the attention of all those who are about to use them.

Straightforward application of these principles would produce child-rearing classes in high school. What would be taught in such classes? It is time to recall the previous reference to the metaphysic of our age. As things now stand, we could not expect the schools to intellectualize the child-rearing question without getting it, according to our lights, wrong—without preaching toleration for natural tendencies, without demeaning the practices of successful parents in the eyes of their own children.

What should be taught in such classes? It is time to recall previous reference to the ignorance of criminologists in child-rearing matters. As things now stand, we could not expect much in the way of consensus among experts in the field. And if we found it, we would have reason to be suspicious of its research base.

Still, I think the matter should be pursued. Research identification of child-rearing practices that separate the families of delinquents from those of nondelinquents should be possible. And promotion of these practices by the school is not as unlikely as previous discussion may suggest. The school, after all, is run by adults whose values and practices seem very close to those of successful parents; furthermore, the school is already deeply involved in child-rearing. If the school and the family are now at odds on the principles of child-rearing, they are not at odds on child-rearing practice. In fact, at first glance the school seems to have advantages over the family. Teachers care about the behavior of children, if only because disruption makes their lives more difficult. By the standards of the family, school monitoring of behavior is highly efficient. As a class, teachers are probably more expert than parents in recognizing deviant (and predicting delinquent) behavior. Finally, the school has, and uses, a variety of means for punishing misbehavior. The fatal flaw in this otherwise ideal system is that the school can punish only those students who see education as important to them. If the student does not like school he or she can, in effect or in fact, quit. In this case, the school's child-rearing system too breaks down, and not surprisingly, "attitude toward school" becomes a major predictor of delinquency. But the failure of the school in dealing with some children should not obscure the fact that it does very well with others; more particularly, it should not obscure the basic compatibility between the school and the family on the child-rearing issue.

Beyond efficiency in child-rearing is the more difficult problem of commitment to the task. There may be no point in training parents to do a better job if the outcome has little significance for them. Historically, the incentives for doing a good job have included the honor of the family, security for oneself, and self-reliance for one's children. Today the major incentive appears to be some form of conspicuous display of one's accomplishments. (A doctor-son is nice to have, as is a Cadillac.) For those who cannot hope for such success, and who have little to fear from failure, the rewards of child-rearing may not be worth the effort.

All proposals in this area come down to efforts to increase the care and concern of family members for each other. Put this way, they seem like a good idea. But in fact such attempts require the state to increase the severity of its sanctions (or to extend them to those responsible for the child), to reduce its own responsibility for family members, or to make more difficult the creation and dissolution of families. In this light, proposals to increase the efficiency of the family as a child-rearing institution are not so attractive. Furthermore, on the basis of presently available information, there can be little assurance that such programs would be effective.

For the moment, then, it seems the best we can do is to encourage research on good child-rearing practices and the conditions favorable to them, with little or no expectation that the results will be of immediate practical benefit. The absence of such benefits should not concern us overly much; after all, the pursuit of immediate benefits is what causes all the trouble for delinquents.

5

JACKSON TOBY

Crime in the Schools

Some public schools in central cities of the United States have become major crime sites no less than some parks, streets, and shops. Unfortunately, society cannot afford to be as tolerant of dangerous schools as of dangerous public parks. Crime in schools threatens social continuity in a basic way. Not merely is cultural preparation of our future citizens at stake; at issue also are opportunities for children from disadvantaged families to achieve a better life than their parents.

Schools by nature provide certain occasions for crime. It is inevitable, for one thing, that some children will become troubled as a result of their failure to learn what schools are designed to teach them. That some students become alienated is predictable; not every youngster can make a smooth transition from the style of socialization available in his or her family to the more impersonal form of socialization characteristic of the classroom. Furthermore, some families do not provide enough encouragement, support, and preschool training to give their children a good chance at competitive success.[1] In this sense, schools help to generate criminal behavior simply because some of their clients develop rebellious personalities in the course of school experiences. Moreover, children in school are exposed not only to the official curriculum but to the tutelage of their schoolmates, who are more numerous than adult teachers. Sometimes peer-group influences reinforce the goals of the official curriculum; at other times, of course, the peer group develops its own goals unrelated or opposed to academic achievement. At worst, schools can become virtual training grounds in theft and other crimes.

Some of these crimes are violent. Stories in newspapers and on television have reported dramatic illustrations of school violence, but the actual extent of the problem was not documented until 1979, when the National Institute of Education published a national victimization survey of 31,373 students and 23,895 teachers in 600 junior and senior high schools throughout the United States.[2] Questions such as the following were asked of students and teachers in 1975–76 to provide an estimate of the amount of theft and violence in public secondary schools:

- In [the previous month] did anyone steal things of yours from your desk, locker, or other place at school?

- Did anyone take money or things directly from you by force, weapons, or threats at school in [the previous month]?

- At school in [the previous month] did anyone physically attack and hurt you?

Tables 1 and 2 show that school crime is, in fact, a problem of national scope, although violence directed at teachers is more common in the inner cities of large metropolitan areas than in small cities, suburbs, or rural areas. Furthermore, school crime is only the most visible symptom of a more fundamental problem in the public schools: the difficulty of maintaining general order so that education can proceed.

Sources of School Disorder

Some schools have high crime rates simply because they are located in high-crime communities. Predatory young adults loiter in the streets and sometimes invade the schools looking for

Table 1

Teachers Victimized in Public Schools over a Two-Month Period in 1976

Size of community	By larcenies		By assaults		By robberies	
	in junior high schools	in senior high schools	in junior high schools	in senior high schools	in junior high schools	in senior high schools
500,000 or more	31.4% (56)	21.6% (59)	2.1% (56)	1.4% (59)	1.4% (56)	1.1% (59)
100,000–499,999	24.5 (45)	22.8 (36)	1.1 (45)	1.0 (36)	0.7 (45)	0.9 (36)
50,000–99,999	21.0 (23)	19.3 (31)	0.2 (23)	0.3 (31)	0.3 (23)	0.4 (31)
10,000–49,999	20.8 (94)	16.5 (75)	0.6 (94)	0.3 (75)	0.5 (94)	0.4 (75)
2,500–9,999	16.9 (41)	19.1 (47)	0.3 (41)	0.2 (47)	0.4 (41)	0.4 (47)
Under 2,500	15.9 (42)	18.5 (53)	0.2 (42)	0.2 (53)	0.0 (42)	0.4 (53)
All communities	22.1 (301)	19.3 (301)	0.8 (301)	0.5 (301)	0.6 (301)	0.6 (301)

Note: Numbers in parentheses refer to the number of schools on the basis of which the average percent of personal victimization was calculated for each cell.

Source: Special tabulation of data from U.S. Department of Health, Education, and Welfare, *Violent Schools—Safe Schools: The Safe School Study Report to the Congress* (Washington, D.C.: U.S. Govt. Printing Office, 1978).

Table 2
Students Victimized in Public Schools over a One-Month Period in 1976

Size of community	By larcenies of more than $1		By assaults		By robberies of more than $1	
	in junior high schools	in senior high schools	in junior high schools	in senior high schools	in junior high schools	in senior high schools
500,000 or more	14.8% (56)	14.9% (59)	8.5% (56)	3.7% (59)	5.7% (56)	2.8% (59)
100,000–499,999	18.0 (45)	16.8 (36)	7.8 (45)	2.7 (36)	3.6 (45)	1.9 (36)
50,000–99,999	18.0 (23)	15.3 (31)	7.7 (23)	2.9 (31)	3.8 (23)	1.3 (31)
10,000–49,999	15.5 (94)	15.8 (74)	6.8 (94)	2.7 (74)	3.3 (94)	1.4 (74)
2,500–9,999	16.1 (41)	14.6 (47)	7.4 (41)	3.1 (47)	3.5 (41)	1.4 (47)
Under 2,500	15.8 (42)	14.2 (53)	6.2 (42)	3.5 (53)	3.8 (42)	2.0 (53)
All communities	16.0 (301)	15.2 (300)	7.3 (301)	3.1 (300)	3.9 (301)	1.8 (300)

Note: Numbers in parentheses refer to the number of schools on the basis of which the average percent of personal victimization was calculated for each cell.

Source: Special tabulation of data from U.S. Department of Health, Education, and Welfare, *Violent Schools—Safe Schools: The Safe School Study Report to the Congress* (Washington, D.C.: U.S. Govt. Printing Office, 1978).

opportunities to steal from staff members and from students. But in these communities crimes are also committed by the students themselves. Families living in high-crime areas tend to be socially disorganized as well as economically disadvantaged. Poorer parents often do not supervise their children as effectively as parents in wealthier neighborhoods because they themselves are beset by personal problems. Children of such families are more likely to rebel against teacher authority than children in middle-class communities. Student attacks on teachers have been reported in disadvantaged neighborhoods not only in the United States but also in Great Britain, France, Sweden, Japan, and even Mainland China.[3] When students attack teachers, order in the schools becomes necessarily precarious.

Several circumstances have helped create an environment where such attacks are likely to occur. First, compulsory education laws have forced schools to retain students who are basically disinclined to be there. Second, because classrooms are so heterogeneous, problem students of various kinds, including the physically and mentally handicapped, are grouped together with more educable students.[4] Third, ideological changes have stripped teachers and principals of the absolute authority they once had.[5] Finally, teachers have had to cope with serious racial and ethnic tensions.

Disorder in inner-city schools takes many forms. Some students arrive an hour or more late, explaining that they were needed at home to babysit, to market, or to translate for their foreign-born mothers. Others come to school on time, are recorded present in the homeroom where daily absences are officially determined, and then wander the corridors for the rest of the day. Technically, such students are cutting classes; they are not truanting. But under the circumstances such technical distinctions have little practical relevance. Where there is destruction of the walls, furniture, and plumbing in the school, it usually reflects the lack of educational commitment of students physically present in the building but psychologically someplace else.

At the same time, enrolled students not interested in learning undermine the motivation of those more committed to obtaining an education. Teachers also get discouraged. When only a handful of students attempt to complete homework, teachers stop assigning it; and of course, it is difficult to teach a lesson that depends on material taught yesterday or last week when only a few students can be counted on to be regularly in class. Eventually, in these circumstances, teachers stop putting forth the considerable effort required to educate. Some quit teaching for other jobs; some get teaching positions in private or parochial schools at a cut in pay; some take early retirement; some hold on grimly, taking as many days off as they are entitled to, including not only sick days but days in which to escape from pressure (known in the business as "mental health days").

Teacher absences are both a symptom of disorder in the school and a cause of further disorder. Schools whose students present serious academic and behavior problems find substitute teachers difficult to recruit. A substitute's pay is not sufficient compensation for the strain of trying to maintain order in an unruly class— not to mention the fear of possible violence in the school or in its surrounding neighborhood and the anticipation that one's car may be vandalized in the school parking lot. If substitutes cannot be found, students will have to be given "study periods," which are misnamed. When substitutes *are* found, neither they nor the students in the class expect much learning to take place.

Students, both black and white, who are committed to learning transfer out of troubled public institutions to private or parochial schools, or they find a friend or relative to live with in the catchment area of a better school. This siphoning out of the better-behaved, more industrious students makes the problem of controlling the remaining students even more difficult. Class-cutting increases, and students wander through the halls in increasing numbers. In the classrooms, teachers struggle for the attention of students. Students talk with one another; they engage in playful and not-so-playful fights; they leave repeatedly to visit the toilet or to get drinks of water. Some are inattentive because they are intoxicated; they become defiant or abusive when the teacher tries to quiet them. Only a quixotic teacher expects students to take home books and study assigned lessons. In such an atmosphere, violence directed at both students and teachers periodically erupts.

Reducing School Crime

How can school violence be ameliorated? The administration of the public schools is a local responsibility, but in this case a federal initiative may be the most judicious way to attack the problem. One reason for this is that new programs are costly, and the federal government has greater financial resources than the states. Another reason is that there are laws at both the state and federal levels enacted for purposes unrelated to controlling school crime that incidentally *promote* such crime by undermining the authority of teachers and principals.[6] Congress is in a position to alter both, redesigning federal laws that incidentally increase school crime while at the same time inducing states to make similar changes by providing grants-in-aid for those that do so. For example, the federal government could provide grants to increase security guards in the high-crime schools of central cities. Security guards are necessary in such institutions to combat the substantial portion of violence and nonviolent theft that is the work of intruders.[7] Unless intruders can be kept out of schools, or apprehended swiftly after getting in, central-city institutions cannot be made safe. The problem of controlling intruders is complicated by the fact that many them are suspended or expelled students or the friends or relatives of current students. Federal funds have been used in the past to pay for security guards under the aegis of the Comprehensive Employment and Training Act, but the Reagan administration cut the CETA budget drastically, thereby forcing big-city school systems either to reduce their force of security guards or to hire guards out of regular educational budgets.[8] Since few central cities have the budgetary resources to finance sufficient numbers of school security guards, a federal offer to supply such resources is a tempting inducement.

The primary use of security guards is to control adolescent male trespassers who enter school buildings for purposes of stealing or settling a grudge—in effect, to secure the periphery of the school building. Security guards may also produce some incidental deterrence of crimes perpetrated by students against their classmates and teachers; this effect is likely but not proven. A security program cannot, however, be the *main* instrument for coping with the problem of internal violence, because there can never be enough security guards to patrol large junior or senior high schools thoroughly. The question arises: what policy initiatives might be likely to reduce the tendencies for enrolled students to commit crimes in school, especially the violent crimes of assault and robbery, which are most fear-provoking?

Before this question is addressed, let me point out that student violence seems to be concentrated in fewer than one-fourth of the high schools and junior high schools of big-city school systems.[9] The reason for this concentration is that, in any given school system, a competitive process of negative selection tends to operate, with the failures and behavior problems of the system accumulating in schools with bad reputations. Large school systems tend to be internally differentiated. The advantage of a differentiated system is that some schools—like the Bronx High School of Science—can be superior to many private schools. Its disadvantage is that some schools become virtual jungles from the point of view of student and staff safety and wastelands from the point of view of education. Although individual students can escape from such bad schools and, by one device or another, transfer to safer schools with higher educational standards, many youngsters remain trapped. Controlling internal violence more effectively means giving students in the worst schools within a big-city system a chance for safe, effective education.

The Role of Compulsory Attendance

For such schools, unwilling students play a major role in producing the characteristic vicious circle of escalating disorder. From this point of view, the state laws most in need of reconsideration are those governing compulsory school attendance. Only five states (Arkansas, Louisiana, Maine, Mississippi, and Washington) have compulsory attendance laws set at 15 years of age or less;[10] the other forty-five states and the District of Columbia set the age of compulsory school attendance at 16 years or more. These laws are more complex than they seem. Even in states like Hawaii and Ohio, where the age is 18, administrative exceptions are made for unwilling students—provided that the child's parents acquiesce and a job for the student can be obtained. If for whatever reason the parents refuse to sign the youngster out, he or she remains enrolled, although sometimes a chronic truant. One disadvantage of this tug-of-war between children who wish to leave school and parents who fail to give permission is that it forces youngsters into a phantom category: they are neither clear-cut students nor clear-cut participants in the labor market. If the federal government were to induce state legislatures to move to a uniform age of compulsory school attendance of 15 years, it would establish, in effect, an unambiguous boundary between voluntary and involuntary students.

Why 15? Why not 18? The age chosen must necessarily be based on assumptions about the balance between the advantages of attempting to compel education and the disadvantages of school disorder caused by unwilling students. From this standpoint, the age of 15 seems an appropriate place to draw the line. By the time they reach the age of 15, unwilling students become disruptive enough to jeopardize the educational process, especially in secondary schools enrolling large numbers of students from impoverished homes. Furthermore, the possibility that coerced attendance will produce educational benefits becomes increasingly unrealistic.

But if the age of compulsory attendance were lowered to 15, wouldn't an enormous number of students drop out? Actually, the numbers of 15-, 16-, and 17-year-old students leaving school would probably be in the tens of thousands, and not, as some might assume, in the millions. I base this estimate on an analysis of 1970 census data on school enrollment in states with varying ages of compulsory attendance. There were only small differences in the enrollment of 16- and 17-year-olds between states with low ages of compulsory school attendance and those with high ages, as table 3 shows. Compulsory attendance laws seem to be a minor factor in enrollment and very likely a less important factor in actual attendance.

Teenagers go to school because they have been convinced by their parents, their friends, and the general culture that it is a good idea. By the time youngsters reach the age of 15, compulsory school attendance laws will do little to persuade those who have not accepted this idea to participate in a meaningful way in the educational process. Conversely, students who consider school valuable to their future lives will not drop out just because the

Table 3

White Males Enrolled in School
by Age and State of Residence, 1970

| Age of white males enrolled in school | State law requires compulsory attendance to: | | Difference |
	Age 15 or less (five states)	Age 18 (four states)	
14	94.6%	97.1%	2.5%
15	93.7	96.5	2.8
16	90.2	94.9	4.7
17	85.8	90.1	4.3
18	70.3	71.3	1.0

Source: U.S. Bureau of the Census, *Census of Population,* vol. I (Washington, D.C.: U.S. Govt. Printing Office, 1973), ch. D, parts 5, 13, 20, 21, 37, 39, 46, 49.

laws no longer insist on attendance. Conceivably, a reduction in the age of compulsory school attendance may *increase* public school enrollments. In Hawaii, for example, where that age is 18, where a tenth of the state's secondary school students are enrolled in private schools,[11] and where the public secondary schools have a reputation for low academic performance and sporadic violence,[12] a lower age of compulsory school attendance might well improve the educational climate in public schools sufficiently to lure back some private-school students.

Effect on School Crime

Even though only small numbers of students would leave if the age of compulsory school attendance were reduced to 15, their absence would make possible a significantly better educational climate. At present, we coerce the attendance of a handful of unwilling students at the price of promoting a climate of violence and fear in many public secondary schools.[13] This in turn makes it especially difficult for public schools to rival private schools in educational accomplishment.[14] By lowering the age of compulsory school attendance, not only would we soon rid the schools of many disruptive youngsters, but the control of teachers and school administrators over unruly students over 15 who remain would be enhanced. In *Goss* v. *Lopez*,[15] the Supreme Court held that in enacting a compulsory school attendance law, a state incurred an *obligation* to educate children until the age specified in the law was reached. Although this ruling did not render impossible the expulsion of disruptive or violent students subject to compulsory attendance, it made it very difficult. As a result, many central-city schools have tended to abandon expulsion as the ultimate enforcer of strict discipline.[16] Thus one consequence of a lower age of compulsory school attendance will be that students who assault teachers or fellow students can, when they pass 15, be forced to choose between adopting acceptable behavior or leaving school. Of course, students under 15 will continue to be protected from expulsion. But presumably younger students with behavior problems are better candidates for reform through counseling than older ones.

Past experience with varying ages of compulsory attendance in different states suggests strongly that such a policy can in fact improve the climates of troubled schools. The National Center for Education Statistics collected data on school crime from the fifty states in the fall semester of 1974–75.[17] Researchers tallied incidents serious enough to result in reports to the police and computed rates per thousand enrolled students for each state. As table 4 shows, higher compulsory attendance ages went hand in hand with higher rates of secondary school crime: in the five states with a compulsory attendance age of 15 or less, the average rate of secondary school crime was 8.0; in the thirty-six states and the District of Columbia with a compulsory age of 16, it was 10.5; in the five states with a compulsory age of 17, it was 11.6; while the four states with a compulsory age of 18 had an average of 20.1. (As would be expected, corresponding rates of elementary school crime differed only marginally.) Crude though these data are— states vary in urbanization, ethnic composition, and economic development—they suggest that the higher the age of compulsory attendance, the more school crime.

There are other advantages to be had from lowering the compulsory attendance age. For one thing, it would simply clarify for many students the difference between being in school and out. At present many mischievous students behave in school much as

Table 4
Referral of School Crimes to the Police
by Age of Compulsory School
Attendance in the State, 1974–75

Age of compulsory school attendance	Average rate per thousand enrolled students		Difference
	In elementary schools	In secondary schools	
15 or less (5 states: Arkansas, Louisiana, Maine, Mississippi, Washington)	3.1	8.0	4.9
16 (36 states and the District of Columbia)	3.2	10.5	7.3
17 (Nevada, New Mexico, Pennsylvania, Texas, Virginia)	3.8	11.6	7.8
18[a] (Hawaii, Ohio, Oregon, Utah)	4.8	20.1	15.3

[a]Because there are so few states in the 18 age group, extreme values for one of them greatly influence the average. Hawaii, for example, had by far the highest rate of school crime on both the elementary and secondary levels. If Hawaii were excluded from the average and the remaining eight states with compulsory ages of school attendance of 17 or higher were averaged, the result would be 4.0 for elementary schools and 11.4 for secondary schools, with a difference of 7.4.

Source: Computed from data published in U.S. Department of Health, Education, and Welfare, *Violent Schools—Safe Schools: The Safe School Study Report to the Congress* (Washington, D.C.: U.S. Govt. Printing Office, 1978), Appendix B, p. 6.

they do in the playgrounds or the streets. In schools where such students predominate, youngsters tend to be pitifully unaware of just how little educational benefit they are obtaining from their presence in the school building. One finding of a study of minority students in San Francisco public schools uncovered a startling discrepancy between the objective inadequacies of student performance in reading and other basic skills and the students' lack of awareness of these handicaps.[18] Youngsters who were barely literate, who attended school irregularly, and who never studied, nevertheless believed that they could attend college and become doctors and lawyers. By establishing high classroom standards and then insisting that studious behavior is necessary, society would clarify the choice presented to youngsters in the public schools. This clarification of the meaning of school already occurs in selective private and public schools where education is taken seriously; it was clear, for example, in Dunbar High School, an all-black high school in Washington, D.C., where from the years 1870 to 1955 black children were selected for their aspirations rather than for their abilities, were made to work hard, and in a majority of cases went on to college.[19]

There are those who decry educational seriousness, who say that children should not stake their self-esteem on academic achievement, and who cite the high rate of adolescent suicide in Japan as the *reductio ad absurdum* of overcommitment to academic achievement. But the junior and senior high schools in the central cities of the United States are in no danger of resembling the high schools of Japan. In general, our secondary school students need to take education far more seriously than they do. Contrary to the impression prevailing among many American youngsters, a school should not be attended for the excellence of its athletic facilities or for the opportunities it offers to meet members of the opposite sex. Making education more voluntary will help to emphasize the true purpose of school attendance.

Of course, every effort should be made to persuade those who decide to leave that they should return to school whenever they feel ready to pursue further education. Scandinavian countries are more successful than the United States at institutionalizing the idea that resumption of education is possible at any age.

Impact Outside of Schools

Even so, the notion of allowing tens of thousands of youngsters to leave school, even temporarily, is daunting. If youngsters are put out of the schools and into the streets, won't they turn to crime? After all, they will have little chance of obtaining employment without experience or education.

In fact, although truants and dropouts have a higher crime rate than high school graduates,[20] the usual inference that dropping out of school leads to involuntary unemployment and eventually to criminality seems to be incorrect. There are two excellent longitudinal studies that follow students carefully throughout their high school years,[21] gathering data covering the entire time period. In one study, official arrest records and self-reported crimes were monitored; in the other, only self-reported offenses. The studies were conducted independently—one in California, the other in the nation as a whole—yet the results were identical. In both cases, the higher delinquency rate of the dropouts was found to *precede* their dropping out of school. In the national study the rate remained at the same high level after the students dropped out of school; in the California study, delinquency actually declined somewhat after the students left. Somewhat surprisingly, dropouts did not appear to be seriously disadvantaged in the labor market compared with high school graduates who did not go on to college.

Apparently, characteristics that lead to higher-than-average delinquency rates manifest themselves while students are still enrolled in school. To put it another way, American society would probably not experience a crime epidemic even if large numbers of youngsters responded to the lower age of compulsory school attendance by dropping out. This conclusion is also compatible with the fact that arrests of juvenile offenders are not appreciably greater during the summer vacation or other holiday periods than when schools are in session. In short, the impact of compulsory attendance laws on antisocial youngsters has probably been exaggerated. Even if delinquent students attended school regularly, which few do, the school day is short enough to leave time and energy for plenty of crime.

In addition to inducing the states to lower to 15 the age of compulsory school attendance, Congress should change federal laws that give youngsters uninterested in education an incentive to remain enrolled in school, such as statutes governing welfare benefits under the program of Aid to Families with Dependent Children (AFDC). Although his family qualifies for AFDC benefits, an older child himself may not. Eligibility for continued benefits for children over 16 and under 21 normally depends on certification by the local school system that the child is indeed enrolled in school. Thus even if a youngster is no longer attending school regularly, continued enrollment is financially advantageous for the family. A study by the Office of Research and Statistics of the Social Security Administration showed that about 90 percent of the AFDC youngsters from 18 to 20 were enrolled in school.[22] Since fewer than 45 percent of the 18- to 20-year-olds in the general population are enrolled in school,[23] it appears that AFDC benefits act as an incentive for continued school enrollment.[24] Section 402(a)(8)(A) of the Social Security Act operates as a similar incentive for AFDC children by excluding the earnings of a dependent child in calculating the eligibility of the family for benefits—provided that the child is enrolled in school.

Of course, it is possible that these provisions persuade youngsters from disadvantaged families to improve their verbal and other skills by continuing in school longer than they otherwise would. But it is also likely that continued enrollment is educationally meaningless for many of these youngsters—even if they are actually enrolled—and serves merely to delay their entrance into the labor market. Meanwhile, there are signs that many youths may be attending school only sporadically and may be contributing to school violence. In the course of a study of the labor market problems of teenagers, the United States General Accounting Office concluded that "consideration should be given to changing the rules of the current AFDC program so as to disregard all the earnings of dependent children (ages 14 to 17), regardless of their school status, when calculating the families' 'entitlement.'"[25] Tying AFDC benefits to school enrollment has an effect similar to that of compulsory attendance laws: pressuring uninterested students to remain enrolled in school. If AFDC benefits were available to children of 14 to 17 regardless of employment status or school attendance, there would be less reason to remain enrolled without a willingness to learn.

No one knows exactly how many students would leave the public secondary schools if there were not financial incentives to stay because of AFDC eligibility and if the compulsory attendance laws were lowered to 15. Although the initial numbers may not be large, as schools succeed in increasing educational require- ments—attendance, homework, a reduction of horseplay—their attractiveness as places in which to socialize with friends may decline. Dropouts will increase further. Can the federal govern- ment do anything to help integrate such youngsters into the larger society?

The Youth Unemployment Problem

Given the high unemployment rate among teenagers, it is not easy for students who leave school to find jobs. They lack the work ex- perience, training, and necessary reading and writing skills,[26] deficiencies that are not easily remedied by government pro- grams. Many teenagers are also uninterested in working. Others are undecided about occupational interests and shift from job to job, thereby creating transitional periods of unemployment. But there are certainly some teenagers eager to find work of almost any kind and unable to do so. Both minimum wage laws and child labor laws contribute to their difficulties.

Minimum wage laws are especially troublesome. Economists have pointed out for years that the minimum wage prices teenagers out of the labor market because unskilled and inex- perienced youngsters are not worth as much to employers as older workers.[27] Minimum wage laws may place legal requirements on employers, but they do not repeal the laws of economics. If employers cannot hire teenagers for what they are worth, they substitute labor-saving equipment or older workers whose skill and experience make them worth the minimum wage or more. On the other hand, if subminimum wages can be paid to teenagers, employers have an incentive to hire them and in effect to offer them training.

Labor unions have traditionally resisted subminimum wages for young workers, fearing that these low rates depress wages for all workers. Most economists regard this fear as exaggerated, because teenage workers are not in competition for skilled, responsible positions. Youngsters can obtain only the entry-level unskilled jobs that most adults do not want.

Moreover, minimum wage laws assume, usually incorrectly, that an adolescent living with his parents needs as high a wage as adults with family responsibilities. As Nathan Glazer notes, "It is because we think of the individual worker alone rather than the family that we find it easy to accept as a public policy that 16-year-old dropouts without experience should be paid the same wages as heads of families—which is the policy of our youth employment programs."[28] Finally, there are good reasons to believe that society's interest in socializing adolescents to adult work requirements may outweigh the benefits to adult workers of reducing competition by low-paid workers.

A lower wage structure for teenagers would only marginally reduce school violence. But a relaxation of the minimum wage laws applicable to teenagers would help all young people to obtain job experience, in part-time as well as full-time work. Hence a sub-minimum wage for teenagers has more to recommend it than its incidental effect on school crime. On the other hand, modifying minimum wage laws does not guarantee that dropouts will make a good work adjustment. The same characteristics that cause some students to be violent and disruptive in school make them undesirable employees as dropouts even if they are willing to work for a low wage. Nevertheless, it is probable that some students who were chronic offenders at school will find in the workplace less frustration and a new chance for self-respect. Thus modification of minimum wage laws could contribute modestly to the rehabilitation of some youngsters whom the schools find intractable. Bear in mind, of course, that abolishing legal barriers to the employment of teenagers at lower than adult wages does not mean that teenagers will actually work for less than adults receive. All such choices are subject to the mechanisms of the marketplace. Some teenagers will spurn low-paid jobs, preferring street crime, dependence on their parents, or welfare. What modification of the minimum wage laws can do is to provide opportunities for work experience to teenagers who might otherwise not be employable, even though eager to work.

The younger the worker, the less valuable he or she will be to an employer—consequently, the greater the incentive should be. One way to accomplish this objective is to establish a graduated minimum wage for teenagers. Fifteen-year-olds might be permitted to work for 60 percent of the adult minimum wage, 16-year-olds for 70 percent, 17-year-olds for 80 percent, and 18- and 19-year-olds for 90 percent.[29] Congress should not only modify federal wage laws but should attempt to induce the states to modify state minimum wage laws along the same lines. (As with congressional efforts to persuade states to lower their age of compulsory school attendance to 15, the incentive could be provided by grants for additional security guards in public schools.)

If the age of compulsory schooling were reduced to 15, if the secondary schools took advantage of the new situation to insist on higher educational standards, and if those teenagers who chose not to remain enrolled in schools had a better chance of obtaining jobs, the school violence problem would surely become less serious, though it would not disappear any more than crime in the larger society would disappear.

There are some continuing causes of school crime that this program cannot adequately address:

• *Intruders.* A considerable amount of school crime, particularly violent crime in central-city schools, is committed by intruders rather than by enrolled students. Not only would intruders continue to be a problem after the above-mentioned measures are taken, but they might become a more serious problem because the population of out-of-school youth would be larger. Former students would tend to retain their interest in friends, including girlfriends, and in the illegal activities that go on in school (e.g., drug traffic). Hence some dropouts would try to enter the school although they would no longer be entitled to do so. Therefore an effective safe-schools program must devote greater resources to security, including additional guards, than most school systems can afford at the present time. Nevertheless, the intruder problem may be made more manageable by federal grants for increased school security.

• *Crime and truancy among younger students.* The new program to reduce school crime, since it is geared to youngsters over the age of 15, addresses mainly the crime problem in the eighth through twelfth grades. Youngsters below 15 will still rob and assault their classmates—and, more rarely, teachers and staff members in their schools. Possibly the improved atmosphere in the high schools and in the upper grades of junior high and intermediate schools will seep down to the lower grades, but this remains to be seen. However, school systems relieved of the problem of coping with the behavior problems of students *over* 15 may be better able to address the difficulties posed by unruly students *under* 15. Consider, for example, truancy, which has reached epidemic proportions in many central-city high schools.[30] If the attendance teachers (truant officers) and counselors now dealing with chronic truants over 15 were to spend their time instead handling the attendance problems of preadolescents, fewer children would miss school on a regular basis. With truancy as with other deviant patterns of behavior, prevention may be easier than cure.

• *Lack of family cooperation.* The new program will not solve the problem of student misconduct stemming from family cultures unsupportive of academic achievement in the early grades. Since poor self-esteem resulting from deficient academic performance has been shown to be related to involvement in delinquency generally[31] and to school crime in particular,[32] the new program will not address the motivational roots of school crime. What it *will* accomplish is to control better the overt expression of these deviant motivations.[33] Of course, a program that addresses the root causes of school failure would be helpful to individual students as well as to schools and communities, but society cannot delay crime control in school until this more basic strategy of school crime prevention becomes practicable.

In America, public education has traditionally functioned as a social escalator, carrying talented children from poorer families into higher-paying business or professional careers.[34] Particularly in the slum neighborhoods of central cities, public schools in former days offered prospects of a bright future for intelligent, diligent children with academic aptitude. Most public schools still offer this opportunity to enrolled students. School violence, however, has reinforced other threats to order in many large secondary schools in central cities. The result is that some schools are schools in name only—from which even able and motivated youngsters cannot learn what they need to know in order to escape from poverty. Children enrolled in such schools will remain at the bottom of the socioeconomic heap; not only will they suffer as a result, but American society will lose the chance to draw upon their talents.

Tuition tax credits and educational vouchers—remedies often proposed for this problem—would indeed enable children from disorderly public schools to find their way to private schools with high academic standards and an orderly atmosphere, but that would also leave large numbers of students behind, trapped in schools that offered no real hope. The approach suggested in this article is designed to improve all schools, including the worst, until they reach minimum standards of safety and education. In this way, children from "bad" public schools, many of whom come from backgrounds of poverty, will retain a chance for social mobility through educational achievement.

6

RICHARD B. FREEMAN

Crime and Unemployment

> Are there people really walking around saying there is
> no relationship between crime and unemployment?
> Are we beating a dead horse here? Is there a
> unanimous consensus on the subject or do we have
> something more to prove?
>
> *Rep. John Conyers, in Hearings*
> *before the Subcommittee on*
> *Crime of the House Judiciary*
> *Committee*

The notion that the labor market, through unemployment, is an important determinant of the crime level has a definite appeal. A person with a full-time high-paying job is, most of us believe, less likely to engage in crime, particularly economic crime, than someone out of work. After all, isn't idle time the devil's handmaiden?

Despite the surface plausibility of this assumption, however, empirical analysis shows at best only a moderate link between unemployment and crime. In some analyses the expected significant positive relation is found, but in others it is not. Similarly, some studies find a significant positive relation between poverty (measured in various ways) and crime, while others fail to show such a correlation. No one would gainsay that there is some correlation between the labor market and crime, but the strength and magnitude of the link are more subtle and difficult to determine than one might expect.

This chapter examines modern research on the relation between the labor market and crime. There have been some reviews of the literature concerning this relationship (especially in terms of unemployment),[1] but in general the subject has not received the same attention as the effect of criminal sanctions on crime rates.[2] This imbalance is unfortunate, for it encourages us to direct attention disproportionately to the "stick" of deterrence rather than to the "carrot" of improved employment prospects, despite the fact that the behavior of potential criminals depends on both.

We will begin with a brief review of the economic rationale for expecting the labor market to influence crime, consider the various methods used by social scientists to study the expected relationship, and then turn to the main issue: the empirical findings of the various studies.

Expected Link between Unemployment and Crime

Modern economic analysis of criminal behavior is based on an individual choice model that treats the decision to engage in crime in the same manner as a decision to engage in any other potentially money-making activity.[3] It postulates that an individual chooses to commit a crime depending on the expected benefits and costs. The benefit from crime depends on the chance of success and money (utility) being obtained; the expected cost depends on the chance of being caught (1 minus the probability of success) and convicted, on the criminal sanctions involved, and on the earnings lost as a result of imprisonment and the time allotted to the criminal activity. In this framework, the labor market is expected to influence criminal behavior on the cost side: workers with high-paying jobs will presumably commit less crime than workers with low-paying jobs or without jobs because the higher paid face a greater opportunity cost from crime. Their time is more valuably spent in legitimate activities, and they risk losing more income from incarceration than the unemployed or persons with low wages. Because crime is risky, attitude toward risk also plays an important role in the decision. Since few would disagree that people respond to incentives in rational ways, the issue in analysis is the magnitude of such responses—whether they are important enough to show up in observed data. It is for this reason that the vast majority of studies have had an empirical orientation.

Methods of Empirical Studies

Social scientists have sought to measure the impact of labor market conditions on crime using four distinct types of studies, each of which has particular advantages and disadvantages for pinning down the relationship.

The first is time series analysis, in which the crime rate is compared to the level of unemployment and related labor market indicators over time. This is the most direct way to examine the effect of the business cycle on crime and thus to answer the broad question of what might happen to crime levels if overall job prospects improved. But time series analysis suffers from a myriad of problems. Most serious is the so-called "collinearity" of variables (the tendency for many variables to move together over time, providing little variation from which to discern the independent effect of each). Time series data also pose a more basic interpretative problem: an analysis that shows that crime varies over the business cycle can be interpreted as indicating that unemployment affects the *timing* rather than the *level* of crime. A person who decides to commit a robbery, for example, may be more likely to rob during a recession because of a lack of alternatives, but might be disposed to commit the crime eventually anyway. The situation is analagous with that of a woman who decides to work one quarter out of the year. When stores hire additional sales clerks for the Christmas season, she chooses, rationally enough, to work then, but even in the absence of such seasonal demand for labor she would still work one quarter a year.

A second approach employs cross-sectional analysis of crime rates and labor market conditions across geographic areas. In contrast to time series analysis, cross-sectional studies are more likely to reveal "permanent" responses of crime rates to unemployment than the timing of decisions, and are generally free from problems of collinearity. But these studies suffer from their own set of inference problems. Areas may differ in both labor market conditions and crime rates for reasons having to do with the unmeasured "nature" of the area. Such a circumstance can produce spurious correlations or hide true ones. Also, the migration of criminals, say from high-unemployment to low-unemployment areas, may eliminate the link of unemployment to crime in area data, despite the fact that high-unemployment conditions create more criminals. Finally, there is the so-called "ecological correlation" problem— the difficulty of making inferences about individual behavior from aggregate relations. It turns out, for example, that in several cross-sectional studies, crime is shown to be inversely related to the percentage of nonwhites in an area. At face value, this would imply either that blacks are statistically less likely to be criminals or that black areas are subject to less crime than white areas—both highly questionable conclusions in light of other data.

Researchers also make use of comparisons of individuals who commit crimes with those who do not. Analyzing the economic model of crime in light of data for individuals has the advantage of focusing on actual decision-makers. For characteristics of individuals that are relatively fixed (race, sex, age, education) it provides a useful tool for inferring differences in crime rates. For variables that change or are potentially controlled by the individual, however, there are serious inference problems. One could, for example, interpret the fact that criminals are more likely to be unemployed than others in two ways: as supporting the claim that unemployment led the person into crime, or as indicating that the person was unemployed because he or she counted on crime as his or her main source of income. The direction of the causal link is, in the absence of other information, impossible to determine.

Finally, there have been actual social experiments in which the government has altered the labor market opportunities for criminals, as in the Transitional Aid Research Project (TARP). (These experiments are described later in the chapter.) One way to test whether jobs will reduce crime among criminals is to provide jobs at specified levels of pay to part of a population released from prison while letting the other part fend on its own. Presumably the group with jobs will have a lower crime rate. Such an experiment can help make clear the direction of causation between crime and unemployment. In fact, most experiments have not "guaranteed" jobs to offenders but rather have provided them with job placement and income support for several months after prison. The effects on behavior can thus be expected to be more complex.[4] Even if experiments were more tightly constructed, there would still be a danger of "experimental contamination," since jobs generated by a governmental program may differ from those generated in a free market.

In short, all of the methods used for studying the labor market/crime link have their limitations. Each provides a potential answer to a somewhat different question. The time series evidence, for example, enables us to determine whether crime varies over the business cycle; the experimental evidence indicates whether providing job assistance to criminals will reduce their incidence of crime but tells us nothing about the link between joblessness and crime among persons who have not committed crimes. Each of the methods, moreover, is subject to the problems of nonlaboratory data analysis. And because each method yields results somewhat at odds with the others, no unanimous consensus on the problem has emerged.

Time Series Results

Table 1 summarizes the results of a variety of time series analyses of the link between labor market factors and crime. In some cases, the studies have also explored the link between crime and variables describing deterrent measures (such as chances of being convicted, length of criminal sentences). The models vary greatly in time coverage, variables chosen, and statistical technique. The latter range from simple regression analyses of the relation between changes in crime and changes in unemployment (Phillips), to sophisticated time series systems models (Phillips and Ray). All but one of the models examine the effect of unemployment rates on crime; some also examine the effect of labor force participation rates. Because of problems posed by the collinearity, or overlapping influence, of the factors involved, comparatively few of the studies look in addition at other labor market variables, such as

Table 1
Contents of Time Series Studies

Author and nature of study	Effects of unemployment	Effects of labor force participation	Effect of other labor market variables	Comparison to deterrence variable
Fleisher, Analysis of Age-Specific Arrest Rates in Three Cities, 1930s–1950s	yes	—	—	—
Phillips, Votey, and Maxwell, Analysis of Age-Specific Arrest Rates, 18–19 Year Olds, 1952–1967	yes	yes	—	—
Phillips, Analysis of Age-Specific Arrest Rates, 18–19 Year Olds, 1964–1977	yes	yes	—	—
Phillips and Ray, Analysis of California Homicide Rate	yes (3⅓ year lag)	—	—	unemployment is weaker
Brenner, Analysis of Homicide, Arrest Rates, and Unemployment, 1940–1973, 1952–1975	yes	—	yes, per capita income	—
Danziger and Wheeler, Analysis of Property Crime Rates, 1949–1970	no	—	yes, income inequality	—
Ehrlich, Analysis of Murder Rate, 1933–1969	yes	yes	yes, median income	unemployment is weaker

Orsagh, Analysis of Crime Rate, 1950–1974	yes		—	—	
Leveson, Analysis of Crime Rate and Youth Unemployment	yes		—	—	—
Land and Felson, Various Crimes, 1947–1972	yes		—	—	— unemployment is weaker

— Indicates did not include variable in analysis.

Sources: B. M. Fleisher, "The Effects of Unemployment on Juvenile Delinquency," *Journal of Political Economy* 71 (December 1963): 543–55; L. Phillips, H. L. Votey, Jr., and D. Maxwell, "Crime and Youth and the Labor Market," *Journal of Political Economy* 80 (May–June 1972): 491–504; Llad Phillips, "Some Aspects of the Social Pathological Behavioral Effects of Unemployment among Young People," in *The Economics of Minimum Wages*, ed. Simon Rottenberg (Washington, D.C., and London: American Enterprise Institute, 1981); Llad Phillips and Subhash Ray, "Evidence on the Identification and Causality Dispute about the Death Penalty," in *Applied Time-Series Analysis*, ed. O. P. Anderson and M. R. Perryman (New York: North-Holland, forthcoming); H. Brenner, Statement on Unemployment and Crime, Hearings before the Subcommittee on Crime of the Committee of the Judiciary of the House of Representatives, 1978; S. Danziger and D. Wheeler, "The Economics of Crime: Punishment or Income Redistribution," *Review of Social Economy* 33 (October 1975): 113–31; Isaac Ehrlich, "The Deterrent Effect of Capital Punishment: A Question of Life and Death," *American Economic Review* 65 (June 1975): 397–417; T. Orsagh, "Empirical Criminology: Interpreting Results Derived from Aggregate Data," *Journal of Research in Crime and Delinquency* 16 (July 1979): 294–306; Irving Leveson, "The Growth of Crime" (Hudson Institute, Croton-on-Hudson, N.Y., 1976, Mimeographed); K. C. Land and M. Felson, "A General Framework for Building Dynamic Macro Social Indicator Models: Including an Analysis of Changes in Crime Rates and Police Expenditures," *American Journal of Sociology* 82 (November 1976): 565–604.

income. Three compare the impact of deterrent measures to that of unemployment. And all of the studies suffer to one degree or another from some of the standard problems of nonexperimental data analysis (poorly measured variables; omission of variables; variation in the magnitude of results depending on the precise specification of the equation, and so on).[5]

Despite differences and weaknesses among the studies, a general finding emerges: namely, that rises in unemployment and/or declines in labor participation rates are connected with rises in the crime rate, but that the effect tends to be modest and insufficient to explain the general upward trend of crime in the period studied. The labor participation rate is, moreover, often found to have a closer link to crime than does unemployment, suggesting that those who actually leave the labor force are the most crime prone. In the few studies that include income variables, higher income in an area (interpreted as a measure of the marginal benefits to be derived from crime) was linked to higher crime, apparently because there is more to be gotten from high-income areas. Income inequality was also found to be positively related to crime. The three studies that included deterrence variables found them to be more closely related to crime than were the labor market variables.

To provide a general picture of the nature of time series evidence, figure 1 graphs the relation between the uniform crime rate and the unemployment rate for the period 1947 to 1980. The crime rate is dominated by an upward trend, but there is also a definite cyclical component related to unemployment, which can be seen in the scatter diagram. The relation is, however, quite weak, as the reader will notice by comparing the levels of crime in the booming late 1960s with the levels in the higher-unemployment early 1960s/late 1950s. In 1961, with an unemployment rate of 6.6 percent the crime rate was just 1.9, compared to a rate of 3.7 in 1969 when unemployment was a bare 3.4 percent. In short, unemployment influences crime, but the post–World War II rate of crime is dominated by an upward trend owing to other factors.

A regression analysis of the effect of the unemployment rate on crime, using a time trend variable to cancel out the upward movement, shows the relation between crime and unemployment to be weak: according to this analysis, a one-unit change in

Figure 1

Relationship of Crime Rate to Unemployment, 1947–1980

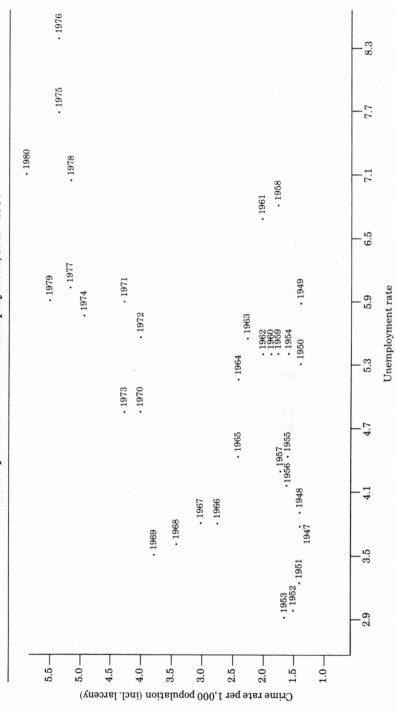

unemployment will result in a rise in the uniform crime rate of 0.05 per 100,000 inhabitants—an increase of moderate statistical significance.[6] Thus, a halving of the unemployment rate from 10 to 5 percent would reduce the crime rate by 5 percent in the 1980s, though whether this would represent a permanent decrease in crime or simply a shifting in crime from a low- to high-unemployment year cannot be determined.

In sum, while not all of the analyses in table 1 yield significant results and while none shows unemployment to be the dominant determinant of crime, they do lend overall support to the notion that crime varies over the business cycle.

Cross Section Results

There have been a large number of studies comparing crime rates across states, cities, or SMSAs (standard metropolitan statistical areas). Sample sizes, variables, and the periods covered differ considerably. In recent years many of the studies have made use of what are termed "simultaneous equations." A typical model includes two equations: one relating crime to criminal penalties or resources spent on police, labor market conditions, and other factors; another relating the level of criminal penalties or police resources to the factors that determine them.

Table 2 summarizes the results of these studies, dividing the findings into four categories: those showing strong (statistically significant) effects in the expected direction (i.e., rising unemployment with rising crime); those showing weak (insignificant) effects in the expected direction; and those showing strong or weak effects in the opposite direction. Because findings are sometimes ambiguous, the categorization is rough. But while one could change some of the classifications, the table provides a reasonably fair picture of the overall results.

The majority of studies show significant relationships between unemployment and crime. Of those that do show significant results, all are in the expected direction, and the majority show a positive relation. Whether this is to be taken as strong or weak evidence for the effect of unemployment on crime is not entirely clear. The preponderance of evidence is more favorable to a positive linkage than not, but if one were anticipating an overwhelmingly strong relation, one would be severely disappointed.

Table 2
Results of Studies on Labor Market Crime Link

	Number of studies showing specified link to crime			
	Strong correct direction	Weak correct direction	Weak incorrect direction	Strong incorrect direction
1. Unemployment	4	7	4	0
2. Income as incentive to commit crime (average income)	5	3	3	1
3. Income as cost of crime (income of poor; percent of population in poverty)	4	3	1	0
4. Criminal sanctions	10	3	4	0

Sources: John P. Allison, "Economic Factors and the Rate of Crime," *Land Economics* 2 (May 1972): 193–96; Ann P. Bartel, "Women and Crime: An Economic Analysis," *Economic Inquiry* 17 (January 1979): 29–51; Isaac Ehrlich, "Participation in Illegitimate Activities: A Theoretical and Empirical Investigation," *Journal of Political Economy* 81 (May/June 1973): 521–65; idem, "Capital Punishment and Deterrence: Some Further Thoughts and Additional Evidence," in *Criminology Yearbook Review*, vol. 1, ed. Sheldon L. Messinger and Egon Bittner (Beverly Hills, Calif.: Sage, 1979); B. M. Fleisher, "The Effect of Income on Delinquency," *American Economic Review* 56 (March 1966): 118–37; B. Forst, "Participation in Illegitimate Activities: Further Empirical Findings," *Policy Analysis* 2 (Summer 1976): 477–92; M. Greenwood and W. J. Wadycki, "Crime Rates and Public Expenditures for Police Protection: Their Interaction," *Review of Social Economy* 31 (1973): 138–51; R. F. Grieson, "The Determinants of Juvenile Arrests," Working Paper no. 87 (Cambridge, Mass.: MIT, 1972); J. A. Gylys, "The Causes of Crime and Application of Regional Analysis," *Atlanta Economic Review* 20 (September 1970): 34–37; Irving Hoch, "Factors in Urban Crime," *Journal of Urban Economics* 1 (April 1974): 184–229; K. C. Land and M. Felson, "A General Framework for Building Dynamic Macro Social Indicator Models: Including an Analysis of Changes in Crime Rates and Police Expenditures," *American Journal of Sociology* 82 (November 1976): 565–604; Vijay Mather, "Economics of Crime: An Investigation of the Deterrent Hypothesis for Urban Areas," *Review of Economics and Statistics* 60 (1978): 459–60; Lee R. McPheters and William B. Stronge, "Law Enforcement Expenditures and Urban Crime," in *The Economics of Crime and Law Enforcement*, ed. Lee R. McPheters and William B. Stronge (Springfield, Ill.: Charles C. Thomas, 1976); J. Nagel, Statement on Unemployment and Crime, Hearings before the Subcommittee on Crime of the Committee of the Judiciary of the House of Representatives, 1978; Thomas F. Pogue, "Effects of Police Expenditures on Crime Rates: Some Evidence," *Public Finance Quarterly* 3 (January 1975): 14–44; Richard Quinney, "Structural Characteristics, Population Areas, and Crime Rates in the United States," *Journal of Criminal Law, Criminology and Police Science* 57 (March 1966): 45–52; D. I. Sjoquist, "Property Crime and Economic Behavior: Some Empirical Results," *American Economic Review* 63 (June 1973): 439–46; Eugene Swimmer, "Measurement of the Effectiveness of Urban Law Enforcement—A Simultaneous Approach," *Southern Economic Journal* 40 (April 1974): 618–30; John C. Weicher, "The Effect of Income and Delinquency: Comment," *American Economic Review* 60 (March 1970): 249–56.

The results with respect to other market variables are similar. Studies normally use the income of the overall population in an area viewed as a measure of the possible gain to the criminal from economic crime, and the fraction of the population in poverty (or some related variable) as an indicator of the opportunity cost of crime. Crime rates vary with respect to these variables in the expected direction and are significant in a fair number, but not a majority, of cases.

For purposes of comparison, table 2 shows results for estimated effects of criminal sanctions on crime. Here, the results are noticeably stronger, with the majority of studies suggesting that relatively severe sanctions are correlated with reductions in crime.

Why should results for criminal sanctions be so much less ambiguous than results for unemployment? One possibility is that considerable effort has gone into estimating deterrent effects of criminal sanctions, while the labor market factors—usually entered solely as "controls"—have not received such careful attention. As a result, the variables for deterrence measures or criminal sanctions may be better measured than are the labor market variables, and statistical models may be more suitable for pinning down deterrence effects than for tracing the impact of unemployment.[7] For example, most cross-sectional studies use a simple aggregate unemployment rate. The level of crime among young people out of work suggests that a youth-out-of-labor-force measure might be better.

A second reason for this divergence of results may be the different character of the variables. Deterrence variables relate *directly* to the options facing potential criminals, while general labor market variables do not: the potential criminal may be quite responsive to his own unemployment (or wage) prospects but those prospects may be only weakly related to aggregate market conditions.

Finally, how should we assess the scorecard results in Table 2? In its evaluation of studies on the effect of deterrence on crime, the NAS–NRC Panel on Research on Deterrent and Incapacitative Effects concluded that "we cannot yet assert that the evidence warrants an affirmative conclusion regarding deterrence ... [although] ... the evidence certainly favors a proposition supporting deterrence more than it favors one asserting that deterrence is absent. . . ."[8] The results for labor market variables are generally less decisive than those for deterrence variables, so readers who agree with the panel's conclusion on deterrence will be even more circumspect in reaching the affirmative conclusion regarding unemployment and other labor market factors. They may agree with Orsagh and Witte that the economic model of crime "as that model relates to unemployment and income is not confirmed by tests performed on aggregate data sets."[9] After all, labor market variables yield more insignificant than significant coefficients. My view is more positive with respect to both the deterrence and labor market results. It is, however, clear that the evidence is not strong enough to yield Rep. Conyers' "unanimous consensus."

Studies of Individuals

Take a group of convicted criminals, and compare their work record with that of other citizens of the same age and sex. Invariably one will find that the criminals will have a much spottier work history: they will have lower skills, lower wages when working, and considerably more unemployment than the average (see table 3). While at first glance this might be taken as clear-cut evidence that unemployment and poor labor market performance are a major cause of crime, interpretation of analyses of individuals in fact yields more ambiguous results than might appear at first glance, for several reasons.

First, instead of showing the effect of unemployment (and other labor market failures) on crime, the data on individuals may reflect the fact that the criminal population consists of people who are unable to succeed in the mainstream society because of "personal characteristics." That is, the cause of both the unemployment and the criminal activity may be a third variable having to do with specific attributes of the individuals. If this were the case, changes in labor market conditions would have little or no effect on the criminal's life of crime, although we would always find poor work records among criminals.

Second, the potential criminal may have chosen unemployment in preparation for criminal activity. He may have had a job but turned it down in favor of such activity. In this case unemploy-

Table 3
Preimprisonment Work Experience of Arrestees

	Georgia	Texas	Washington, D.C.
Proportion unemployed at time of arrest	48%	47%	46%
Type of employment:			
Unskilled labor	45%	15%	41%
Semiskilled labor	48%	62%	11%
Reported wages earned per week	$136	$148	
Percentage earnings below $3.00 per hour			50%

Sources: Statistics for Georgia and Texas from P. H. Rossi, R. A. Berk, and K. Lenihan, *Money, Work and Crime* (New York: Academic Press, 1980), table 7.6, p. 131; statistics for Washington, D.C., from "A Supplemental Report by the Office of Criminal Justice Plans and Analysis," in *Unemployment* and *Crime,* Hearings before the Subcommittee on Crime of the Committee of the Judiciary, House of Representatives, 95th Congress (Washington, D.C., 1978), pp. 111–12.

ment per se is not the cause of crime, though the overall rewards from work relative to crime may have influenced the individual's decision.

Third, while potential criminals are in fact responsive to unemployment and legitimate earnings opportunities, their specific economic choices may be only weakly linked to the overall performance of the economy, so that aggregate analyses fail to capture relations at the individual level. This is especially the case to the degree that criminals come from the back of the "job queue," so that their employment chances are only vaguely affected by the overall level of unemployment. To the extent that this is true, employers will hire other workers before the potential criminal, with the result that it will take huge swings in the overall level of unemployment to raise the potential criminal's employment chances.

Together these three observations suggest that the link between unemployment and crime found in the comparison of criminal and noncriminal work records cannot be used to infer what will happen to criminal activity when overall labor market conditions change. However, the implications of the first two explanations differ fundamentally from the third. The first two hypotheses suggest that changes in job possibilities for potential criminals are (within normal ranges of variation) likely to have little impact on their criminal behavior, whereas the third suggests that the potential criminal will indeed respond measurably to these opportunities.

Studies of recidivism among actual releasees provide one, albeit imperfect, way of analyzing the response of one set of potential criminals, ex-offenders, to their own labor market experience. Anne Witte studied the work experience of 641 men who were in prison in North Carolina in 1969 or 1971. For this group, a comparatively high wage level received on the first job out of prison tended to decrease the subsequent chance of conviction. But the variable measuring unemployment had an unexpected negative effect, giving a rather mixed picture of the effect of labor market performance as a whole on the behavior of these offenders. The Rossi-Berk-Lenihan analysis of TARP participants in Texas and Georgia (see table 4) showed a significant trade-off between number of arrests and weeks employed, with those employed longer having fewer arrests. In addition, however, researchers found a weak or anomalous relation between their measure of the labor market (unemployment in the county of the release) and the individual's employment experience. In short, the aggregate market variable had no effect on the individual's behavior.

At present there are too few studies of individual behavior to reach any overall assessment.

Results of Social Experiments

In recent years several social experiments have been developed to evaluate the responses of ex-offenders to job market incentives. The programs have varied: some offered job placement; others provided money to ex-offenders as financial security until they found a job; others attempted to provide them with a social environment encouraging work as opposed to crime. Because of recidivism and the concentration of crime among a small subset of the population, ex-criminals are part of a group that can be assumed to cause a large proportion of crime. These studies give us an indication of how they respond to their *own* labor market incentives. Here there is also the advantage that the incentives are controlled by the experimenter, providing a truly exogenous labor market variable for study. If these analyses showed a strong link between unemployment (and other labor market factors) and crime, the case for the connection would be greatly enhanced.

Unfortunately, like the other evidence in the field, these studies, while generally supportive of the link, do not give a uniform picture either of our ability to reduce crime by altering labor market opportunities or even of the relation between unemployment or earnings and crime. As table 4 shows, some studies have successfully altered behavior (e.g., the Baltimore Living Insurance for Ex-Prisoners [LIFE] experiment) while others have not (e.g., Parole Reintegration Projects, Supported Work, the diverse manpower programs surveyed by Taggart).

The recent and statistically sophisticated study of the TARP experimental program by Rossi et al. showed essentially no difference in recidivism between the experimental group (who received unemployment compensation so that they could better search for jobs after release from prison) and the control population. Rossi and his colleagues explain the failure of the program to reduce crime as resulting from the combined effects of the unemployment compensation on acceptance of jobs and of employment on crime. That is, they interpret the evidence as showing that if you give money to ex-convicts to look for work, they will take a longer time finding jobs than if you do not; in addition, because people without jobs commit more crimes, you will also have a higher crime rate as a result. Viewed in this light, the TARP experiment supports the link between unemployment and crime, but fails to support the notion that crime can be reduced among ex-criminals by giving them aid after they are released.[10] By contrast the Baltimore LIFE experiment (see table 4), on which TARP was modeled, found a stronger link between unemployment in the city and crime than between the individual's own work experience and crime. While these two studies lend some support to the notion of a link between unemployment and crime, there are enough failed experiments to call into question our ability to predict how the link will operate in any particular instance.

Table 4
Some Experimental Studies on the Effect of Economic Incentives on Recidivism

Program (analysis)	Results of providing economic incentives
1. TransitionalAid Research Project: prisoners given up to six months of unemployment insurance to reduce economic incentive for economic crime.	Work disincentives of TARP reduced employment, increasing crime, while payments reduced crime for those with some employment, with no net effect. Large unemployment/crime relation.
2. Baltimore Living Insurance for Ex-Prisoners (LIFE) project: ex-prisoners given financial aid and job placement services	Financial aid reduced crime; unemployment in city at time of release also affected crime; no job placement effects.
3. Supported Work experiment: ex-offenders provided with subsidized employment and social support for working.	No sizeable significant effects on crime.
4. Diverse manpower programs for ex-offenders: a variety of vocational training and placement programs.	Programs generally ineffective.
5. Parole Reintegration Projects: stipends or grants given to parolees to ease transition to work.	Little positive impact.

Sources: (1) P. H. Rossi, R. A. Berk, and K. Lenihan, *Money, Work and Crime* (New York: Academic Press, 1980); (2) Ibid.; D. C. Mallar and V. D. Thornton, "Transitional Aid for Released Prisoners: Evidence from the LIFE Experiment," *Journal of Human Resources* 13: 208–36; K. Lenihan, *Unlocking the Second Gate*, Research and Development Monograph, U.S. Department of Labor (Washington, D.C.: U.S. Govt. Printing Office, 1977); (3) Manpower Demonstration Research Corporation, *Final Report on the National Supported Work Demonstration* (New York: MDRC, 1981); (4) Robert Taggart, *The Prison of Unemployment* (Baltimore, Md.: Johns Hopkins University Press, 1973); (5) Ibid.; Irving Piliavin and Rosemary Gartner, "Assumptions and Achievements of Manpower Programs for Offenders: Implications for Supported Work," Institute for Research on Poverty, Discussion Paper no. 541, University of Wisconsin at Madison, 1979.

So what in fact do we know about the relation between the labor market and crime? The bulk of the studies examined here show some connection between unemployment (and other labor market variables) and crime, but they fail to show a well-defined, clearly quantifiable linkage. We know:

• There is a cyclical pattern to the crime rate, with crime rising over the cycle with unemployment—but only weakly, so that changes in crime rates are dominated by other factors.

• There is evidence that criminals have poorer work records than noncriminals, but only limited evidence that, once a person embarks on crime, moderate changes in these market opportunities will cause him to choose legitimate earnings channels.

• The widely different crime rates of various cities and states are loosely linked to labor market conditions.

• In studies that include measures of criminal sanctions and labor market factors, sanctions tend to have a greater impact on criminal behavior than do market factors.

There is nothing in the empirical evidence to cause anyone who strongly believes that unemployment causes crime to abandon that belief. On the other hand, in light of the stronger evidence available concerning the deterrent effect of sanctions, the "stick" looks relatively more important than the "carrot."

So while it seems safe to say that there is some difficulty in measuring the relationship between crime and unemployment, the various job experiments with individual crimes offer little optimism about the effect of job creation on the behavior of persons already embarked on a career of crime. It may be that the key to the unemployment/crime relationship is to be found in the behavior of young persons who have yet to embark on such a career. We have, as yet, little information on the effect of labor market forces on their behavior and no experiments regarding ways in which we can reduce the probability that they will engage in crime.

7

CHARLES A. MURRAY

The Physical Environment and Community Control of Crime

Common sense and everyday experience tell us that the physical environment has a lot to do with the risk of crime: we avoid poorly lighted streets, cul-de-sacs, run-down neighborhoods, etc. This assumption often goes hand in hand with another widely shared belief—namely, that a basic secret of crime control in the past has been the informal self-protection of the small, homogeneous community. In the old days, people watched out for their neighbors; and as crime rose in the 1960s, so did nostalgia for the seemingly safer bygone era.

The disappearance of such self-protective neighborhoods was generally assumed to be an inevitable consequence of social change. Tightly-knit ethnic communities were dispersing. People moved in and out of urban areas so rapidly that new bonds had no time to form. The anonymity of the postindustrial city induced apathy. These and other factors, ranging from racial tensions to television, were said to leave the urban planner helpless to preserve the safety features of past community arrangements.

In the last decade, the hopes for such informal crime control through community design have been dramatically revitalized. The catalyst for the new discussion, and a spate of experimental projects that followed, was a single book by Oscar Newman, *Defensible Space*.[1] The essence of Newman's message was that people will defend themselves given the right physical framework. While Newman was not the first to make this point (Jane Jacobs[2] was his most notable predecessor), his book has had by far the greatest impact on the public imagination.

The widespread media attention that greeted Newman's work was undoubtedly encouraged by his memorable term "defensible space"—but the idea was also immediately plausible. In the broadest sense, Newman had to be right. In the narrower sense— using the specifics of defensible space theory as an approach to reducing crime—what have we learned?

Defensible Space Theory

I will use the phrase "defensible space theory" as shorthand for three propositions about the relationship between people's physical environment and crime: territoriality, natural surveillance, and "image and milieu."[3]

Territoriality. The instinct to demarcate and defend territory has long been observed among animals. In the mid-1960s, Robert Ardey popularized the theory that territoriality characterizes human behavior as well.[4] Newman applied Ardey's thesis to crime, arguing that people perceive certain areas as their own space, which can and should be defended. A family that has a sense of territoriality about the entryway to its apartment will be more likely to defend it against intruders than a family that does not. A community that has a shared sense of territoriality will be more likely to act in concert against intruders than a community that has none. Proper design can establish real and symbolic barriers and demarcation lines that foster this sense of territoriality.

Natural surveillance. The "observability" of crime can likewise be improved by designing the use of space to increase the number of friendly "eyes on the street." The greater the number of observers, the greater the probability that an offender will be seen in the act, thereby aiding law enforcement and deterring criminals.

Image and milieu. Proper design can alter the visual impact of a neighborhood or housing project. Offenders are alert to visual cues, and can be deterred from or encouraged to invade a given space (housing project, neighborhood, residence) on the basis of them. A vandalized, run-down housing project, for example, looks disorganized and vulnerable.

At the heart of these propositions about the relationship of the man-made environment to crime is the concept of "informal social control"—the means other than police and jails whereby a community exerts pressure to prevent violations of its norms. Defensible space increases the effectiveness of informal social control, which in turn reduces crime. This two-step process distinguishes defensible space theory from "target-hardening"—i.e., the more prosaic ways in which the design of the physical environment can deter crime through better locks and stronger doors.

Research Findings

Defensible Space was published in 1972. By 1974, major demonstration projects were already under way in public housing projects. The Law Enforcement Assistance Administration (LEAA) funded a multimillion-dollar "Crime Prevention through Environmental Design" (CPTED) undertaking to extend defensible space theory to environments other than public housing projects (a commercial strip, a residential area, a school, and a transportation system). Street-lighting projects proliferated. By 1975, plans were proceeding for an application of defensible space concepts to an entire neighborhood in Hartford, Connecticut. Defensible space was in vogue.

Researchers followed in the wake of the planners and designers, sometimes evaluating the effects of the demonstration projects, sometimes using natural variation as a means of comparing crime in environments that were and were not "defensible" according to Newman's precepts.

In the late 1970s LEAA's successor, the National Institute of Justice, decided to pull together the lessons that had been learned from the experience. Two major reviews of the work to date were prepared. One, conducted by the Center for Metropolitan Planning and Research at Johns Hopkins University as part of a study of informal social control, prompted its authors to write:

> Our review of the theory and evidence leads to rather sobering conclusions. First, although defensible space theorizing has improved considerably, further conceptual clarification is needed. The interplay between social and physical elements of the environment deserves closer attention. Second, the impact of varying sociocultural contexts needs tu be specifically addressed.
>
> Although research has improved dramatically, there are still problems. In many studies the critical intermediating variables have not been measured, or have not been measured adequately. . . . Those studies that do assess different types of sites (housing versus apartments) find a different result for each. In addition, it has not yet been determined if potential offenders perceive defensible space features.
>
> Although defensible space theory is lacking, and research to date inconclusive, we do not feel it is appropriate to abandon the ship. Rather, we suggest that defensible space theory can be clarified, and that an updated model may be of use in understanding crime-related outcomes in residential environment.[5]

The point of this report was merely to propose a research agenda and not to prescribe new policies.

The second major review, conducted by the American Institute for Research, examined all types of changes in the "built" environment (including traditional target-hardening strategies as well as defensible space theory) and summarized its conclusions in three points:

- First, available evidence does suggest that changes in the physical environment (and especially combinations of changes) can reduce crime and fear of crime. This does not happen consistently; but it does occur.

- Secondly, the available evidence does not illuminate the dynamics. Except for simple, almost self-evident relationships (e.g., that stronger doors reduce the risk of burglary), the links remain obscure. Tests of the hypotheses that underlie the surveillance rationales (e.g., the "eyes on the street" hypothesis) have resulted in contradictory findings. The behavioral changes predicted by the community-building rationales (e.g., increased social cohesion) have consistently failed to appear.

- Third, because of this lack of cause-effect information, the present knowledge base cannot be used to prescribe solutions. It does not tell whether a given strategy is likely to be effective in a given situation. It does not suggest the kinds or numbers of strategies to use. It does not identify the conditions (if any) under which a design strategy is cost-effective.[6]

From a scientific perspective, these cautious conclusions are entirely appropriate. Much research has been done on defensible space, but the studies are of widely varying quality and low generalizability, and their findings are contradictory. Despite recent valuable contributions to the literature, no one is yet in a position to write a college textbook on the relationships among the physical environment, informal social control, and crime. Too little is known.

For policymakers, however, some lessons can be formulated. The basic policy question is practical: is there reason to believe that physical design changes can significantly affect the crime problem? If the literature has not pinned down precisely the nature of the relationship between the environment and crime, we do know much more now than ten years ago about the limits and potentialities of attempts to manipulate the physical environment. I will review the history of these attempts, then conclude with a brief look at the practical implications of the results.

Crime Reduction Potential

The initial attraction of defensible space theory lay in its potential for reducing crime independently of other measures. The lament of the 1960s was that crime was so embedded in basic social and economic conditions that little could be done until those conditions were changed. Newman said this was too pessimistic—that physical design changes could in and of themselves "release latent attitudes in tenants which allow them to assume behavior necessary to the protection of their rights and property."[7] *Ceteris paribus,* a housing project or neighborhood that scored "low" on defensible space could reduce its crime by increasing the defensibility of its space. Changes in the physical environment would be the necessary and sufficient condition for releasing the "latent attitudes" that Newman hypothesized.

This expectation, the most optimistic of the hopes for defensible space theory, was soon abandoned by most planners. The evaluations of the public housing projects were especially discouraging. Public housing projects represented both the worst problem and (it was thought) the most likely place for defensible space theory to have an effect. But none of the early public housing experiments produced evidence of the kind of response anticipated by defensible space theory—a substantial, lasting decrease in crimes because the inhabitants began defending their turf or because offenders began steering clear of better-defended targets.

For that matter, there was little evidence of any decrease in crime in the public housing experiments, for whatever reason. Scattered anecdotal claims were advanced, especially in the early years of the experiments, but the documentation was scanty.[8] When formal evaluations were undertaken, the rumored crime reduction effects could not be found.

The major demonstration efforts during this period were at two public housing projects in New York City, Clason Point and Markham Gardens. The design changes included establishment of play areas, improvements in the appearance of the projects, better lighting, fencing to divide areas into semi-private spaces, and barriers and channels for pedestrian traffic. The evaluation found a few optimistic, albeit ambiguous, signs of more "neighboring" and a greater sense of territoriality because of the design changes; but the general improvement that had been anticipated in crime-related outcomes did not materialize. The changes were either trivial or inconsistent. In one of the sites, burglary and robbery decreased—but vandalism doubled. After installation of street lights at Clason Point, crime decreased between 5:00 and 9:00 P.M.—but increased between midnight and 5:00 A.M., for a total net increase.[9] At best, the early demonstrations of defensible space in public housing could point only to highly selective, tenuous examples of success in reducing crime—examples that had to be ignored when crime went up. The simple explanation seemed to be that the evaluators were observing fluctuations that had little to do with the design changes.

Much of the same frustration was encountered with the other

leading type of design change during the mid-1970s: street-lighting projects. One offshoot of the general interest in environmental design had been a spate of anecdotal reports of major reductions in crime because of better street-lighting, and a number of cities undertook their own experiments. However, upon close examination the claims became less impressive. In a review of all the recorded street-lighting experiments up to 1977 (forty-one, of which fifteen were deemed important enough to warrant a full-scale assessment), researchers concluded that there is no statistically significant evidence that improved street lighting has an impact on the level of crime.[10] Although immediate but short-lived reductions were occasionally observed, evidence of permanent improvement had proved elusive.

By 1975 or 1976, a modified view of the role of defensible space had taken hold. Changes in design were no longer expected to reduce crime in and of themselves; but they could, it was believed, be one important component in a package of crime reduction measures. Changes in defensible space could facilitate greater social cohesion and thereby increase informal social control—but only if that cohesion were catalyzed by community organization, better policing, improved police-community relations, and the like.

There has been one good test of the merits of this approach.[11] The Asylum Hill project in Hartford, Connecticut, was an ambitious application of defensible space theory, implemented more or less as planned and evaluated through a careful longitudinal study. The demonstration project was implemented in 1976 and the evaluation (in two stages) took place through 1979.[12]

Asylum Hill is a working-class, racially mixed residential neighborhood surrounded by commercial areas. The physical changes introduced by the project consisted of alterations in the streets and intersections—closing some off to create cul-de-sacs, narrowing the openings at intersections to create the effect of a "gateway" into the residential area, and using one-way streets to discourage commercial traffic. The purpose of the changes was to reduce "outsider" vehicular traffic, increase pedestrian use by the neighborhood's inhabitants, and demarcate the boundaries of the neighborhood—all changes in accord with defensible space theory about how to encourage territoriality, natural surveillance, and a safer image and milieu.

The physical changes were implemented in North Asylum Hill. Other components of the project, implemented in both North and South Asylum Hill, consisted of a neighborhood police team permanently assigned to the neighborhood, a police advisory committee composed of local residents, and other formal neighborhood organizations.

Neither the physical nor the social changes were focused on a particular crime prevention activity: "The program was simply designed to create an environment which would increase the likelihood that residents could begin to control their own neighborhood and solve their own problems."[13]

The evaluation found much evidence to vindicate defensible space theory. Three years after the changes were put in place, there were significant increases in the residents' use of the neighborhood, ability to recognize strangers, intervention in suspicious situations, and positive perceptions of their neighbors as a resource against crime. All of these results were interpreted as intermediate links between the design changes and crime reduction through better informal social control. However, the project did not reduce crime. Burglary and robbery decreased significantly after the first year of implementation but rose thereafter, "returning approximately to the levels that one would have predicted from the city-wide trends."[14]

This evaluation, the most thorough and objective assessment to date of a defensible space project, was encouraging in that the project was found to have fostered territoriality and improved social order—an effect that, as the authors correctly pointed out, had not been demonstrated elsewhere. As for crime, the evaluation stated the case fairly:

The fact that burglary rates and robbery rates increased significantly in the face of significantly increased social control is a very important observation with which theorists must deal. In essence, the project emphasizes the need to focus on offenders and on police activities, as well as informal social control, in order to predict crime rates.[15]

This observation applies not only to Asylum Hill, but to the results of all attempts to reduce crime through defensible space.

Reducing the Fear of Crime

There is, then, no evidence that changing a neighborhood's physical environment according to defensible space theory can produce major crime rate reductions. However, reducing crime was not the only goal of the demonstration projects. Early in the experimentation with defensible space, the objective of reducing *fear* of crime began to be perceived as just as important as reducing crime itself.

The rationale for giving "fear" equal emphasis with "crime" has two main elements: fear can affect everyone, whether or not victimization occurs; and fear is often exaggerated, bearing little relation to the level of crime.[16] When people have an unreasonably high fear of crime, it is good (according to this line of argument) to reduce fear independently of success in reducing crime. I have separated consideration of the crime reduction and fear reduction effects of defensible space projects to avoid confusion between them, for the picture is quite different when we consider fear.

Again the Asylum Hill project provides the best evidence among the experiments to date. The results were that fear of robbery and burglary held steady through the three years of observation, during a period when fear was rising markedly in the rest of Hartford. The authors concluded that the fear of crime in North Asylum Hill was significantly lower than it would have been without the project. Because this effect was observed during the same three-year period that the residents' sense of territoriality and willingness to assert social control increased, the authors further concluded that "the apparent intimate relationship between people's fears and concerns about crime and the degree of social organization and informal social control in a neighborhood is a critical finding."[17]

The assumption that fear levels that are "holding steady" constitute evidence of improvement is open to argument. However, evidence from another source, street-lighting projects, does indicate that changes in fear levels can in fact be produced by simple physical changes.[18] In the review of street-lighting projects, it was found that improved street lighting sometimes was followed by short-term—and occasionally large—reductions in the fear of crime. In Baltimore, 66 percent of the residents interviewed said they felt safer after street-lighting was improved. The comparable figure was 82 percent in Milwaukee. Smaller or unspecified decreases in fear were found in Tucson, Denver, and Norfolk.[19] The Clason Point project found evidence of a markedly increased sense of safety among the residents, which they attributed to the improved lighting (but not to any of the other defensible space innovations).[20]

It would appear that reduced fear of crime is linked to the specific design change of better lighting.[21] Inferences about the role of other defensible space innovations in reducing fear must rest on the Asylum Hill experience. But there remains reason for optimism that the fear of crime can be reduced, at least temporarily, by making physical changes. The AIR (American Institutes for Research) report, which included target-hardening changes in its review, went further, stating that "we believe that *changes in the physical environment are probably the fastest way of reducing fear of crime.* Since the response is to the program's inputs (lighting, fences, security stations) rather than its outcomes, almost instantaneous impact can be expected."[22]

But that is the problem, as the AIR report noted. If the reduced fear is independent of real reductions in the risk of being a victim, where is the advantage? At Asylum Hill, street crime and robbery were increasing between 1977 and 1979, while the fear of crime was holding steady. Whether lower levels of fear are good or bad depends mainly on whether the existing level of fear is unrealistically high. Insofar as reasonable fear leads to reasonable precautions, it seems dubious wisdom to reduce fear without reducing crime as well.

The Physical Environment and Community Crime Control

I began by stating that in some broad sense Newman had to be right: we all recognize from personal experience that the physical environment affects our behavior in relation to crime. We all know from experience that informal social control is a real phenomenon. Yet attempts to reduce crime through environmental design have fallen far short of expectations. Was the relationship between crime and the physical environment overstated? Misstated? Illusory? Or have we failed to try the right modifications, the right "treatment," or the right environment?

Only the demonstration projects provide a direct answer to the salient policy issue of whether *changes* in defensible space design can produce *reductions* in crime. However, the great bulk of research in the last ten years has dealt not with attempts to manipulate the environment but with "natural variation" in design settings. The task has been to understand first, whether the differences in design settings are associated with differences in crime; and second, if so, why.

Much of the early work was of marginal quality or worse, as described in the syntheses of the research cited earlier.[23] But enough has been learned, especially in a handful of studies completed since 1980, to discern patterns in the findings. Together, they point toward some increasingly plausible speculations about why we have seen so little effect from the demonstration projects, and what might be expected if we pursue efforts to reduce crime through environmental design. I will put these speculations in the form of two simplified propositions:

- Those elements of defensible space theory that bear on the offender's perception of the *real risk* of apprehension are the most critical in deterring crime.

- The effectiveness of defensible space features depends crucially on the preexisting social environment; as a general rule, defensible space theory applies least to places with the worst crime problems.

Defensible space and the offender. Perhaps the biggest lacuna in the data on defensible space has had to do with the criminal's point of view. How does the offender—especially the offender who victimizes the inner city—choose his targets? A recently published ethnographic study of a housing project in a Northeastern city helps fill this gap. The researcher, Sally E. Merry, was able (after prolonged residence in the community) to obtain detailed, apparently candid information from seven young men who lived in the project and were responsible for many of the robberies there.[24] Their calculations, strategies, and eventual decisions about where and when to commit robberies were generally consistent with the expectations of defensible space theory, with two noteworthy caveats.

First, the offenders were extremely pragmatic. Their calculations seemed to be based on a hard-headed appreciation of the facts. *Real* risk of being observed, *real* risk of someone calling the police or intervening, and *real* risk of being cut off without an escape route loomed largest in their thinking. Symbolic barriers and demarcation lines, symbolic evidence of the site's cohesiveness, and symbolic increases in risk of observation and apprehension seemed to be of little deterrence value.

Second, the offenders knew the project intimately—the residents and what kind of people they were—as indicated in this passage:

One street is considered good robbing space because the people who live there are thought never to look out. A plaza outside the elderly housing is poor because the old people are always looking out their windows. Some people are thought to look out their windows only after they hear a noise while others watch all the time. Only the latter concern the robbers. Some are known to do nothing and are ignored; others are reputed to intervene actively. Of this latter group, some shout and tell the criminal to stop but do not call the police: these succeed in moving the crime around the corner. Others are believed likely to call the police, and robbers are very cautious about committing crimes within sight of these apartments.[25]

Merry's account suggests that providing more and better windows will indeed have a deterrent effect, *if*—an important qualifier— the residents are "nosy," unafraid witnesses.

The accounts in Merry's interviews are consistent with the indirect evidence from several studies that have examined the effects of neighborhood isolation from major traffic arteries and commercial land use.[26] Each of these studies adds evidence that neighborhoods that are "out of the way" experience lower burglary rates even after demographic and socioeconomic factors are taken into account. This is an outcome predicted by defensible space theory: the less the traffic, the easier it is to recognize strangers (natural surveillance). Isolation from major arteries and commercial centers also may be expected to foster a sense of identity within the neighborhood, which in turn increases territorial behavior and thereby informal social control.[27]

The conclusions are plausible and the logical link with defensible space theory is clear; but it is doubtful that the *actual* link has much to do with territorial or any other active social control behavior. One study that addressed this issue directly examined both natural surveillance and territorial control variables and concluded:

By and large, the dimensions of territoriality were not found to be distinguishing characteristics of low crime neighborhoods. In fact, informal social control, such as movement governing rules and surveillance, appeared to be more characteristic of high crime than of low crime areas.[28]

The authors found a better explanation in the fact that "[r]elative to high crime neighborhoods, the flow of outsiders into and out of low crime neighborhoods appeared to have been limited by more homogenous land use, fewer major arteries, and by the nature of boundary streets."[29] They speculated that this inhibited opportunistic crimes by outsiders. Yet one need not invoke opportunism. Merry's informants might be expected to have another explanation: criminal offenses are not a matter of opportunism (for the crimes in Merry's study were generally quite deliberate) but of preferring not to "work" in an area where they have a difficult escape route, no natural cover, and no local knowledge.

Where might defensible space work? What then of the relationship between physical design and informal social control? Is it illusory? Two ambitious recent studies argued that it is not—that connections have been detected and are robust. Both employed quantified measures and a sophisticated (and controversial) statistical approach called "path-modeling" to assess their findings. One, part of Oscar Newman's continuing involvement in defensible space theory, examined archival and interview data from sixty-three low- and moderate-income housing sites in three cities.[30] The other study examined sample survey data from twelve neighborhoods in Baltimore.[31]

The two studies came to many of the same conclusions. Both found evidence of relationships between defensible space features and crime-related outcomes, between territorial variables and crime-related outcomes, and between defensible space features and territorial variables. Researchers have concluded that the similarities in findings far outweigh the differences, and that these similarities exist despite the differences in sites—public housing projects in one case and residential neighborhoods in the other.[32]

But what are the implications for using informal social control to reduce crime? Does the presence of a statistical relationship at a specific moment in the history of a neighborhood suggest that changes in the physical environment would engender lasting changes in behavior and crime rates?

With regard to this issue, the importance of the preexisting social context stood out. The Baltimore study concluded that physical and social contexts are, as social scientists put it, "interactively" bound up with each other: the data did not permit a clear distinction between overall social context and the crime-reducing effects of specific design features.[33] The tri-city study called attention to the importance of the proportion of welfare families, the ratio of teenagers to adults, and whether residents own their apartments.[34] The universal "latent attitudes" of which Newman's early work had spoken were far in the background.

What does an "interactive" relationship between the social context and physical environment mean? In the quantitative studies, it is explicated by means of path coefficients and quantified variables. To clarify the concept, let us return to Sally E. Merry's ethnographic study on where crime happened, to whom, and what the victims did about it. Her findings are congruent with those of the quantitative studies, and her evidence is far easier to assess.

Many of her observations conform closely to defensible space theory: people tend to fear the places that the theory would predict they should fear; they do believe that a lack of clarity about "ownership" of space contributes to crime and a sense of danger; and in some instances natural surveillance can be severely inhibited by design features, much as Newman stated. Yet despite such shortcomings, the housing project as a whole was well-designed for defensible space, which provides an opportunity to ask why over half of the robberies occurred "in areas which are architecturally defensible."[35]

Merry identifies four reasons for lack of intervention by onlookers: subtle violations of defensible space principles, lack of effective modes of intervention (the police often do not arrive in time and intervening personally can be dangerous), fear of retaliation by offenders who live in the immediate area, and unwillingness to help strangers. An analysis of the instances in which people *did* intervene is also revealing. Almost all of the interventions occurred in areas that were "defensible" in design—which supports defensible space theory—but the people who did the intervening were a very distinctive group, persons who in Merry's analysis were "highly committed to the neighborhood in terms of their length of residence, social networks, and time spent in daily social interaction inside the project."[36]

Merry describes the ethnic and cultural loci of these attitudes— the pervasive differences among the Chinese, the blacks, and the Syrian-Lebanese in their stances toward "territory," toward intervening, toward their roles in the housing project themselves. Her conclusion would seem to be consistent with the inferences to be drawn from the quantitative studies:

Even if buildings are low, [with] entrances and public spaces clearly linked to particular apartments, residents will not respond to crimes if they feel that the space belongs to another ethnic group, if they believe that the police will come too late or they will incur retribution for calling them, or if they are unable to distinguish a potential criminal from the neighbor's dinner guest. Residents often fail to intervene because of the fragmented social organization of the project, its pervasive anonymity and fear, the prevalence of stranger relationships among bystanders, and a sense of futility about calling the police.[37]

That the preexisting social context has such a strong influence on the use of design characteristics does not diminish the need to explore the relationships among crime, informal social control, and the physical environment. That influence helps explain, however, why changes in the physical environment have done so little to reduce crime. It is difficult to imagine a community organization effort that would change the deeply embedded social characteristics of the housing project that Merry describes—or, for that matter, the sites described in the quantitative analyses. Can such conditions be changed under any circumstances? Perhaps. Can they be changed by the combinations of physical design and community organization that are realistically possible? It seems extremely unlikely.

Thus we can see why it is likely that defensible space improvements may have the least effect in places with the worst crime problems. If indeed it is true that the worst crime problems are found where the offenders are predominantly "insiders" with intimate local knowledge, and if it is also true that the worst crime problems exist in places where preexisting, hard-to-change social characteristics militate against informal social control, then defensible space improvements in high-crime areas face two nearly insuperable obstacles.

This does not mean that the principles of defensible space should be ignored. Many of the innovations proposed by Newman still seem to be sensible, appropriating design features that can be incorporated when new housing is being built, with little if any additional cost. If nothing else, the innovations tend to make the housing more attractive and livable. But when it comes to deciding whether to alter existing housing or neighborhoods, the question of how best to allocate scarce resources arises.

Defensible space improvements can, it seems, help forestall deterioration in a low-crime area that is threatened with encroachment by outside offenders. They may also be of some help in a place such as North Asylum Hill that already has a severe crime problem, but one that has been caused largely by outsiders.

In other, more difficult environments, the problem comes down to the two faces of defensible space. Where neighbors are allies, measures that make it easier for them to see who comes and goes from each other's houses may serve an important burglary control function. In neighborhoods where the neighbor may very well *be* the burglar, the same measures can be a menace.

IV

The Criminal Justice System

8

MARK H. MOORE

Controlling Criminogenic Commodities: Drugs, Guns, and Alcohol

Crime control policies ultimately contend with human nature. Since human nature resists "social engineering," and since American society hesitates to manipulate character even where it might succeed, this simple fact dampens hope for any easy solution to the crime problem. But optimism is endemic to the American culture. So is confidence in cleverly designed technical interventions. At various times, then, the idea of controlling crime by regulating "criminogenic commodities" (such as heroin, guns, or alcohol) has attracted public interest.[1]

The basic logic of such proposals is clear. Drugs, guns, and alcohol (and people who use them) all figure disproportionately in criminal attacks. Plausible hypotheses giving these commodities a *causal* role in generating crime are supported by intuition, analytic reflection, and empirical observation. An apparent implication is that if these commodities could be prohibited (or at least tightly regulated), crime could be reduced.

The appeal of such policies is also apparent. To the extent that the commodities are criminogenic, government crime control policies could focus on a narrow slice of commerce and escape the frustrations of the principal alternatives—restructuring society on the one hand, incapacitating or rehabilitating individual offenders on the other.[2]

The purpose of this essay is to probe the practical potential of policies regulating criminogenic commodities for reducing violent street crime. This involves a brief examination of the evidence linking these commodities to criminal offenses, and a somewhat closer look at plausibly effective reforms of existing policies towards drugs, guns, and alcohol.

Relationships between Criminogenic Commodities and Crime

The important empirical observations establishing a link between drugs, guns, alcohol, and criminal attacks can be easily summarized. With respect to drugs:

- Drug users are disproportionately represented among people arrested and incarcerated for street crimes such as robbery, assault, and burglary.[3]

- Levels of criminal activity (measured by arrests and self-reported crimes) are much higher for daily heroin users than for those who use heroin less frequently, or for those who use no drugs.[4]

- Levels of criminal activity among heroin users increase during periods of daily use and decrease in periods of abstinence.[5]

- Drug users commit violent offenses (assault and sex crimes) at about the same rate as other offenders and commit property crimes (robbery, burglary, and larceny) much more frequently (2–10 times as often) than non-drug-using criminal offenders.[6]

With respect to guns:

- Large fractions of violent criminal attacks are committed by people using guns—primarily handguns.[7]

- The presence of guns in assault situations increases the likelihood that a homicide will occur.[8]

- The presence of guns in robbery situations also increases the likelihood that a homicide will occur, and shifts the distribution of victimization away from weaker targets such as the elderly toward more lucrative, better-defended targets such as bars, stores, and young men.[9]

With respect to alcohol:

- Large fractions (more than half) of those arrested for felonies report that they were drinking prior to the crime, and have high levels of alcohol in their blood.[10]

- In more than half the criminal homicides, the offender, the victim, or (most commonly) both were drinking at the time of the crime.[11]

- A large fraction of the aggravated assaults that occur among strangers in public locations occur in and around places where alcohol is served.[12]

These facts, combined with the perception that drugs, guns, and alcohol undermine sobriety and civility while contributing little redeeming social value, explain the shady social reputation of these commodities. However, they fall short of guaranteeing that tighter control of such commodities could substantially reduce crime. The reason is that the facts do not necessarily establish a causal link running from these commodities to criminal offending. It could be, for example, that the sorts of people who commit crimes also happen to drink, take drugs, or collect guns. Alternatively, people who intend to commit crimes may prepare themselves by drinking, taking drugs, or acquiring a gun. Since the determination to commit offenses could exist independently of the commodities, and since substitute equipment may be available, restricting their availability need not have any appreciable effect on crime.

Such cautions are appropriate and helpful in gauging the crime reduction potential of controlling criminogenic commodities: they suggest that the benefits will be both smaller and less certain than a naive interpretation of the available facts would indicate. But the evidence linking the commodities to criminal offenses is suffi-

ciently compelling to require explanation. Moreover, the most persuasive explanations *do* suggest that these commodities have
criminogenic effects. The causal relationships turn out not to be
the simple ones we imagine, however.

   Drugs and crime. When we consider the criminogenic effects
of drugs such as heroin, marijuana, cocaine, barbiturates,
amphetamines, LSD, and so on, we sometimes imagine a direct
physiological link: the drugs transform ordinary people into
vicious offenders. Despite the public vitality of this conception,
supporting evidence has been sparse. Bits of evidence establish a
link between "aggression" and the use of stimulants (such as
amphetamines, methamphetamines, and cocaine).[13] But even if
this link exists as a physiological phenomenon, it is not epidemio-
logically significant in that these drugs rarely appear among
people arrested for violent crimes.[14] Ironically, the drugs that
seem to be the focus of the most intense public concern—heroin
and marijuana—operate physiologically to make people passive,
not aggressive.[15] And barbiturates work like alcohol—they make
people clumsy and inattentive.[16]
   The main reason we tend to link physiological characteristics of
drugs to criminal attacks is the image of "dope fiends" willing to
do anything to get their next "fix."[17] But this image applies only to
heroin. The machinery that links heroin addicts to high rates of
offending is an intricate combination of three conditions: 1) that a
person is addicted to heroin; 2) that heroin is expensive; and
3) that the addicts' best sources of income are criminal offenses.[18]
As a logical matter, if any of these conditions were absent, then
the link between addiction and crime would weaken. If "junkies"
are not highly addicted, they can make discretionary decisions
about committing crimes. If heroin is not expensive, addicts may
satisfy their habits by panhandling, as public drunks now do.[19] If
heroin addicts can hold high-paying jobs with discretionary hours
(as do musicians and physicians), then they need not turn to crime
to finance their habits. The implication is that the current link between heroin use and crime is established partly by the fact that
we make heroin use illegal (therefore both expensive and irregularly available), and partly by the fact that it (for a variety of
reasons) is concentrated among those least able to afford it.[20] So

heroin use probably does cause crime, but only when it occurs among certain groups confronting certain social policies.

Alcohol and crime. The link between drinking and crime is also somewhat circuitous. The theory of a simple relationship—that drinking itself causes people to become aggressive—is probably not correct. The physiological evidence suggests that alcohol makes people distractable and clumsy, but not necessarily aggressive.[21] The sociological evidence indicates great variability in "drunken comportment": while drunkenness is associated with belligerence and aggressiveness in the U.S., it is linked with sleepiness and giddiness in other cultures.[22] The most important connections between alcohol and crime are probably twofold.

First, drinking may produce criminal offenses by "disinhibiting" potential offenders, granting them a personal or social license for their offense, or making them clumsy and negligent. It has been hypothesized, for example, that bullying husbands get drunk so that they can excuse assaults on their wives.[23] It must also be true that the potential for "accidental" offenses increases as people get reckless and clumsy. Cars can hit people, fires from neglected cigarettes can destroy buildings, guns can actually go off, a heavy glass ashtray can crash against a head rather than a wall, and so on.

Second, drinking can create victims and provocative situations as well as offenders. Public drunks are notoriously vulnerable to criminal attack. Moreover, anyone who has been in a drunken quarrel or has read police files describing domestic homicides, assaults, rapes, and child abuse must realize that offenses can be created by *situations* as well as by the intentions of offenders.[24] Therefore, reducing instances of drunkenness could conceivably have an effect not only on drunk driving, but also on a variety of criminal offenses ranging from homicide, through robbery, to minor assaults.

Guns and crime. The simple idea linking guns to crime is that for any given potential offender, guns bring a larger (and more varied) set of targets within reach, and therefore increase the likelihood that offenses will occur.[25] Armed juveniles can attack gas stations, convenience stores, and even bars as well as elderly people and women. A frightened wife, equipped with a gun, can stand up to a bullying husband. Because more attacks are possible, more attacks occur.

The empirical evidence on the effects of gun availability on levels of criminal attack is now fairly clear and opposes this simple conception: the ready availability of guns seems to increase the *seriousness* of criminal attacks, but not the overall *levels*.[26] Because more assaults and robberies become homicides in areas where guns are readily available, guns seem to influence levels of homicide.[27] But apart from converting more assaults and robberies into homicides, ready gun availability seems to exert little influence on the frequency of these attacks. What does happen is that guns alter the distribution of victimization. Where guns are available, commercial targets are robbed more than individual citizens, and young men more frequently than elderly women.[28] Similarly, in domestic assaults husbands are more frequently the victims. Thus the most important effects of guns on crime are that they increase the seriousness of criminal attacks and affect the distribution of victimization; they do not seem to markedly increase overall levels of criminal attack.

Controlling Criminogenic Commodities: General Considerations

Given commodities with plausible criminogenic effects, it sometimes seems but a short logical step to conclude that the commodities should be tightly controlled in the interest of reducing crime. This apparently small step is in fact, however, a heroic leap across crucially important questions of fact, value, and institutional feasibility.

The crucial factual question is how much crime can be reduced, or lessened in severity, by controlling criminogenic commodities. To a degree, this is answered by understanding the *current* relationship between the criminogenic commodity and crime. And it is the current relationship that inspires those who would control the commodities. But this relationship need not remain constant. When policies tighten control over the commodities, their relationship to crime may change. As noted above, the link between heroin use and crime is primarily the result of tight controls over the availability of heroin, which concentrates its use among people who must respond to the high cost by committing crimes. If controls over heroin were weakened, an important relationship between heroin use and crime would still exist but it would resemble the one that now exists between alcohol and crime: the crime would emerge from periods of psychological disinhibition rather than from economic need.[29] Similarly, if controls on alcohol and guns were tightened, it is possible that they would become much more closely associated with crime than they now are. This might occur because their use would be increasingly concentrated among people who commit criminal offenses, or because the identification of the commodities with violent crime actually would increase the likelihood that people would use them in the commission of violent offenses. In effect, if these commodities were perceived as criminogenic, and controlled as though they were criminogenic, they not only would become more closely linked to criminal activity, but they also might increase the criminal activity among those who continued to possess and use them.[30]

Such concerns may seem exotic, but they stem from a basic uncertainty about the exact nature of the causal mechanisms that link the commodities to crime. These uncertainties cannot be banished. The implication is that crime may decrease less than simple extrapolations from reduced use of the commodity would suggest.

In fact, in some areas, tight controls of criminogenic commodities will increase rather than reduce crime. To the extent that "tighter controls" over criminogenic commodities includes criminal sanctions against distribution, possession, and use, "crime" will, of course, increase: acts that were previously perfectly legal will have become criminal. But prohibiting distribution, possession, and use will probably create some real criminal violence as well. Tight restrictions generally create "black markets," and illicit markets depend on violence to enforce contracts, to prevent employees, customers, and others from informing on the illegal activities to enforcement agencies, and to seek monopolistic advantages in the illegal markets. Thus the existence of these markets will lead to new assaults and homicides.[31] Much of this violence will be "internal" to the illegal markets, and may therefore seem less important than comparable violence directed at less culpable citizens. But such violence may occasionally spill over the boundaries of the illegal markets, and, at any rate, the number of assaults and homicides will be increased.[32]

It is not clear, then, that restricting criminogenic commodities will produce a large net decrease in criminal violence. Crime will be reduced as use of the commodity declines in the general population, and fewer people and circumstances are subject to the various criminogenic effects. But among those who continue to use the commodities, the criminogenic effects may be strengthened. In addition, the act of restricting the commodity may create black markets that will spawn criminal violence. It seems very unlikely that the initial crime reduction benefits of restricting availability would be entirely offset by the mechanisms generating increases; but these offsetting mechanisms will operate to reduce the practical benefits of controlling criminogenic commodities.

The crucial question of value overlooked in the leap from criminogenic effects to a policy of tight control is how much weight should be given to protecting safe and legitimate uses of the commodities. Of course, some deny that guns and alcohol have any legitimate uses, at least none that compares in significance with the social interest in controlling crime. Many others, however, accord great value to these commodities and insist on their right to convenient access. Recreational shooters, gun collectors, and frightened home owners rally to protect the legitimate uses of guns. Recreational drinkers defend low prices and convenient access to alcohol. Even heroin has defenders, many of whom urge that it be made available to terminal cancer patients. Since restrictions on criminogenic commodities almost necessarily sacrifice some portion of legitimate use, society must decide whether and how to regulate them so as to balance its interest in protecting such use against possible reductions in criminal violence.

Current institutional arrangements are also a critical consideration in gauging the practical potential for controlling crime through tighter regulation of criminogenic commodities. To the extent that more restrictive policies are politically unsupportable, there is little practical reason to consider them. Moreover, to the extent that such policies depend on bureaucratic, regulatory, and enforcement capabilities that do not now exist and cannot be easily created, the restrictive policies are also of little or no practical interest. Finally, even if the policies are politically and bureaucratically feasible, they will involve costs, and adequate resources must be committed to enforce their provisions.

Thus in moving responsibly from a *factual* determination that some commodities have criminogenic effects to a *policy* determination about whether and how best to control their availability, at least three additional considerations must be taken into account: the possibility that apparent crime reduction benefits associated with tighter regulations may be partially offset by increased crime associated with black markets; the certainty that legitimate uses of the commodities will be sacrificed by tighter regulations; and the institutional feasibility and cost of more restrictive regulatory regimes. Because these considerations bear differentially on practical proposals to control drugs, guns, and alcohol, it is necessary to explore each area separately.

Controlling Heroin and Other Drugs

For the last decade, federal policy applied across many drugs has been "balanced" between "supply reduction" efforts designed to restrict availability, and "demand reduction" efforts designed to discourage people from beginning drug use and to treat those who have become intensive users.[33] A parallel structure exists at state and local levels.

To a great degree, this elaborate and expensive apparatus is justified as a crime reduction policy. The implicit assumption is that drug users are very likely to commit crimes, and that the number of drug users can be minimized by supply reduction and demand reduction policies. Moreover, the image of drug policy as oriented toward crime control is reinforced by heavy involvement of the criminal justice system. After all, supply reduction policies depend on drug agents' battling criminal conspiracies, and demand reduction policies depend on both the generalized pressure of the criminal justice system and specific referrals from courts to motivate drug users to seek treatment. If the criminal justice system is so heavily involved in drug policy, it must be that the aim of that policy is to reduce crime.

This account of drug control policy as crime control policy has a certain coherence. It also has widespread appeal. It may even be an accurate account of what we think we are trying to accomplish with drug control policy. But as a logical and empirical proposition, it fails. Two anomalies are particularly striking.

First, if our drug control policy were really focused on violent street crime, it would presumably concentrate on those drugs that are most closely linked to such crime. This means heroin. It is true that both supply reduction and drug treatment policies currently do emphasize heroin. But the *degree* of emphasis is far short of heroin's relative importance in producing violent street crime. Cocaine, marijuana, and other hallucinogens all compete effectively for enforcement, prevention, and treatment resources even though they currently have no close connection with violent crime. In short, if our drug policy were narrowly designed to control violent street crime, it would be much more sharply focused on heroin, and would neglect cocaine and marijuana.[34]

Second, it is at least arguable that our current drug control policies *increase* rather than reduce crime.[35] All the mechanisms through which tight controls of a criminogenic commodity might increase crime operate with a vengeance for heroin. Because heroin is addictive and users earn money largely through criminal activity, the high prices for heroin created by stringent control policies may increase the violent crime committed by users. Because current policies outlaw the manufacture, distribution, possession, and use of various drugs, they create criminal offenses where none previously existed. And because a black market in heroin has arisen, some violence has been created by our control policies. In effect, we could reduce crime by *decreasing* rather than *increasing* the stringency of controls over heroin.

Current drug policy is much easier to understand if we resist thinking of it as a short-term crime reduction policy, and see it more as a policy designed to promote social welfare by minimizing the number of people who emerge as chronic, intensive users of drugs. This goal may have some long-run impact on criminal activity, because such users frequently engage in criminal conduct. But it is important to keep in mind that their behavior is partly shaped by current policies. If drugs were less stringently regulated, we might end up with a larger but less frequently criminal population of chronic, intensive drug users. Since it is probably valuable to discourage very heavy drug use even if it is *not* linked to violent crime, and since our policies probably do reduce the number of heavy users in the society (even though they make the behavior of those that do exist more criminal), it is easier to understand our drug policy if we think of it in broader terms than anti-crime policy.

If we want to turn drug policy more toward the objective of controlling violent crime without sacrificing the other social objectives tied to drug policy, probably the most effective approach would be to step up efforts to arrest, control, and treat frequent heroin users who commit offenses. There is ample evidence that some heroin users are unusually active criminal offenders.[36] Moreover, there is also evidence that their level of criminal activity can be noticeably reduced by relatively inexpensive forms of supervision and treatment such as methadone maintenance—at least as long as the addicts remain in the program. Current evidence indicates that if heroin addicts can be induced to reduce or eliminate their heroin use for any period of time, their criminal activity—including violent crime such as robberies as well as larcenies and drug offenses—will also decrease, but not disappear.[37] This may sound like a minor benefit, and certainly falls far short of being a "solution" to the "drug problem," but compared with many other ways of controlling crime, it is an attractive and not yet systematically exploited opportunity.

This idea differs from current conceptions about how to use drug policy to control violent crime. It is not a stepped-up attack on drug dealers (the usual "supply-side" approach). Nor is it a proposal to expand treatment to all drug users who want it (the usual "demand-side" proposal). Instead, it proposes to focus supervisory and treatment resources on a limited segment of the drug-using population: heroin addicts who commit street crimes at very high rates.

It is also important to notice that some institutional machinery exists for implementing this reform. For at least a decade, the Law Enforcement Assistance Administration supported a program called Treatment Alternatives to Street Crime designed to divert drug addicts from jail to treatment.[38] At the time it was created, the project was justified primarily in terms of rehabilitation. Yet whatever its success in rehabilitating drug offenders, the program was probably even more effective as an inexpensive, well-targeted form of "incapacitation." If I am right, this program should be reinvigorated and expanded.[39]

Gun Control

The basic thrust of current federal gun control policy is to keep guns out of the hands of criminal offenders through regulation of gun commerce. The Gun Control Act of 1968 requires people who "engage in the business" of selling guns to acquire a federal license, and prohibits these dealers from knowingly selling guns to certain proscribed categories of people (e.g., convicted felons, fugitives with outstanding warrants, drug addicts, mental defectives, minors, and out-of-state residents).[40] The law is enforced primarily by the Bureau of Alcohol, Tobacco, and Firearms in the U.S. Department of the Treasury (hereafter called ATF).[41]

In addition to the federal legislation, a large body of local laws regulates not only the buying, selling, and transferring of guns, but also their use—for example, whether they can be carried, how they must be stored, and so on.[42] These laws are enforced primarily by local police departments—though there are remarkable disparities in enforcement depending on the political and bureaucratic conditions in local departments.[43]

At various times, proposals have been made to effect deep cuts in the national inventory of guns, particularly of handguns. Sometimes these proposals are directed at withdrawing the existing stock (estimated at 25–50 million handguns) through "buy-back" programs or "bans" on gun ownership with limited grace periods when guns can be voluntarily surrendered. Occasionally a small jurisdiction experiments with one of these approaches and finds it most difficult to defend its program against the flow of inter- and intrastate commerce.[44] At the national level, however, there has been little interest in such radical ideas.[45] The proposals most likely to be effective are designed to limit the *supply* of guns (rather than their distribution and use) and have been directed at the *flow* of new gun production rather than at established inventories. The most radical of these call for a ban on all new production or importation. Narrower proposals attack special *kinds* of guns—

those that seem well-suited to crime and less well-designed for legitimate purposes, or those that lack a powerful domestic constituency.[46] In fact, the only guns that have been recently prohibited in the U.S. combined these traits: the Gun Control Act of 1968 banned foreign guns that could not meet a "sporting arms" test.[47] Thus, while one can still imagine that attacks on the supply of guns or handguns could be an effective way of controlling violent crime, such measures seem politically hopeless: decades of political struggle have created little more than a bitter impasse between gun owners and gun controllers.

An alternative approach would be to focus less on federal legislation to restrict the production of guns or shrink the existing national inventory, and turn instead to stronger enforcement of existing statutes designed to keep guns out of the hands of criminal offenders and off congested city streets. While current federal and local statutes leave some important loopholes, they also provide scope for stepped-up enforcement against illegal transfer, carrying, and possession.

The Gun Control Act of 1968 implicitly establishes a national licensing system. The system is "permissive" in the sense that the presumption is in favor of gun ownership: a person has to show clear evidence of dangerousness or irresponsibility before he is denied the right to acquire and own a gun. However, in denying the right to acquire guns to convicted felons, fugitives, addicts, and minors, the act clearly seeks to keep guns away from people who seem unusually likely to use them in criminal offenses.

Unfortunately, the regulatory system established to implement the act has limited powers. On the bright side, everyone "engaged in the business" of dealing in firearms is required to obtain a federal license. As federal licensees the dealers are required to keep records and are prohibited from knowingly selling to proscribed persons. This prohibition is enforced by requiring the customer to sign an affidavit attesting to his lack of disqualifying characteristics. In addition, regulations spell out what kind of identification can be accepted by the dealer; but they do *not* require the dealer to verify any of the customer's statements.

Three obvious loopholes create problems for the system. One is its incompleteness: not everyone who sells or transfers a firearm is required to obtain a federal license—only those who are "engaged in the business." This leaves an unregulated "private transfer" sector: people who transfer only a few handguns a year have no federal responsibility to avoid proscribed persons. A second problem is the vulnerability of the legitimate system to fraud and collusion. Proscribed customers, with or without the collusion of the dealer, may lie in filling out the necessary affidavit. This makes them guilty of a crime but absolves the dealer. The third loophole involves thefts from manufacturers, licensed dealers, collectors, and private owners. The thefts may be directly routed to proscribed persons, or they may be mediated by the appearance of more or less elaborate black market institutions. Thus, proscribed persons can acquire guns from the legitimate sector through a variety of means.[48]

Efforts to close these loopholes take many forms. The attack on private transfers and diversion of guns to proscribed persons would require a broadened and intensified regulatory program, since the obligation to acquire a license would have to be widened to include more private owners. And the licensees would have to face closer scrutiny—perhaps even undercover approaches to see if they were willing to ignore clear evidence of disqualifying responsibility.

The attack on thefts and black markets *could* be the responsibility of ATF, but might more effectively be delegated to local police departments. Local police have the resources and the mandate to attack thefts of all kinds—including handguns. They may seem less well suited to attacking sophisticated black markets or interstate gun smuggling operations. But it seems likely that the illegal market in guns would be composed of many small transient businesses or generalized fencing operations rather than of a few large, stable firms.[49] This theoretical conclusion is supported by a small amount of research on the characteristics of illegal businesses encountered by ATF.[50] If the illegal firms turned out to be indeed small and transient, there is no reason that the local police could not deal with them. Thus the major approaches for attacking important loopholes in firearms control are federal regulatory efforts directed at licensed dealers and local criminal enforcement targeted on thefts and black markets.

Which of these alternative thrusts should be most emphasized depends on which supply sources are currently most important for criminal offenders, and which can be most easily closed. Again, a small amount of research indicates that the offenders who commit robberies with guns are most likely to be supplied by thefts and black markets. Those who commit assault are most likely to be supplied by the legitimate sector.[51] Indeed, many of the assaulters are licensed to own weapons. This suggests that if violent street crimes like robbery were our main priority, the most important loophole to close would be thefts and black markets. This depends primarily on local police.

Keeping guns out of the hands of criminal offenders is one part of the recommended approach. The other part involves keeping guns off congested city streets. The basic logic of this idea is that some uses of guns are more dangerous (and more "offensive") than others, so we should regulate the dangerous uses more stringently than the less dangerous ones. Carrying a gun in the city is arguably more likely to be an offensive act than possessing a gun in one's home or place of business; the inherent danger of guns in crowded areas was recognized in the frontier tradition of checking guns when one came into town or entered a saloon. More recently, this danger has been recognized in the elaborate system created to deter airline hijacking. And most importantly, it is reflected in the tighter restrictions governing licenses for carrying (as opposed to owning) a gun in many metropolitan areas. In effect, tight regulations effectively enforced against carrying guns in cities might prevent street muggings and assaults among strangers while leaving a citizen's capacity to protect business and home unaffected.

If the goal of keeping handguns off city streets were adopted as an important part of gun control policy, then the natural organizations to assume responsibility for this task would be local police departments. The method would probably involve stepped-up pedestrian and auto checks in which the police ask people if they are carrying weapons. It might even involve technologies such as hand-held magnetometers like those used at airports, to reduce the intrusiveness and increase the specificity of searches for hidden dangerous weapons. Whether local police could be successful in deterring the carrying of illegal weapons without harming important constitutional rights is presently unclear and the question is a suitable subject for experimentation.[52] In advance of the needed experiments, however, one should note that enforcement against illegal carrying of guns should be easier and less intrusive than enforcement against marijuana and other drugs. Despite this fact, the police make many more arrests for drugs than for weapons.[53] This suggests some unexploited enforcement potential.

Note that the argument being made here tends to shift the focus of the gun control debate: it moves the debate from calling for new federal legislation restricting the supply of guns to managing the ownership and use of guns through local enforcement agencies. This is neither the position of the gun controllers (who want federal legislation regulating the supply), nor the position of the gun advocates (who want only enhanced penalties for crimes committed with guns). It challenges the gun controllers to test the practicality of their ideas in a world where 25–50 million handguns are already in circulation and strong political currents run against tighter control. It challenges the good faith of the gun advocates, for it forces them to accept some burdens and responsibilities associated with goals they have always supported— namely, keeping guns out of the hands of dangerous people and minimizing their dangerous or irresponsible uses. Again, while it is not obvious that the approach recommended here would work, it is worth trying, and offers one way out of the current gun control impasse.

Drinking and Crime Prevention

It is ironic that while alcohol seems to occupy the most secure place as a "criminogenic commodity" (since it is involved in half to two-thirds of all homicides), it is the commodity that is now least frequently the focus of policy discussions. The explanation, no doubt, is that alcohol was once a major topic of public discussion, the result of which was Prohibition. Revisionist views of Prohibition are now being written that show the "Great Experiment" to have been both more successful in controlling alcohol consumption and less badly motivated than the earlier historians indicated.[54] Despite the revisionists, however, the conviction that Prohibition was a textbook case of how not to regulate a commodity remains almost universal. As a result, politicians and government officials run great risks when they renew discussion of more stringent alcohol control policies.

As a logical matter, however, strictly regulating alcohol could be justified and accomplished in ways similar to those proposed for drugs and guns. Even more interesting is the fact that a regulatory structure continues to govern alcohol and is available for use despite the abandonment of Prohibition. Alcohol is the only "criminogenic commodity" that is now taxed at federal, state, and local levels. There is evidence suggesting that increases in taxes can influence total consumption of alcohol and the corresponding incidence of cirrhosis and traffic accidents.[55] This may imply that taxes could also decrease the frequency of drunken episodes that lead to violent attacks at home and in bars. In addition, the commerce in alcohol is tightly regulated at the state level: liquor stores are sometimes state operated, and if not state operated, usually state licensed. Bars and drinking establishments are also licensed.[56] Finally, local statutes and ordinances regulate drinking conduct by prohibiting drunken driving, public drunkenness, drinking by minors, and drinking in public locations after certain hours.[57] In principle, this elaborate structure of regulation could be turned to the purpose of reducing crime by reducing the incidence of drunkenness leading to violent attacks. In practice, however, these regulations are made to serve a variety of other purposes such as generating tax revenues, limiting competition among liquor stores and bars, and so on.[58]

The regulatory policy directed at alcohol that could most plausibly have an effect on violent crime would be reinvigorated enforcement of laws against public drunkenness. In recent years, a "decriminalization" movement has resulted in revisions of the statutes governing public drunkenness in a score of states. The aims of the movement were to provide treatment and avoid stigmatizing those arrested for public drunkenness, and to prevent unfair discrimination in police enforcement.[59] Yet the police were not wholly removed from the scene. Because they were often the only available agency, they continued to respond to incidents of drunkenness, and police intervention was sanctioned by provisions allowing limited periods of "protective custody." The decriminalization movement did, however, succeed in reducing police activity; and the police were happy to escape their responsibilities for managing public drunks.[60]

It is wise, no doubt, to manage a nuisance offense without invoking the full apparatus of a criminal enforcement response, and to provide treatment rather than custody. But several aspects of the decriminalization effort seem questionable. First, it is possible to see laws against public drunkenness not as efforts to enshrine idiosyncratic views of public decorum in the criminal law, but instead as attempts to prevent crimes that could occur when people are intoxicated, including drunken assaults *by* as well as robberies and thefts *from* intoxicated people. This makes the laws against public drunkenness similar to the laws against carrying guns, possessing burglary tools, or speeding. They are designed partly to protect the drunk from being victimized, and partly to prevent him from victimizing others. To the extent this view is accepted, one of the major ideological objections to these laws disappears: they do have a legitimate social purpose.

Second, I think it is an error to encourage (or allow) the police to reduce their efforts to regulate public drunkenness. It is all very well to say that public drunkenness is a health or social problem rather than a crime (a view I share), but until physicians and social workers begin roaming the streets at night, the police are going to be in the best position to see and manage the behavior. To the extent that they fail to respond because they no longer think of drunkenness as police business, some potential crime prevention benefits may be sacrificed—to say nothing of a good deal of therapeutic potential.

In sum, while the movement to decriminalize public drunkenness was well motivated and created greater flexibility in the official response, it had at least two slightly negative effects: it broke the link in people's minds between public drunkenness and criminal violence, and it discouraged the police from actively managing public drunkenness. Among the alternatives for regulating alcohol production, distribution, and use in order to reduce violent crime, I would pick renewing police interest in managing public drunkenness. One cannot be very optimistic that this would have a substantial crime reduction effect, since it is certainly true that only a few incidences of public drunkenness produce criminal violence. But short of inducing major changes in American drinking habits, it seems to be the most promising way to reduce crime through alcohol control policies.

Policies for Intractable Problems

Americans have often blamed social problems on the "evil" objects or substances associated with them. This is not only true when we think about public health threats associated with unsafe cars, impure foods, and toxic chemicals, but also even when we think about crime. It is testimony to the enduring appeal of this mode of thought that we have often looked for the solution to the crime problem in the more restrictive regulation of criminogenic commodities, specifically guns, drugs, and alcohol. Indeed, this interest has contributed to the development of laws and institutions regulating each of these commodities. A fresh look at such policies leads to new perspectives about their current impact, and to some specific proposals for increasing their effectiveness.

With respect to drugs, for example, it seems clear that our policy is designed less to reduce crime than to reduce the number of chronic, intensive drug users in society. This may have a long-run effect on crime, and it is almost certainly a desirable social policy. But the immediate effects of current drug regulations are to *increase* rather than decrease street crime. To the extent that we want to use policies in this area to control street crime, we should emphasize heroin over other drugs, and should focus existing capacity for supervising and treating drug users on heroin addicts who commit street crimes at very high rates.

With respect to guns, the great legislative struggles over policies aimed at the national inventory of handguns are distracting attention from a narrower but plausibly useful policy. Much statutory authority now exists to support a policy of keeping guns out of the hands of likely criminal offenders, and off city streets. Moreover, all one needs to do to make this statutory authority effective is to rouse large city police departments to take their responsibilities in this area more seriously. They are in a good position to prevent gun thefts, disrupt illegal gun markets, and discourage illegal carrying. One can reasonably doubt that such efforts will be markedly successful, but if local police cannot succeed at this task, it is hard to understand how more radical federal legislation would succeed, since any effort to shrink the existing national inventory of guns will ultimately depend on local enforcement capabilities. Given this fact, we might as well start by seeing what local enforcement agencies can do with their existing authority.

With respect to alcohol, opportunities to pursue crime reduction through tighter regulation of drinking practices have been neglected because of the shadow of Prohibition. There is reason to believe that higher taxes and other generally restrictive policies would reduce instances of public drunkenness and consequently some drunken violence. The price of such general approaches, however, is that a great deal of legitimate drinking is inconvenienced as well. A more surgical approach would be to renew police interest in public drunkenness laws, in order to prevent drunken people in public from being victimized, or from victimizing others.

Great hopes for effective crime control through broad regulation of criminogenic commodities are almost certainly unwarranted. They are dashed by continuing empirical uncertainties about the net effect of such policies on crime, a strong interest in protecting legitimate uses as well as discouraging harmful uses of the commodities, and limited institutional capacities for adopting and implementing more restrictive policies. To the extent that tighter control of criminogenic commodities does represent a possible approach to controlling crime, it is probably along the narrow paths described above. In all likelihood, while these measures hold only limited potential for crime control, they have one important virtue: they are probably feasible.

9

LAWRENCE W. SHERMAN

Patrol Strategies for Police

Few developments are more indicative of public concern about crime—and declining faith in the ability of public institutions to cope with it—than the burgeoning growth in private policing. In the past decade, reliance on private security personnel by businesses and individuals has increased markedly. Between 1972 and 1977, revenues for detective agencies and private protection services rose by 84 percent.[1] In many affluent neighborhoods, residents now pay commercial security firms $40 a month or more to patrol their streets, check their homes, or respond to their burglar alarms. In some less affluent neighborhoods, citizens have organized themselves into nighttime auto and foot patrols. According to a recent Gallup poll, 17 percent of Americans surveyed nationally reported some sort of organized volunteer crime prevention effort in their neighborhoods.

The upsurge in private policing bears witness to the persistence in modern life of an age-old, commonsensical conviction about public safety—namely, that "watching" is one key way of preventing crime. At the same time, the recent emphasis on voluntary watching efforts suggests a diminishing public confidence in the ability of publicly empowered police to perform this traditional task. Experience and research have both contributed to these public doubts. As recently as the late 1960s, the public tended to respond to rises in crime by calling for more police. Yet crime continued to climb despite rapid increases in police manpower. By the mid-1970s, municipal fiscal crises brought sizeable cutbacks in city police, and doubts about police effectiveness set in. At present, voters still seem reluctant to approve funding requests for additional police officers. Moreover, empirical research has tended to corroborate public skepticism concerning police effectiveness. A number of influential studies in the past decade have called the efficacy of traditional patrol methods into question.

In short, while common sense and experience strongly suggest that "watching" ought to be the centerpiece of any anti-crime strategy, there is little consensus about how and to what degree it actually works. Questions about the effectiveness of watching are becoming especially pressing in the 1980s, as the U.S. approaches a turning point in the quantity, financing, and organization of watching. Major changes in watching strategy have already occurred, and more seem to be in store. These changes raise important public policy issues: How much watching do we need? Who should pay for it? How effective is watching by volunteers? Should traditional police even do much watching, or should they rather work simply to organize and stimulate private efforts?

Watching is actually one of three basic strategies that human society has employed from the earliest times to prevent crime; the other two are "walling" and "wariness." "Walling" includes the use of locks, bars, fences, and similar obstructions to deny criminals access to person and property. "Wariness" includes all the adjustments in personal behavior that people make in order to avoid criminal attack (staying home at night, taking self-defense classes, leaving lights on when no one is home, etc.). "Watching," in contrast, refers to the various methods of observing people and places that criminals might attack, as well as apprehending the criminal in the act if an attack does occur. It includes police patrolling, the work of private security guards, and voluntary citizen efforts, as well as the informal natural watching that people do when looking out their windows and observing their neighbors.

Of the three strategies, watching raises the most difficult public policy questions because it consumes by far the largest amount of public financing and an increasing share of private resources. It is also the most controversial of the strategies because it is the most intrusive. Neither walling nor wariness poses threats to individual liberty, but watching conjures up specters of dictatorship and oppression.

History of "Watching" Strategies

In earlier preindustrial societies, natural watching played a key role in social control. Both Malinovsky's Trobriand Islanders and Sinclair Lewis's *Main Street* neighbors spent a good deal of time watching each other. Their watching was not their job or their duty; it was more a form of entertainment in the absence of other diversions. As social roles became more specialized or differentiated, watching became the specific responsibility of certain people, although informal efforts persisted. By the 15th century, for example, English village society had adopted a rotating system of assigning watch duties to adult males on a mandatory basis and without pay. This system soon degenerated as poorly paid watchmen were hired to take the place of wealthier men assigned to the duty.

The era of transition from volunteer watchmen to full-time specialists produced the stereotype of the drunken, sleeping night watchman. After almost two more centuries of highly literate (and well-documented) debate over the issue, the English finally decided to hire a full-time police force paid by public taxation. American cities shortly followed suit, and the quasi-military watch forces of Western Europe eventually moved toward this civilian police model.

The 19th-century foot patrol officer probably provided a highly informed and socially integrated kind of watching; while he was watching his beat, the beat was watching him. There is little detailed record of how police officers interacted with the public in the 19th-century cities, but folklore holds that the officers were familiar figures who knew the people on their beats. High-density neighborhoods provided ample opportunities for informal watching, and the proximity of the foot patrol officers meant they were available for gossip and conversation. Both police and the public probably watched with a great deal of contextual knowledge about people on the street—aware of who was familiar, who was not, who was dangerous, who was untrustworthy.

Three social changes in the 20th century reduced both the quantity of watching and the contextual knowledge that police and citizens brought to it: the emergence of the automobile, the spread of the suburb, and the growth of two-income households. Industrialization had already taken the male breadwinner out of the home for his work (which among other things profoundly changed the structure of child-rearing, leaving young males under less male surveillance and more prone to commit crimes). The car made possible greater distances between work and home, culminating in the low-density suburb, which made both formal and informal watching much more difficult to accomplish. After suburbanization came a substantial increase in the number of working wives, which for all its benefits had the tremendous cost of leaving two-career family homes vacant all day long, a factor strongly correlated with burglary.

Of these changes, the emergence of the automobile was perhaps the most significant. Together with the telephone, it reduced the need to rely on neighbors for companionship and communication. Social networks expanded over much larger geographical areas and lost their function as crime prevention surveillance systems. The automobile was also harmful to neighborhood relationships based on pedestrian traffic, although air conditioning and television also played a role in getting people off the front porch and away from watching (or hailing and chatting with) their neighbors; the disappearance of the front porch in modern home design reflects this change. Frequent job transfers also contributed to the post—World War II erosion of the social fabric of residential neighborhoods.

The automobile produced an equally great decline in public police protection. Taking police off foot patrol to put them into cars had the seductive appearance of increasing the level of watching by increasing the amount of distance police could cover in a shift. Cars also appeared to have the benefit of bringing police more quickly to crimes in progress, enhancing the intervention and apprehension side of the watching strategy. In fact, however, the watching that police do from inside a car is so different in character from the watching police did (and still do) on foot that it is questionable whether it should really be called "watching" at all.

What the patrol car officer sees is familiar buildings with unfamiliar people around them. What the public sees is a familiar police car with an unfamiliar officer in it. The public has little chance to tell the officers what is going on in the community: who is angry at whom about what, whose children are running wild, what threats have been made, and who is suddenly living above his apparent means. Stripped of this contextual knowledge, the patrol car officer sees, but cannot truly observe.

By assigning patrol officers to much larger beats, and by reducing the number of officers per capita, the regimen of automobile patrols created the further problem that even if the officer talked to citizens, there would be too many citizens to keep track of in sufficient detail. That is, in cases where police actually could obtain contextual knowledge, they would tend to suffer an information glut.

The greatest damage to the public police watching strategy, however, was produced by the use of the telephone in combination with police use of the automobile. The rise of telephone dispatch transformed both the method and purpose of patrol. Instead of *watching* to *prevent* crime, motorized police patrol became a process of merely *waiting* to *respond* to crime. Typically our society rewards those who deal with emergencies after the fact more than those who quietly prevent them: surgeons earn fortunes, while public health doctors are poorly paid. In a similar way, the modern "dial-a-cop" system has led police to forsake the routine work of crime prevention for the glamour of responding to "emergencies," many of which turn out to be long over and done with by the time police arrive.

In general, as the level of crime prevention watching has declined, the level of crime has risen, and so has public dissatisfaction with the public police. Rather than approving funds for more police, the voters have turned to volunteer and paid private watchers, while at least three cities have explicitly rejected a special tax designed solely to pay for more public police. The one exception to this pattern supports the thesis that the public wants more watching: Flint, Michigan, voters approved a tax increase specifically earmarked for neighborhood *foot* patrols by public police.

The recent growth in private watching has arisen from more than a desire to supplement reduced police watching; it has also been spurred by the civil courts. A growing trend of civil litigation holds businesses responsible for crimes committed against customers on or near business property if their security measures are "negligently" inadequate. Hotels, banks, shopping centers, and apartment complexes are under increasing threat of suffering large (some of them multimillion-dollar) civil damages if they do not hire private security guards or take other reasonable steps to prevent foreseeable kinds of crime. Corporate investment in watching parking lots and areas near businesses will probably continue to increase in response to this pressure.

Even without the spur of litigation, some businesses are striving for more watching. A group of Oakland, California, corporations, for example, recently agreed to pay several million dollars to fund public police to serve the corporations' private need for better watching in the downtown area. Again, the money was specifically earmarked for patrol strategies other than waiting for calls: foot patrol, horse patrol, scooters, etc. Given the money the corporations had spent on new office construction, their executives viewed the cost of watching as a prudent investment.

The public police response to the growth of private watching has been less than forthcoming. A recent survey of police executives found marked distaste for commercial private security guards. Rank-and-file police officers have long held their poorly paid private-sector colleagues in contempt. Auxiliary police volunteers have been the subject of even greater scorn by police, but police executives have welcomed the opportunity to keep auxiliary patrols under the control of the police department. The growth of citizen patrols outside the scope of public police control concerns many police executives (despite their public endorsements) as well as members of the rank and file.

This resistance to the growth of private watching can be understood in two ways. One is that public police are understandably concerned about the competence and trustworthiness of private watchers. They see many volunteers as "nuts" or cop "buffs" looking for cheap thrills. They see many private guards as badly screened and unqualified, a poor reflection on the police vocation. Unfortunate incidents of volunteer "vigilantism" and private guards' misuse of force reinforce their concerns.

The other way to understand public police resistance to private watching is as an attempt to preserve a monopoly. Public police unions have called auxiliary police "scab labor" (which they in fact were during the 1919 Boston police strike). Recent resource choices have clearly reduced the "market share" of watching held by public police, even though the size of the market has expanded. The more that police can discourage private watching, the larger the market share they may be able to retain.

Findings on Police Effectiveness

Methods of police watching are also undergoing changes, largely in response to research findings. In general, rigorous empirical research on police patrol methods has cast doubt on their effectiveness. Research on *private* watching efforts has been more sanguine, but less rigorous in method. The most positive findings about police patrolling suggest that police should move away from the waiting and responding (dial-a-cop) strategy to a more focused and goal-directed set of watching tactics.

Strikingly, researchers have discovered that police officers spend about half of their time *waiting* for something to happen. Some researchers describe this as "doing nothing"; others call it preventive patrol. But the empirical observations of police on duty in Kansas City (Mo.), Lansing (Mich.), and elsewhere show that much of this time is spent on matters other than watching—conversations with other police officers, parking on side streets without talking to citizens, and even personal errands. It is safe to say that very few urban police officers are aggressive "watchers" when they have no calls to answer.

This may help to explain another major finding, from the Police Foundation's well-known Kansas City preventive patrol experiment.[2] In a one-year study, automobile patrols were increased in five areas, virtually eliminated (except for responses to citizen calls) in five areas, and held at the same levels in five areas. Using both reported crime figures and the more comprehensive citizen surveys of crime victimization, the experiment found almost no difference in crime across the three groups.

The suggestion that differences in levels of police patrols do not produce differences in crime outraged many police executives and provoked a storm of controversy. But much of the controversy may have missed the point. The Kansas City experiment did not necessarily prove that police watching is ineffective; indeed, it may have suggested the opposite—namely, that a minor increase in police patrol does not deter crime precisely because it features so *little* watching, or so little watching backed up by contextual knowledge.

In fact, the modern theory of preventive patrol has stood the watching theory on its head, stressing the visibility not of criminals to police but rather of police cars to criminals. Patrol theorists argue that criminals see the police and are therefore deterred. The Kansas City experiment may have disproved that theory, but it said little that is conclusive about the converse ability of police to watch for criminals and catch them in the act.

Nor did the Kansas City study examine the effects of massive increases in manpower. Tripling or quadrupling patrol presence in an area would be too expensive to maintain for very long. But some quasi-experimental findings from New York City's subway system and 25th precinct suggest that massive changes might affect crime. Conversely, the apparent increases in crime prompted by police strikes suggest the effects of massive reduction (or a perception of massive reduction) in police strength.

The ability of the police to catch criminals in the act was tested by a second Police Foundation study in Kansas City,[3] which evaluated a police program of "perpetrator-oriented patrol." Police in plainclothes and unmarked cars were supposed to shadow serious repeat offenders. In fact, this method yielded little improvement in the number of arrests. But at the same time, researchers discovered that police were so inexperienced at watching serious criminals that they made numerous mistakes, allowing the criminals to recognize and elude them. (A more recent project in New York turned up similar problems.) Thus these project evaluations were not a fair test of the watching theory, once again because so little watching was done.

A third study in Kansas City[4] provided the strongest evidence against the wait-and-respond, dial-a-cop approach to modern policing. The study measured the impact of police response time on the chances of officers' intercepting a crime in progress and arresting the criminal. It found that the difference between police arriving in two minutes or twenty minutes was generally nil, because citizens took so long to call the police after a crime occurred. For "involvement" crimes—i.e., those in which the victims confronted the criminals—the average citizen delay in calling the police was fifty minutes. These findings were generally confirmed when the study was expanded beyond Kansas City and citizen delay was monitored in Peoria (Ill.), Jacksonville (Fla.), Rochester (N.Y.), and San Diego (Calif.). For police chiefs who had stressed the importance of rapid response for public safety, the conclusions were far from welcome.

The response-time findings suggest at least three options for police. One would be to maintain the same speed of response (and number of police officers), while educating the public to call police more quickly. A second option would be to reduce drastically the number of police officers on patrol needed to maintain an unnecessarily rapid response time. And a third would be to maintain the same number of police officers, but to reallocate them to more systematic kinds of watching in place of unstructured waiting.

Three studies provide evidence in support of the third option. All were designed to test a more intrusive kind of watching, drawing on richer police contextual knowledge of smaller areas. One was an experiment in "field interrogations," in which suspicious-looking people were aggressively sought out and questioned about their purpose for being in a neighborhood.[5] In neighborhoods where police halted that practice, certain kinds of crimes (notably juvenile vandalism) increased in comparison to neighborhoods where the practice was maintained. The limited implication is that field interrogations by police can deter minor offenses, especially the kinds that contribute to public fear of crime: visible signs of disorder in public places.

A Police Foundation experiment in Newark, New Jersey, found encouraging results for the use of foot patrol as a supplement to automobile patrols.[6] In a one-year comparison of similar areas with and without officers assigned to foot patrol, there was no difference in the levels of crime. (A recent Michigan State Univer-

sity study in Flint, Michigan, however, yielded preliminary findings of a reduction in crime produced by foot patrol.) Yet the
Newark experiment found that there was significantly less public
fear of crime in the areas with foot patrol officers. The public also
perceived lower levels of disorder—panhandling, rowdy play by
juveniles, drunks lying on the sidewalks, prostitutes soliciting
customers—in areas patrolled on foot. Since disorder has been
shown by other studies to increase fear of more serious crime, it
appears that foot patrol officers reduced fear by reducing disorder.
And since fear of crime is an important factor in residential and
business flight from central cities, reducing public fear of crime is
an important achievement.

The foot patrol experiment also suggested a solution to one of
the biggest problems of watching: boredom. Interviews of automobile officers and foot patrol officers (some of whom were volunteers) suggested that the foot patrol officers were more satisfied
with their jobs. This supports the findings of a third study, the San
Diego Community Profile Project.[7] The Police Foundation evaluation of this project found that when officers were assigned the
task of learning about the social fabric of their patrol beat, they
tackled the job with great relish and learned a great deal by inter-
viewing citizens and businessmen, analyzing crime, and compiling
demographic statistics. While the study did not examine the impact of this knowledge on the officers' ability to reduce crime, it
did show that officers can acquire the contextual knowledge they
are likely to need to watch more effectively and become more interested in their watching.

The limited research on the effectiveness of watching by private
citizen volunteers who are familiar with their neighborhoods is
even more encouraging, if somewhat harder to believe. A great
deal of press coverage quotes leaders of volunteer programs (not
social scientists) claiming dramatic crime reductions, especially
for burglary, as a result of the volunteers' efforts. Many factors
can affect reported crime rates, however, and in the absence of a
rigorously controlled experiment it is hard to be sure that the
reductions in crime figures are due to the volunteers.

More careful studies also suggest a short-run reduction in crime
rates when a neighborhood adopts volunteer watching, especially
when watching is combined with better efforts at walling and

wariness. But these studies also reveal a tendency for citizen interest in voluntary watching, at least from behind windows inside a house, to decline after an initial burst of enthusiasm. The classic example of this was a well-evaluated project in Seattle, in which a substantial decrease in crime was achieved. Shortly after the evaluation was completed, volunteer organizers noticed that citizen interest was waning, and the crime rate increased.

Another difficulty with the apparent short-term success of these volunteer programs arises from what may be termed their displacement effect. New watching efforts drive some criminals to areas with less watching, and consequently it is unclear what would happen if all areas were equally protected; criminals might just accept a higher level of risk, eliminating any effect of watching on crime.

A volunteer approach that is less common than watching from behind windows is watching on citizen patrol. The studies of these efforts have been less detailed, shedding little light on such problems as displacement and persistence of citizen interest. But there is at least some evidence that citizen patrols may be effective in apartment buildings.

There is virtually no systematic evidence about the crime prevention effectiveness of private watching in uniform, by commercial uniformed private security guards, uniformed volunteer auxiliary police, or uniformed volunteer patrols such as the Guardian Angels. (One exception is a nonexperimental study that claims private guards help prevent bank robbery, but other evidence contradicts this finding.[8]) Nor is there any study of the alleged "vigilantism" or other problems (including injuries to volunteers) that the existence of these groups may create. The absence of such knowledge may at least partly explain why both participants and residents are eager for these patrols, since it "makes sense" that they should deter crime. But it also "made sense" to argue that increased police patrols and rapid responses deterred crime, until systematic evidence suggested the opposite.

The ironic law of evaluation is that the more carefully a strategy is evaluated, the less likely it is to be found effective. This bit of gallows humor by social scientists, who take the heat for delivering bad news, is relevant to some, but not all, studies of watching. While the studies of current police practices are rigorous and have arrived at largely negative conclusions, studies pointing toward a new strategy are not very rigorous and the findings have been positive. The findings on private watching, while generally positive, are far from reliable. Much more research is needed before we can be very conclusive about whether and how watching can prevent crime, through either public or private efforts. But the empirical findings now available do raise important public policy questions—and the answers cannot wait for more research.

Patrolling and Crime Prevention

The basic policy issue facing watching efforts concerns goals and focus. Do we want to prevent crime, or do we want to do something about criminals? British criminologist Leslie Wilkins has suggested that modern public policy has badly confused these two very different tasks. For even though catching and punishing criminals may have some deterrent effect on crime, there is much more to crime prevention than punishment—and in any case we are simply not able to catch and punish most serious criminals. Yet arguably modern crime control efforts, especially by the public police, have focused too exclusively on a punishment strategy at the expense of others. The growth of private watching may be an indication of public preference for broader strategies of prevention.

To the degree that the primary policy goal should be crime prevention, it will be necessary to alter policies governing both public and private watching.

With regard to the police, policymakers have traditionally been preoccupied with questions of quantity—i.e., how many police are needed and how big a police budget is required for public safety. But answers to such questions depend crucially on what the police need to do. For the past two decades police executives have lobbied for more personnel on the grounds of reducing response time in order to catch criminals more effectively. Now that empirical findings have shown little connection between response time and arrest, one needs to ask whether officers are needed for rapid response. Police executives have also lobbied for more personnel on the grounds that the increased visibility of automobile patrols will act as a deterrent to crime. Here, too, empirical findings offer little support for this policy perspective.

At the same time, adopting the goal of crime prevention does not necessarily imply a reduction in police personnel. Indeed, it may imply an increase. We have not yet even begun the research needed to learn what methods are most effective for public police to prevent crime, let alone how many police are needed to do it. But if police are to develop a strategy of watching neighborhoods closely with detailed knowledge of social context, then more officers per capita could well be required.

One way of getting more watching without increasing the size of the police force would be to deemphasize police responses to citizen calls for service. Police executives are very reluctant to cut back on the dial-a-cop service, because each caller who is not served in this way may well become a critic and complainer about the police department. Still, a public education effort could stress the benefits to the many of cutting back on service to the few; most people never call the police, even though they are bothered by the same minor problems (noise, rowdy kids, family arguments) that produce most complaints. If police restricted their responses to true emergencies and crimes in progress, very few officers would be needed for the wait-and-respond strategy. Most patrol officers could be freed for crime prevention.

Despite the political problems with such an approach, there are some signs of movement in this direction. The National Institute of Justice has funded the design of a "call-screening" system, in which police telephone operators gather more detailed information about the nature of the caller's problem. The operator then decides whether or not a police car should be sent to the citizen, and if so, how quickly. Some callers may have to make an appointment to see police the next day; others, who have only a minor crime to report, may be told that they have to visit or phone a police station to report the crime. The system is now being field tested in several sites.

The adoption of a call-screening system is the first step away from the maxim that 911 (the emergency police telephone number in many cities) runs the police department. It implies that police will no longer let individual complaining citizens—an unrepresentative sample of the population—decide how the police will spend their days. It commits the department to using analysis and planning to decide on crime prevention strategies and to carry them out on its own initiative. It is the first step in transforming the public police from a primarily reactive force into a more goal-seeking organization.

A decision to take more initiative, however, raises many difficult questions about which strategies to use. One strategy is to have the police themselves do more watching. If that watching is to be based on contextual knowledge of an area, much of it should probably be done on foot. That does not necessarily mean police must give up their patrol cars. They can park the cars and walk near them. With modern radio equipment strapped to their uniforms, police no longer need to be in the car to maintain radio contact in case of emergency. Nor do they even have to be available for responding to calls all the time if call-screening is taken seriously. Most police in most big cities could probably spend four hours of most eight-hour tours on initiatives of all sorts that would not be interrupted by calls for service.

Yet there is some question whether the police themselves should be the primary providers of watching services. Given the low density of most residential neighborhoods, the assignment of highly trained and highly paid public police officers to patrol them is probably an inefficient way of performing watching services. Instead of trying to do all or most of the watching themselves (and viewing other watchers as a threat), police might become organizers and coordinators of private watching efforts, both commercial and volunteer.

Public police officers are in an excellent position to coordinate private watching. They stand at the peak of a hierarchy of watchers, commanding the most legitimacy, authority, and respect. They have access to reported information about crime patterns and trends in small areas—information that could help focus watching efforts more productively. And with more personal contact with area residents and business people, public police could gather even more information about the social life of an area, providing the context for understanding crime patterns and doing more informed watching.

One model for this coordinating role in residential areas would be a "cop-of-the-block" plan currently under development in Minneapolis. Under this plan, one officer would be assigned to a block club as a permanent liaison. The officers would still have many other duties, and might serve multiple block clubs. Their work would include attending the club meetings several times a year, in order to stimulate and maintain citizen interest in volunteer watching. The cop of the block could suggest strategies the club might follow for dealing with its own local problems, such as pressing the parents of unsupervised juveniles to bring them under stricter control.

The growing numbers of commercial security firms providing neighborhood watching services could benefit from closer coordination with public police. Instead of resisting (and sometimes harassing) the private guards, public police could meet with them regularly. They could review crime patterns, suggest locations needing special attention, and discuss possible suspects or descriptions of unknown suspects. The coordination efforts would also allow public police to exercise tighter control over their private counterparts, training and regulating them while helping them provide better service to their paying customers.

As organizers and coordinators of private watching, police would require very different skills. Each police officer working with neighborhoods would have to become adept at community organizing, running meetings, motivating and training volunteer leadership, conducting crime analyses, and planning crime prevention strategies. Few urban police officers have ever engaged in any of these activities. The transition to this kind of role would be a painful process, perhaps even an impossibility under current constraints of police union power. But the potential payoff in total watching efforts from a small amount of police "leverage" may be worth the attempt. From the investment of one public police officer's time for a few hours, hundreds of hours of focused private watching could result. This seems to be a better bargain than paying public police to do all the watching by themselves.

To be sure, there are some types of watching that should not and cannot be entrusted to citizen volunteers. Two of the most important are watching for repeat criminals and for the carrying of concealed weapons. Little police watching for these problems is currently being provided, but a conscious decision to cut back on dial-a-cop services would allow police to invest more of their highly trained resources in these tasks, with a great payoff in potential reduction in crime.

Watching repeat offenders is important because they seem to account for such a large portion of serious crime. According to some estimates, as few as 5 percent of all offenders may account for over half of all robberies and other violent crimes for gain. If police can catch repeat offenders in the act, they are more likely to obtain convictions and incapacitating prison sentences.

The problems that surfaced in the Kansas City and New York experiments with watching repeat offenders are not insurmountable. The Washington, D.C., police, for example, recently launched a similar effort with apparent success at disguising both the officers and their automobiles. Whether these programs can prove to be effective is still unclear, but at least they can be implemented more carefully, and they do not even necessarily require the creation of a special unit. In another recent program in Brooklyn, pictures of local repeat offenders have been posted in the station house so that all police officers on patrol can watch out for them. After years of posting pictures of the ten most wanted criminals nationwide in every police precinct, we have finally discovered the much more useful technique of targeting the most serious *local* criminals—whom police have a much better chance of catching.

Perhaps an even more important kind of watching that police should do themselves is watching for guns carried illegally. To restrict the carrying of guns (as distinct from their ownership) is extremely important, because most guns crimes are committed by people who have had to carry them in public illegally. Moreover, the Massachusetts experience with mandatory sentences for gun crimes suggests that reduced carrying of guns may reduce gun crime. If police can seek out and apprehend a larger percentage of people carrying gun illegally, they may be able to reduce gun crime even more.

There are major constitutional, technological, and political obstacles to watching for guns. "Roadblocks" of pedestrians to search for guns, dogs on street patrol that can smell ammunition, and metal detection devices all offer possibilities for new police initiatives in gun detection. But any major effort in this area may require a conscious public policy to allow the police to become more intrusive in order to reduce the rate of gun crime.

Use of Volunteer Patrols

Different policy issues arise for volunteer and paid private watching. Volunteer watching raises the question of how much public support and control it should receive. The millions of dollars in U.S. Justice Department funding that helped spark the volunteer efforts in the 1960s are now gone. Some communities have picked up the costs of supporting volunteer programs out of other federal or municipal funds, but many other programs have died with the end of federal funding.

Some may question the need for *any* funding for volunteer programs. The costs of walkie-talkies, gasoline for car patrols, street signs warning criminals away, and other expenses may be viewed as unnecessary frills. Alternatively, one could argue that the volunteers should raise the funds for these expenses through donations, car washes, and the like. But the biggest expense is neither a frill nor something that can be paid for with bake sales: the salaries for professional community organizers.

The key problem in starting and maintaining volunteer watching efforts is motivation. Technical guidance on how to watch is also helpful, but watching is not very complicated. One cause of the poor maintenance record of volunteer efforts may be the simple fact that, in the context of modern culture, watching is just boring. Motivating volunteers to continue watching, year in and year out, is a major need that community organizers can fill—but without public funding, it is unlikely that this job will get done. Voluntarism may be on the rise, but for people to spend many hours a week (or month) guarding their neighborhoods will require a major change in modern life-styles.

With a different kind of public mandate it might be possible for police to serve as the community organizers maintaining block clubs. But under present conditions, it is probably unrealistic to expect police officers to use salesmanship and persuasion to create block clubs out of a collection of strangers. Even the cop-of-the-block role would depend on community organizers' creating the block clubs for police officers to work with. And even community organizers may be unable to elicit the necessary community motivation.

Three policy choices are available for funding community

organizers: federal, local public, or local private funding. Both federal and private funding are too precarious for institutionalizing these efforts, given their abrupt fluctuations from year to year. Local public funding makes more sense as a continuing source of support. If more watching for crime prevention is a legitimate public policy goal and the public shows some willingness to participate, then a reduction in the police department budget necessary to cover the costs of community organizers would be a reasonable trade-off.

Still, some issues in organizing volunteers must also be addressed: whether neighborhoods should be organized around a broader set of problems than just crime, whether the police department rather than an independent agency should control the organizing, and whether volunteers on patrol should be trained and certified by police to avoid unfortunate mishaps. The most basic question is still effectiveness. Before substantial public funds are committed to supporting volunteer efforts, rigorous experimental evaluations of this strategy should be conducted.

The policy issues facing commercial private security primarily concern regulation. Some critics have attacked the boom in private security as "the new feudalism," whereby rich companies and individuals are able to hire personal armed retainers. Although the image is extreme, this development raises legitimate questions of accountability, such as whose interests are to be served by state licensing of private employees to carry arms and to exercise limited or "special" police powers. The legitimacy of these questions is reflected by the debate within the security industry about whether private guards should be armed, how much background screening and training should be required of each guard, and how much monitoring of private security companies should be done by local police agencies. The effectiveness issue also needs to be addressed. In the absence of empirical research on the crime prevention effects of private security guards, it seems at least questionable to hold companies liable for millions of dollars in legal damages for failing to provide them.

We still do not know to what extent watching can prevent crime. But before moving more resources into walling or wariness, we should at least give watching a chance—and current public police strategies are not a fair test. Implementing a total watching strategy that is more likely to succeed will be difficult, but at least the basic elements required of such a strategy are fairly plain.

One point seems clear. We should not change the current numbers of public police. Instead, we should redirect their efforts away from waiting and responding toward analyzing, coordinating, and watching. Police should spend more time on foot talking to citizens, and do more to stimulate and guide volunteer watching efforts. They should focus special attention on repeat offenders and illegal gun-carrying. They should gain the time to do this by refusing to handle certain kinds of requests, despite the political storm it may provoke.

Public and private watching efforts in all their various forms should be subjected to rigorous testing in field experiments. The results should be used to guide policy choices between public and private watching, and among the different strategies now in use. Funding for community organizers to initiate and maintain volunteer watchers on an experimental basis should be provided from municipal budgets by slight reductions in police funding, at least until the organizers' effectiveness can be evaluated.

None of this guarantees reduced crime. But trial and error is the only path open to us. If all these efforts fail, we will at least have learned more about what *not* to do, and we can move on to test other strategies for fighting crime.

10

BRIAN FORST

Prosecution and Sentencing

It is well known that most crimes are not reported to the police, and that most of those that are reported do not result in arrest. The cases that do survive to the arrest stage are nonetheless plentiful in absolute number: during the latter part of the 1970s, an average of 1.5 million arrests for serious crime (homicide, forcible rape, robbery, burglary, aggravated assault, and grand larceny) were presented to prosecutors in the United States each year.[1]

What ultimately happened to those arrested? The standard statistical reference texts tell us little about that. Readily available statistics indicate only that new imprisonments nationwide (for terms of at least one year) ran between 125,000 and 130,000 annually for the period from 1975 to 1978.[2] From these figures we can conclude only that about one in ten persons arrested for felony offenses is sentenced to a term of imprisonment in the United States. The statistics say nothing at all about what happens to the other nine arrestees, and very little even about the one who is imprisoned.

This chapter attempts to provide a better understanding of what happens in the criminal justice system after arrest and before incarceration. In particular, it tries to answer the following questions: What determines which cases are accepted by the district attorney and then advanced to subsequent stages of prosecution? What determines the sentence that a convicted offender receives? What are the primary incentives that confront the actors in this process? Is justice done in this set of arrangements? What is currently being done to improve prosecution and sentencing? What policies and procedures appear at this time to be most in need of reassessment?

Typical Case Dispositions

Thanks to recent improvements in the record-keeping technology of prosecution and adjudication, we are beginning to learn what happens to suspects arrested in the United States.[3] Figure 1 depicts the outcomes of one hundred typical arrests for felony offenses in a large cross section of jurisdictions in this country. To begin with, over one-third of all felony arrests involve juvenile offenders. Statistics about the outcomes of these cases are not readily available, largely because of a widespread reluctance to maintain juvenile records. To the extent that we do know about the dispositions of the half million or so felony cases involving juveniles annually, we can say that as compared with adult felony cases, they tend to involve more variation in case-handling from jurisdiction to jurisdiction and, generally, fewer long-term commitments.[4]

We know considerably more about what happens to adults arrested for felony crimes. About 40 percent of these cases are either rejected outright at the initial screening stage or dropped by the prosecutor soon afterward; 60 percent are accepted for prosecution (or a total of forty of the original one hundred felony arrests displayed in figure 1). In about four of these forty, the judge dismisses the case due to evidence insufficiency, procedural difficulty (e.g., the prosecutor is not prepared), or the triviality of the offense; two more are eventually dropped because the defendant fails to appear in court after having been released on money bond, personal recognizance, or third-party custody. (Approximately

Figure 1
Typical Dispositions of 100 Felony Arrests
in the United States, 1974–1980

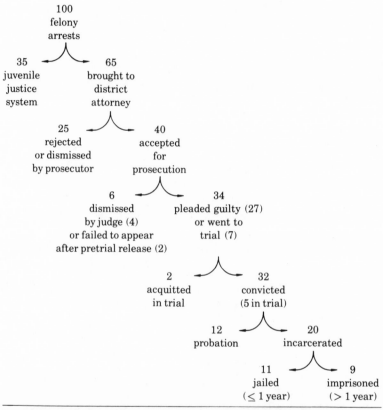

Sources: Brian Forst, Judith Lucianovic, and Sarah Cox, *What Happens after Arrest?* (Washington, D.C.: Institute for Law and Social Research, 1977); Kathleen Brosi, *A Cross-City Comparison of Felony Case Processing* (Washington, D.C.: Institute for Law and Social Research, 1979); Federal Bureau of Investigation, *Uniform Crime Reports* (Washington, D.C.: U.S. Govt. Printing Office, 1980); Bureau of Criminal Statistics, *Adult Felony Arrest Dispositions* (Sacramento, Calif.: 1981); Mary A. Toborg, *Pretrial Release: A National Evaluation of Practices and Outcomes* (Washington, D.C.: U.S. Department of Justice, 1981); Barbara Boland, Elizabeth Brady, Herbert Tyson, and John Bassler, *The Prosecution of Felony Arrests* (Washington, D.C.: Institute for Law and Social Research, 1983).

thirty of the forty defendants whose cases are accepted for prosecution are released prior to trial, and five are rearrested before the first case is resolved.[5]) About twenty-seven (80 percent) of the thirty-four remaining defendants plead guilty, usually to obtain a lighter sentence than if found guilty in trial; the other seven go to trial and are most often found guilty. Most of the thirty-two defendants thus convicted are incarcerated, with the majority of those given jail terms of less than a year.

Factors Associated with Conviction and Incarceration

These numbers tell us nothing about the factors that determine *which* cases are selected for prosecution and harsher sanctions. Note in figure 1 that three-fourths of the adult felony cases that fail to end in conviction are weeded out by the prosecutor and never seen by a judge. To learn about the factors that influence felony case dispositions, we would do well to begin by focusing on these dropped cases and on the reasons given by prosecutors for rejecting them.

It turns out that the vast majority of all felony cases dropped by the prosecutor are rejected due to insufficiency of evidence—the police fail to produce adequate physical evidence (e.g., stolen property, implements of the crime) or testimonial evidence from victims or eyewitnesses.[6] The next major reason given by prosecutors, although far less common than evidentiary insufficiency, is triviality of the offense. The defendants in cases involving trivial offenses are generally not viewed as serious threats to the community. Most of these cases are dropped outright, while others are "diverted"; in the latter circumstance, the defendant is often required to complete a light program of counseling or instruction aimed at rehabilitation.

Many of the cases dropped or diverted are not trivial, however. Cases of assault, in particular, are frequently dropped by prosecutors—often cases involving serious injury—because they arise from communal circumstances. For example, studies of felony arrest processing in New York and the District of Columbia have shown that in the majority of violent offense cases, the assailant is known to the victim, and many even involve members of the same family.[7] Prosecutors usually regard such cases as unattractive; the victims, after having called the police to arrest the offender, are frequently uncooperative.[8] Because of uncooperative witnesses, prosecutors reject arrests for crimes of assault within families at a rate of over 40 percent—nearly three times the rate for assault cases involving strangers.[9] Husbands who make a habit of assaulting their wives may actually commit serious crimes in the home as frequently as other offenders with more serious criminal records do on the street. Prosecutors nonetheless traditionally have been loath to give the attention to such cases that may be warranted by conventional standards of justice.

It is widely believed that many, if not most, felony cases presented to prosecutors are dropped for another reason—legal "technicalities" related to Fourth Amendment exclusionary rule violations. In fact, fewer than 1 percent of all felony arrests are dropped on such grounds.[10] While the exclusionary rule may retard the ability of the police to arrest a large number of offenders, it does not appear to play a major role in the prosecutor's decision to reject or dismiss cases.[11]

Of course, the reasons for case rejections officially recorded by public agents are not necessarily to be believed. On this question, however, independent empirical evidence exists to validate the prosecutors' official reasons. Convictions are systematically more likely to follow arrest when police produce and document physical evidence in the case than when such evidence is not produced. Likewise, when police produce information about two or more witnesses (including victims), convictions are more likely to follow. Finally, when police are able to make the arrest soon after an offense occurs, physical evidence is more likely to be found, and thus convictions are more likely to follow, than when more time elapses between the offense and the arrest.[12]

There is nothing surprising in the finding that arrests with the strongest tangible and testimonial evidence are most likely to produce convictions. Anyone brought up on Perry Mason knows that the evidence needed to convict in a courtroom must be sufficient to prove guilt beyond a reasonable doubt. More important is the fact that the *police* are responsible for obtaining physical evidence and information about witnesses, as well as for providing information to witnesses that induces them to support the prosecutor in convicting offenders. It turns out that some police officers consistently produce arrests that end in convictions at a rate that substantially surpasses random chance. In a study of arrests made by about 10,000 police officers in seven jurisdictions in 1977–1978, it was found that as many as half of the convictions were the product of arrests made by a mere 12 percent of the officers; nearly twice as many officers (22 percent) made arrests that failed to yield a single conviction.[13] The pattern held up even after researchers accounted for the officer's assignment, the number of arrests made by the officer, the normal conviction rate associated with each officer's offense mix, and randomness associated with the small number of arrests made by most of the officers.[14] Interviews in two of the sites suggested that officers with high conviction rates tended to be more persistent about finding witnesses and more conscientious about follow-up investigation than officers with low rates of conviction.

In short, whether an arrest ends in conviction depends in the first place on factors over which the prosecutor has no direct control: the strength of the evidence as presented to the police officer, the effectiveness of the officer in bringing the evidence (both tangible and testimonial) to the prosecutor, and the seriousness of the offense. Nonetheless, prosecution resources and practices do play a significant role in determining whether arrests lead to conviction.

District attorneys normally exercise considerable latitude in choosing the approximately 60 percent of felony arrests brought by the police that will prosecuted—so much so that the district attorney has been said to exercise "the greatest discretion in the formally organized criminal justice network."[15] The typical urban prosecutor's office, presented with about one hundred felony cases per attorney each year, obviously cannot give Watergate-level attention to each and every case.

In fact, for many (if not most) cases, the decision whether to prosecute is virtually automatic—cases in which the evidence is either extremely weak or strong and cases involving either trivial or very serious offenses. Numerous studies agree that prosecutors' case-screening and handling decisions have been influenced primarily by the strength of the evidence and the seriousness of the offense.[16] More recently, prosecutors in many jurisdictions have instituted programs to "target" their resources on cases involving repeat offenders.[17] Prosecutors' decisions on these questions are assuredly not random.

Within these boundaries, however, there is substantial discretion. In deciding whether to accept cases, in selecting charges to file with the court, in negotiating pleas with defense counsel, in preparing cases more or less extensively for trial, and in recommending sentences to judges, prosecutors have a good deal of room to maneuver. Written policies used even in the most rule-conscious offices do not provide unambiguous instructions about how to handle every type of case. Because of this discretion, even the best statistical models of prosecutors' decision-making are incapable of accurately predicting screening, charging, or plea-bargaining decisions in particular cases.

When asked to explain the rationale behind the decisions, most prosecutors are inclined to say that case-handling decisions, like medical decisions, involve both science and craft, and that experienced prosecutors know how to blend the technical requirements of the law with the good judgment that comes from years of practice. Unfortunately, this tells us nothing about the underlying goals that influence their decision-making process. Nor do we know whether prosecutors consciously make case selection and handling decisions with such goals in mind. Most prosecutors argue that while justice, crime control, and speedy case-processing are all worthy goals, each case is unique. Whether to accept a case, what charges to file, how much time to spend preparing it for a court proceeding, what charge or charges to allow the defendant to plead to in return for dropping other charges (or what sentence to recommend to the judge if the defendant pleads guilty to a particular charge) in any given case cannot be determined by pondering over abstract goals or resorting to a formula derived from such goals.[18] Until a strong argument can be made for instituting a more explicit set of rules (or guidelines) for making case-processing decisions based on well-established empirical links between the rules and such tangible goals as reduced case-processing time and crime control through incapacitation, decisions about individual cases are likely to continue to be made in a subjective and largely unpredictable manner.

Sentencing decisions are not substantially more predictable. The seriousness of the offense, an important factor in prosecution, is also important in sentencing.[19] The offender's prior record has been found to predict sentence severity, especially since the institution of "career criminal" programs.[20] And there is a third predictor of sentence severity: offenders who plead guilty tend to receive lighter sentences than those similarly charged who take their chances and are found guilty in trial.[21]

The sentencing decision is shaped most decisively, however, by the sentencing judge. In fact, recent research on sentencing variation has found the sentence to be affected more by the sentencing judge than by all other factors combined. This finding has been confirmed both in studies in which identical cases were presented to several judges and in studies based on analysis of sentences in light of detailed case descriptions in presentence investigation reports.[22]

Judges are responsible for several kinds of unwarranted sentence disparity. Some judges simply give generally more severe (or lenient) sentences than others. It has been found that judges who support rehabilitation as the primary goal of sentencing tend to give more lenient sentences, while those who support the more strictly utilitarian goals of deterrence and incapacitation have been found to give harsher sentences.[23] There are also more selective kinds of variation; a judge who is neither especially tough nor lenient on the whole may be more lenient than most judges, for example, with defendants found guilty in trial or with persons convicted of forgery. And finally, there is a natural element of inconsistency among the sentencing decisions of an individual judge.

What about the effect of racial or sexual discrimination? After reviewing the available research evidence on the effect of the defendant's race on the sentence he receives, a National Academy of Sciences panel recently concluded that "factors other than racial discrimination in sentencing account for most of the disproportionate representation of blacks in U.S. prisons. . . . Blacks are overrepresented in prison populations primarily because of their overrepresentation in arrests for the more serious crime types."[24] The panel did acknowledge the likelihood of racial discrimination in the decisions of some individual judges in some jurisdictions, and stated clearly that any such discrimination, however small, is unacceptable.[25] Similarly, the disproportionate number of males in prison is primarily the result of the disproportionate number of males arrested for serious crime. When studies do find gender differentials in sentencing, they are usually to the advantage of women offenders.[26] There are other kinds of variation in sentencing, such as that among urban, suburban, and rural courts in the same jurisdiction, but such discrepancies are rarely regarded as "unwarranted" in the same sense as the variations discussed above.

Incentives of Prosecutors and Judges

With a few exceptions, therefore, contemporary case selection and sentencing practices generally accord with our commonsense idea of justice. Prosecutors and judges tend to act in such a way as to ensure that those offenders who pose the greatest threat to the community are convicted and incarcerated—a tendency consistent with the utilitarian principle of crime control through incapacitation and deterrence. The practice of reserving the most severe sanctions for the most serious offenders is consistent both with the notion of "just deserts" and with the principle of deterrence. Likewise, the inclination of prosecutors and judges to conserve scarce court resources by assigning relatively lenient sentences to offenders who plead guilty serves the interests of speedy justice and economy. Arguably, there are other notions of justice, such as those emphasizing restitution and rehabilitation, that could be given more emphasis; nonetheless, current practices are not necessarily incompatible with these notions.[27] Given the substantial obstacles confronting prosecutors and judges—large case loads, limited resources, and broadly conflicting views about what the system ought to be accomplishing—it would be inappropriate to conclude that they are not acting in the interests of justice.

It would be even more inappropriate to assert that prosecutors and judges are not responding to incentives. Like other professionals, they care about their professional reputations; they tend to operate in a way that induces both their peers and the public they serve to respect their judgment and take note of their effectiveness.

As publicly elected officials, district attorneys in particular are usually inclined to conduct themselves so as to appeal to the general public. Unfortunately, public assessments of the effectiveness of district attorneys may have little to do with the actual achievement of justice. One district attorney may be especially conscientious, for example, about taking on cases involving highly active offenders, even when these cases require the commitment of additional resources (e.g., giving extra attention to the needs of reluctant witnesses). If as a result the crime rate were reduced by 10 percent, our inability to prove cause and effect would prevent even the district attorney from knowing with certainty whether his conscientiousness paid off. Another district attorney may routinely drop cases involving repeat offenders unless they happen to be easy cases, taking on only cases that do not require so much attention; and then he may even boast of a 90 percent conviction rate for the narrow subset of cases that went to trial or resulted in guilty pleas. Since information about cases dropped by the prosecutor is not generally made available to the public, a prosecutor's legitimate crime control efforts, or lack of such effort, may thus go unnoticed.

What does give public visibility to the district attorney? Most conspicuous are the outcomes of the handful of exceptional cases that appear in the newspapers and on news broadcasts. Also important is the image that the D.A. projects in press conferences and public appearances on a variety of issues; for example, the D.A. can gain visibility by announcing crackdowns on organized crime and drug-dealing. If a prosecutor says he is tough on criminals and wins the exceptional cases that make the news, his failure to manage his office efficiently or to deal effectively with most of the cases involving predictably dangerous offenders— cases that rarely make the news—will not jeopardize his prospects for reelection or advancement to higher political office.

The "career criminal" prosecution programs, created in 1975, illustrate the tension that can arise between the goals of justice and crime prevention, on the one hand, and the incentives facing prosecutors on the other. These programs were initiated by the Law Enforcement Assistance Administration (LEAA) to deal with the problem posed by those relatively few offenders who, as researchers were beginning to find, account for a disproportionate share of cases involving serious crimes.[28] It had been perceived generally that prosecutors did not give extra attention to cases involving these more criminally active offenders—cases that were often otherwise unattractive. This perception was later validated empirically.[29] To provide an incentive for prosecutors to target more attorney time on such cases, LEAA offered additional resources to local prosecutors for the creation of career criminal programs. Many prosecutors, interested in the additional resources, applied for and obtained them.

Subsequent evaluations of these programs have shown mixed results, however. On the one hand, career criminal units have been found to allocate a much greater concentration of resources to cases involving potential career criminals—perhaps four or five times more than would be conventionally applied.[30] On the other hand, the criteria used by the prosecutors to identify career offenders have tended to be less than optimal. Rather than pinpointing the most criminally active suspects, most jurisdictions have developed criteria that are designed to be easy to administer and to produce interesting cases. Typically, a career criminal unit will target offenders with at least one prior felony conviction and current charges involving a serious crime—often homicide, rape, or assault. These criteria are better than none, but prosecutors can do even better by basing case selection on criteria that correspond more closely to the actual characteristics of dangerous, high-crime-rate offenders: prior arrests for serious crime, a juvenile record, youthfulness, drug use, and known involvement in robbery or burglary. These characteristics have been shown to be the strongest known predictors of predatory crime in research at the University of Pennsylvania, the Rand Corporation, and INSLAW,[31] yet for the most part they fail to appear in career criminal targeting criteria. The public has been deeply concerned about crime and generally supportive of career criminal programs, but in practice career criminal units have employed criteria that focus largely on criminals in the twilight of their careers, bypassing the offenders likely to inflict the most harm on society.

One measure of the enormity of the prosecutor's discretion is revealed in figure 1: for every felony case that a judge presides over in trial, nine felony cases are brought to the prosecutor by the police. Ironically, however, public scrutiny appears to be directed more at judges than at prosecutors and their case selection criteria. Yet since judges are less often elected officials and usually have judicial tenure, they tend not to place as high a premium as the district attorney on public sentiment. Judges do typically wish to establish reputations of fairness in their exercise of discretion and efficiency in clearing the court docket, but these reputations are established primarily among peers (despite frequent disagreement among peers about the goals of sentencing) rather than with the public. At the same time, however, judges are not oblivious to public sentiment. No judge cares to read in the newspaper that a defendant he or she released on personal recognizance was re-arrested for murder.

The incentives of prosecutors and judges, in short, are consistent with accepted standards of justice, but leave substantial opportunity for disparity and inefficiency in the exercise of discretion. The goals of prosecution and sentencing have not been made sufficiently clear, and information about the decisions made by prosecutors and judges has not been made sufficiently accessible, to cause prosecutors and judges to make decisions about individual cases that correspond closely or consistently to any particular standard of justice or efficiency.

Reform in Prosecution and Sentencing

Aware of room for improvement, many prosecutors, judges, and criminal justice reformers have set out to introduce procedures designed to produce greater accountability, uniformity, and efficiency in the decisions and practices that follow arrest. In the 1970s prosecutors began to rely on computers for tracking individual cases and case loads of individual attorneys, printing subpoenas, producing periodic reports showing various aggregate dimensions of office performance, and providing data so that office policy could be analyzed in depth.[32] While lack of information about prosecutor operations prior to the use of computers limits opportunities to measure the benefits of improved information technology, the proliferation of management information systems in a setting that traditionally has been ambivalent about such technology suggests that prosecutors gain benefits from these systems that exceed the costs. And despite the limitations of career criminal programs noted in the previous section, the adoption and retention of these programs after the withdrawal of federal support further attests to a growing consciousness among prosecutors about the importance of aggregate concepts such as crime control. Prosecutors, like other lawyers, have tended to focus traditionally on individual cases and litigation related to those cases rather than on aggregate concepts of performance.[33]

Notably, these reforms have been initiated with the full involvement of prosecutors. Other attempts to reform prosecution practices have been less successful. For example, attempts to abolish plea bargaining that have not enlisted the full support of the prosecutor have proved subject to circumvention through the replacement of charge bargaining with sentence bargaining and through an increase in the rate at which cases are dropped by the prosecutor.[34]

Sentencing reform has received considerably more attention than procedures to improve prosecution. A dozen or more prominent studies have reported finding variation in sentencing patterns among judges in individual courts and jurisdictions.[35] A variety of proposals to make sentencing policy more explicit and uniform have followed those findings. These proposals range from entirely voluntary schemes (sentencing institutes, sentencing councils, and voluntary guidelines), to schemes that attempt to limit sentencing discretion while maintaining moderate latitude for judges (presumptive guidelines and appellate review), and finally to programs that sharply narrow sentencing discretion (mandatory sentencing laws and rigid guideline systems).

Voluntary sentencing reform schemes are especially attractive, for several reasons. First, effective policy reform requires sensitivity to the attitudes of those who will administer the policy in order to minimize the risk of circumvention. The voluntary schemes most certainly succeed by this standard. Second, deliberate reform requires progress in small steps in order to minimize the risk of harmful unintended side effects, such as shocks to prisons or to probation systems. The three common types of voluntary schemes—sentencing institutes, sentencing councils, and voluntary sentencing guideline programs—appear successful by this standard as well. Sentencing institutes and councils are designed to make sentencing more uniform by inducing communication among judges about sentencing policy. Sentencing institutes, which operate at the federal level and in several states, bring judges together periodically, typically in large groups, to dis-

cuss sentencing policy generally; the discussion often applies
general sentencing principles to individual case studies. Sentencing councils, which operate in a few federal districts and in some
state and local courts, bring judges together in smaller groups to
reach consensus on actual cases before the court for sentencing.
Each participating judge studies the presentence investigation report for each case up for sentencing prior to the council meeting,
and then the judges meet to discuss their views, sometimes in the
presence of the probation officers who conducted the presentence
investigations, so that a specific sentence can be arrived at for
each case. Communication among judges about sentencing
typically occurs also in jurisdictions that do not have institutes or
councils, but the dialogue in such jurisdictions is likely to be un-
systematic and may exclude some judges altogether. The empirical evidence on sentencing councils suggests, however, that the
councils, at best, produce a small reduction in sentence disparity.[36]

Voluntary sentencing guidelines, developed in the mid-1970s as
an outgrowth of guidelines created for the U.S. Parole Commission,
aim to attract the support and participation of judges in two ways:
guidelines are explicitly formulated on the basis of "the collective
wisdom of experienced and capable sentencing judges,"[37] and compliance is voluntary. The guidelines are designed typically to reflect
average sentences given to various combinations of offense and offender seriousness, and are presented in the form of a matrix that
has the offense and offender seriousness levels displayed along the
columns and rows. For all that is good about voluntary sentencing
guidelines, they have not yet passed the most important test of all:
the most extensive evaluations of these sentencing systems to date
have not produced findings of significantly reduced variation in
sentences under voluntary guidelines.[38]

Compliance with sentencing guidelines may be stronger when
the guidelines are "presumptive," i.e., established by a legis-
latively created sentencing commission. The first major attempt
to bound the exercise of sentencing discretion in this way, by the
Minnesota state legislature, requires the judge either to give
guideline sentences or to provide reasons for giving other sentences. Like the voluntary guideline systems, presumptive guidelines are presented in a matrix defined by the seriousness of the
offense and the criminal record of the offender. While the reduc-

tion in sentence disparity has not been validated empirically at this time, one would expect less variation in sentences after the institution of presumptive guidelines than before.[39]

One aspect of existing presumptive guideline systems that discourages sentence disparity is appellate review. Sentences that fall outside the guidelines may be appealed by either the defendant or the state. In such cases, two factors are available to the appellate judge that facilitate the sentence appeal process: an explicit sentence guideline sanctioned by law and an explicit rationale for diverting from the guideline given by the sentencing judge. Appellate review of sentencing otherwise has not been an important factor in most jurisdictions of the United States, which do not have presumptive guidelines, even though it plays an important role in virtually every other common-law nation.[40]

More stringent restrictions appear to have been less successful. Rigid sentencing guidelines with strict enforcement have not been legislated, largely due to strong judicial opposition, and harsh mandatory minimum sentencing laws appear to have been easily circumvented. Studies of mandatory sentencing laws have found that they tend to induce dismissals, acquittals, and other outcomes that make the laws ineffective, so that the longer average sentences for those convicted are approximately offset by increases in the number of persons not convicted and sentenced. Thus, sentence disparity actually increases under mandatory sentencing.[41]

Directions for Further Reform

Until very recently, prosecutors and judges operated in a statistical void—a circumstance uncharacteristic of the other major components of the criminal justice system and inconsistent with contemporary standards of management and public accountability. Now statistical information on prosecution and sentencing is beginning to accumulate, and district attorneys and chief judges are tending to shift their thinking from the single-case litigation perspective instilled by conventional legal training to an orientation that considers the aggregate information in the context of goals of prosecution and sentencing. Thus the most fundamental and revolutionary aspect of reform in prosecution and sentencing appears to have begun.

The work that remains has to do primarily with the further development of guidelines for decision-making by prosecutors and judges and the further production, dissemination, and use of sound statistical information to support those decisions. The process of developing guidelines for prosecution and sentencing is itself important for its tendency to induce more systematic consideration of the means of achieving the goals of justice. Once developed, the guidelines serve as explicit statements of policy — primarily to render decision-making by prosecutors and judges more uniform, but also to provide essential information to other decision-makers. Defendants and their counsel, for example, should be less likely to accept inferior offers from prosecutors when the sanctions associated with a particular combination of conviction charges and prior record are explicit.[42]

Guidelines also provide standards against which data can be used to assess criminal justice performance. If the data indicate that the guideline standards are consistently too high — for example, stringent screening standards and harsh sentencing guidelines may produce high arrest rejection and case dismissal rates — a conscious choice can then be made either to make the guidelines less stringent or to improve performance (e.g., to improve evidence by using investigative resources available to the prosecutor more efficiently and to increase witness support by maintaining better contact with witnesses, perhaps using paralegal assistants).

The data can also be used effectively to assess and improve existing criteria for case selection, targeting, bail release, and sentencing decisions. Recent research has produced evidence that criteria derived from empirical analysis of computerized data maintained by prosecutors and courts can yield results that substantially surpass those associated with conventionally derived criteria at each of these important stages of criminal justice decision-making. We have noted the need for such criteria in career criminal case selection; if only nine out of one hundred felony arrestees are to be imprisoned, they should be truly the most dangerous of those with convictable cases. A similar example is provided by bail decisions. Many of the persons who are detained in jail pending trial have been found to have characteristics that make them predictably less prone to pretrial misconduct than others arrested for felony offenses and released. It is clear that by using pretrial re-

lease criteria derived from existing data to select persons for pretrial release, jail populations could be reduced substantially without increases in either pretrial crime or failure to appear in
court.[43]

If they are to use such criteria, prosecutors and judges must
first have reliable data about each of the factors germane to
screening and sentencing decisions. Prosecutors are usually quick
to express concern, as they should, about the need for prompt, reliable information about evidence from investigators, forensic lab-
oratories, and lineups. A crime control–oriented prosecution
system should show as much concern about data indicative of defendant dangerousness, including arrest history ("rap sheet") information, juvenile record, and a urinalysis test result (to indicate
whether the defendant was on drugs at the time of arrest).
Prosecutors and judges have not been conditioned to seek out such
information to support prosecution and sentencing decisions,
despite widespread concern about "false positives"—people selected for incarceration who in fact would not commit another
crime if released. The availability and use of reliable rap sheets,
juvenile records, and urinalysis test results, when combined with
existing information, would provide demonstrably more accurate
assessments of defendant dangerousness than current information alone is capable of providing; more accurate assessment
means fewer false positives.[44]

Data used by prosecutors and courts, properly processed, can
also help improve performance in other areas of the criminal
justice system. For example, district attorneys can induce the
police to bring better arrests by periodically providing information
to police supervisors about the outcomes of the arrests brought to
prosecution, broken down by department, precinct, and officer.
This information could include data about the frequencies of each
major type of outcome (such as those displayed in figure 1) and the
reasons for case rejections and dismissals. Information about case
outcomes could also be given routinely to the victims and witnesses in those cases. The systematic dissemination of information can also nurture cooperation between prosecutors on the one
hand and police, victims, and witnesses on the other. Public support of the criminal justice system is not enhanced by the routine
failure of prosecutors to provide feedback to victims and wit-

nesses; similarly, police incentives to produce better evidence are weakened if prosecutors routinely fail to provide information about arrest outcomes to police officers and their supervisors.[45]

Public and police support of prosecutors and judges is, of course, important, but more support is not absolutely essential. The criminal justice system has demonstrated that it can function without strong public support, without tight cohesion among its components, and with minimal levels of accountability and efficiency. Despite a host of reforms, prosecutors and judges can still find ways of conducting business more or less in the traditional manner, with a disproportionate focus on cases that go to trial and a low level of consciousness about performance in the aggregate. Improvements such as those that have been suggested above—further development of prosecution and sentencing guidelines and additional use of sound data to support the decisions made by prosecutors, judges, and others—can be largely ignored.

Yet they are not being ignored. Guidelines are gradually gaining acceptability, and statistical information about prosecution and sentencing is becoming almost abundant. Why? One apparent reason is that information technology has advanced to a stage that makes it irresistible even to those who are ordinarily reluctant to modify their familiar way of doing business. This technology in turn produces the data that, when analyzed, often make the need for guidelines more apparent. A second inducement to reform in prosecution and sentencing is pressure—from peers in other jurisdictions, legislative bodies, the media, and, especially in the case of prosecutors, political opponents. It is simply no longer respectable for a prosecutor to reject sound principles of management or for a judge to reject reasonable attempts to structure the exercise of sentencing discretion. The incentives of prosecutors and judges appear, in short, to be coming into closer alignment with the broader goals of prosecution and sentencing, and this is a hopeful development.

11

STEVEN R. SCHLESINGER

Criminal Procedure in the Courtroom

The question to be addressed in this chapter is what changes in the laws and rules governing criminal procedure in the courtroom can best improve the administration of justice—can, that is, make it more likely to distinguish accurately and speedily between the guilty and the innocent, and to strike a fair balance between the rights of the accused and those of society.[1] Changes involving the bail system, the exclusionary rule, and habeas corpus petitions will be discussed.

The Bail System

Bail is "a sum of money posted by the defendant or his representative to secure his release from jail until the disposition of his case."[2] The primary purpose of bail is to ensure a defendant's constitutional rights to due process of law and the presumption of innocence, by providing a way to avoid unnecessary incarceration when there has been no conviction. The primary practical objective to be achieved by bail is that the defendant appear for his trial. A second objective in some cases—although its propriety is disputed—is to set bail sufficiently high that a dangerous defendant must remain incarcerated and is thereby prevented from committing crimes prior to his trial.

Typically, shortly after his arrest the defendant is brought before a magistrate or judge who fixes a sum of money that must be deposited with the court in order for him to obtain release. In some cases, the amount of bail is determined by a schedule that sets bail for each offense depending on its gravity; usually, however, judges have a great deal of discretion in fixing the amount. Where there is discretion, judges must consider the likelihood of the defendant's appearance for trial, and in some jurisdictions the suspect's dangerousness to society may also be taken into account. Defendants who are unable to post the entire amount of bail[3] can turn to professional bondsmen who, for a non-refundable fee usually of 10 percent of bail, will deposit the full amount of the surety.[4] If the defendant does not appear for trial, the bondsman forfeits the entire sum.

Under the present bail system, a number of arbitrary factors operate to determine which defendants will remain incarcerated before trial—thereby thwarting the system's objectives. First, because pretrial liberty is denied to those who do not have the money to meet bail, the system discriminates against the poor. Second, the bondsman has a problematic role in the present bail system. Bondsmen "hold the keys to the jail in their pockets"[5] because by accepting or rejecting clients, they can effectively overrule a judge's decision to grant bail.

To the extent that there exist such factors unrelated to the likelihood of the defendant's appearing for trial—thereby resulting in unnecessary incarceration—the bail system entails a high social cost. Defendants who are unable to post bail and are consequently incarcerated are disadvantaged at trial and at sentencing. Pretrial detainees are disadvantaged because they are not completely free to aid in the preparation of their own defense, locate evidence, assist their attorneys, and hold a job (both to earn money to pay counsel and to prove reliability at their trials). Studies have shown that defendants held in jail because they cannot make bail are more often convicted and, when convicted, go to prison more often and receive longer sentences than those who make bail.[6] In fact, the data indicate that only 33 percent of defendants free on bail, but 60 percent of those detained, are convicted.[7] There may be a causal connection between the denial of bail on the one hand and conviction, frequency of incarceration, and length of incarceration on the other. This has not been shown empirically, but the possibility does deserve serious consideration. In any case, one group of researchers has called the higher conviction rate for jailed, as opposed to bailed, defendants the "most serious, disabling and inevitable effect of the bail system."[8] In addition, plea bargaining is encouraged by the system, since suspects who are not granted or cannot post bail are under pressure to make bargains and accept nonvoluntary pleas of guilty to gain release. One study indicates that jailed defendants plead guilty in about 90 percent of their cases as compared with 70 percent for those released on bail.[9] From a budgetary viewpoint, the direct economic costs of detaining the accused in jail, paying welfare benefits to his dependents, and providing state-supplied defense counsel are enormous. The *Task Force Report* on the courts concludes that pretrial detention expenses for the nation exceed $100 million annually.[10] In addition, prospects for rehabilitation may be unnecessarily eroded because pretrial detainees are often exposed to unhealthy influences in jail.

Conversely, the bail system usually does not restrict the liberty of those who are wealthy enough to meet the terms set by the court but likely to continue committing crimes. Thus, certain classes of suspects who have the financial resources to post bail— particularly gamblers, drug dealers, and those involved in organized crime—easily gain release and return to their crimes.[11] There is evidence that some suspects released on bail do commit serious crimes. Indeed, one study suggests that 11 percent of those on pretrial release are arrested on another charge while on bail.[12]

Release on recognizance and preventive detention. The combined effects of two major reforms—release on recognizance (ROR) and preventive detention—would go far toward rationalizing the process of setting bail and, ultimately, the decision as to which suspects should be incarcerated before trial.

ROR programs free selected defendants based on their affirma-
tion or promise that they will appear for trial. The suspect is interviewed by a staff member of a pretrial release program who ob-
tains and verifies information on his residence, family and community ties, employment, and prior criminal record. Based on
these factors, a recommendation is made to the court as to
whether or not the suspect should be released on recognizance,
which the court accepts or rejects.[13]

Greater use of ROR programs in the administration of criminal
justice would have the following advantages:

1. Defendants released on ROR appear at least as often at trial as
    those on money bail. The Manhattan Bail Reform Project re-
    ports that its ROR failure-to-appear rate of 1.5 percent was
    three times better than that for those released on bail in New
    York City,[14] and Wayne Thomas reports that in twenty Ameri-
    can cities the "intentional failure to appear rate" is about 5 per-
    cent for both bail and ROR programs.[15] Other studies have
    reached conclusions similar to those of Thomas.[16] Of course,
    appearance rates are higher for ROR defendants in part
    because careful screening eliminates suspects who pose high
    bail risks.

2. The cost of administering ROR programs is less than one-third
    the cost of detaining arrestees in jail before trial;[17] ROR can
    also free up to 40 percent more prison space for the convicted.[18]

3. ROR operates more quickly and efficiently than bail programs
    because release under ROR is granted at the first court ap-
    pearance; there is no waiting to raise bail money or to secure
    the services of a bondsman.

4. ROR eliminates for selected defendants an increased risk of
    conviction and incarceration due simply to their having been in
    jail before trial; judges and juries frequently know whether the
    defendant has been in jail. A 1970 study tends to document this
    by pointing out that 21 percent of convicted ROR defendants
    were sentenced to prison, compared with 96 percent of a group
    that qualified for ROR but was detained in jail as a control.[19]

5. Because ROR depends on community ties rather than on a fi-
    nancial incentive to appear, it does not discriminate against
    the poor.

6. Defendants are not exposed to the legal, social, and economic hardships of jail and to the resulting pressure to plea bargain.

7. The bondsman and the problems he introduces are eliminated.

8. Because ROR programs are "wiser and fairer than reliance upon the enterprise of commerce insofar as providing assistance for release and avoiding flight before trial,"[20] they will tend, at least over time, to increase the public's confidence in our criminal justice system.

Successful ROR programs require a well-organized pretrial release program capable of providing rapid and accurate information to the court. These programs must continue to meet the challenge of attracting financial support, especially as private monies diminish, conducting effective and fair interviews with suspects, verifying information, avoiding undue delay, and utilizing the best criteria for determining who should be released.[21]

While it seems that increased use of ROR would effectively improve the administration of criminal justice for suspects who are not particularly dangerous or violent, the public remains legitimately concerned about crimes committed by those on pretrial release and, generally, about the crimes of especially dangerous and violent repeat offenders. Therefore, we need to explore another reform designed to protect society from recidivists and dangerous criminals.

The statistics are frightening: according to eight separate studies, somewhere between 7 and 20 percent of persons under pretrial release commit crimes, and for some crimes the figure is as high as 34–70 percent.[22] One recent analysis finds that one of every six defendants studied was rearrested before trial, and one-third were rearrested more than once.[23] A study conducted by the National Bureau of Standards concludes that defendants in the dangerous crimes category "can be expected to produce a much higher recidivist rate—about 3 to 4 times as high as for those in the nondangerous category."[24]

In order to deal with these problems, courts should be given the power to deny release pending trial to a "small but identifiable group of particularly dangerous defendants as to whom neither the imposition of stringent release conditions nor the prospects of revocation of release can reasonably assure the safety of the community or other persons."[25] Known as preventive detention, this reform is incorporated in the District of Columbia Court Reform and Criminal Procedures Act of 1970:[26] it permits judges to consider danger to the community in granting or denying bail.[27] The D.C. act permits detention of a suspect for up to sixty days (1) if he is charged with committing a dangerous crime, *or* is charged with committing a crime of violence and has been previously convicted for the commission of a violent crime, *and* (2) if there is "substantial probability" established through an evidentiary hearing that he committed the crime for which he is charged, *and* (3) if no other conditions of release can assure the community's safety. Preventive detention is also incorporated in the Bail and Sentencing Reform Act of 1982 (S 2572), a bill passed recently by the United States Senate that would institute the practice in the federal system.

Similar legislation should be adopted elsewhere for the following reasons:

1. Preventive detention does not violate the Eighth Amendment, but simply extends the concept of nonbailable offenses that is firmly rooted in our legislative and judicial tradition. The Judiciary Act of 1789 stated that in capital cases the decision to grant bail rests with the judge; today, judges generally have discretion to deny bail in capital cases. In addition, the Supreme Court has held that the Eighth Amendment means that bail may not be excessive, *when it is set,* and that Congress may decide which offenses are bailable. In short, the Court has never established an absolute right to bail.[28]

2. The kinds of procedural safeguards that are provided in the D.C. act described above, and that should be provided in any preventive detention legislation, have the important effect of balancing carefully the defendant's interest in remaining free against the need to protect society. These or similar safeguards[29] constitute the "due process of law" required by the Fifth and Fourteenth Amendments before official restraints on liberty can be imposed.[30]

3. Pretrial detention for the purpose of maintaining the security of the community does not violate the constitutional right of a defendant to be presumed innocent until proven guilty,

because the presumption of innocence "has never been applied to situations other than the trial itself. To apply it to the pretrial bond situation would make any detention for inability to meet conditions of release unconstitutional."[31]

4. The District of Columbia Court of Appeals has upheld the constitutionality of the preventive detention provisions of the 1970 District of Columbia Court Reform and Criminal Procedures Act. The majority in *U.S.* v. *Edwards* concluded that pretrial detention on the basis of dangerousness is constitutional and that it should be used to deal with those who pose serious threats to the community.[32] The Supreme Court has not yet ruled on the constitutionality of preventive detention.

5. It can be forcefully argued that preventive detention is justified because those who have been convicted of committing the kinds of crimes that would subject them to preventive detention have forfeited what would otherwise be a presumption favoring bail, at least when the prosecution can show a "substantial probability" that they committed the crime with which they are charged.

6. We know that a relatively small group of criminals is responsible for a large percentage of American crime. Since preventive detention will tend to incarcerate members of this group, the most dangerous recidivists, it should be of substantial value in reducing serious crime.

7. Because the defendant is detained, this reform encourages defense attorneys not to delay the trial. The defense often has motivation to delay because, among other reasons, the prosecution's witnesses may become unavailable, evidence might disappear or become tainted, or adverse publicity may be forgotten by potential jurors.

8. The Judiciary Committee of the United States Senate in its report on the Bail Reform Act of 1981 concluded that "while predictions which attempt to identify those defendants who will pose a significant danger to the safety of others if released are not infallible, the Committee believes that judges can . . . make such predictions with an acceptable level of accuracy."[33] Indeed, a 1980 INSLAW (Institute for Law and Social

Research) study in the District of Columbia revealed that the nature and seriousness of the charge, the history of prior arrests, and the presence of drug addiction all have a strong positive relationship to the probability that a defendant will commit a pretrial criminal act.[34] In part because earlier studies raise doubts about the ability of judges to make such predictions,[35] it seems clear that more empirical analyses in this area are needed. Finally, the courts are not currently forbidden from making judgments about future conduct—they predict appearance in all release decisions and consider future behavior in sentencing. A requirement of total certainty as to these and other judgments would immobilize the system.

9. It is "considerably fairer to detain a defendant without bail after a full hearing on the issue of dangerousness than to detain him on a judicial hunch of dangerousness through the deceitful practice of setting bail beyond his financial capabilities."[36] Because community safety in fact underlies most bail decisions—even though most current statutes permit judges to consider only the likelihood of appearance—if there is no legal authority to deny bail on grounds of dangerousness, judges will continue to set high money bail as a "sub rosa form of preventive detention."[37]

10. Preventive detention "may help to lessen the oppressive fear of crime that hangs so heavily over the American society and is inhibiting the life of American cities."[38]

Three problems have arisen with the D.C. preventive detention statute. First, more judges, courtrooms, support staff, and prosecutors, perhaps specifically detailed to preventive detention work, are needed to conduct preliminary hearings and meet the procedural requirement that a detained defendant be brought to trial within a specified number of days. It does seem evident, though, that adequate resources should definitely be allocated to this area of criminal justice, because offenders subject to preventive detention are among the most dangerous and violent. A second problem is that D.C. prosecutors have been overly cautious about asking for preventive detention hearings because they have not wished to disclose evidence against the accused; they have preferred to surprise the accused and his counsel at trial. However, competent prosecutors should not have to rely on evidentiary surprises in order to win guilty verdicts;[39] prosecutors should be instructed by their superiors not to oppose detention hearings in order to prevent disclosure of evidence to the defense. Third, prosecutors in the District of Columbia have argued that the procedures of the D.C. preventive detention statute—especially the hearing procedures—are too cumbersome. These complaints have recently been considerably reduced, however, because prosecutors have become more familiar with the statute's provisions and their practical impact, and because *U.S.* v. *Edwards* has resolved many of the questions about which prosecutors were concerned. For example, before *U.S.* v. *Edwards* there was a question as to whether the prosecution need produce the crime victim for cross-examination at the detention hearing. Finally, it is worth noting that in D.C. some of the prosecutors' objections to detention hearings have been reduced by an amendment to the preventive detention statute that lengthens the permissible period between hearing and trial from sixty to ninety days, thereby giving prosecutors additional time to prepare for trial.

A third important reform is not related directly to the bail system but concerns effective implementation of the requirement for a speedy trial. One of the most important factors influencing the defendant's behavior while he is on bail is the amount of time between arrest and trial. The defendant's likelihood of avoiding both nonappearance and rearrest depends to a high degree on how long he remains on pretrial release—the shorter the wait, the better. One study reports that only 30 percent of pretrial crimes were committed within sixty days of the original arrest.[40] Reducing the amount of time between arrest and trial, thereby imposing the deterrent of "swift and certain judgment," reduces both nonappearance and rearrest rates for those awaiting trial.[41] This reform would of course involve the costs of increasing the number of courtrooms, judges, support personnel, and prosecutors.

The importance of bail reform should not be underestimated. In addition to the obvious social costs of the present system, the public perception of the difficulties contributes to general disenchantment with the criminal justice system. To the extent that reforms less sweeping than ROR or preventive detention are expedient, they should also be encouraged. For example, some jurisdic-

tions have initiated citations in lieu of arrest, whereby police are
authorized to issue tickets in the field or at the station house to
those arrested for misdemeanors when explicit conditions are met.
The citation instructs the offender where to appear for arraign-
ment. Two advantages of this practice are that judicial involvement is unnecessary and any period of confinement is avoided.[42]
Another available option is the 10 percent cash bail system, in
which the defendant personally deposits with the court 10 percent
of the amount of bail set. Ninety percent of the deposit is returned
upon his appearance and the remainder is used to fund the program. Such a plan places the entire incentive to appear upon the
accused.[43] These developments, while not sufficient in themselves,
are salutary; each step toward a rational bail system is important.

The Exclusionary Rule

The exclusionary rule renders inadmissible in criminal proceedings evidence that is obtained illegally or improperly by law enforcement officials.[44] The United States Supreme Court has imposed the rule on federal courts since 1886 and on state courts
since 1961.[45] It continues to be in effect although the public policy
justifications advanced for it cannot be sustained, and although it
has many serious social costs and disadvantages. Moreover, there
are alternatives to the exclusionary rule that would accomplish its
purposes and eliminate its drawbacks. For these reasons, the rule
should be abolished.

Since 1886, the two primary public policy justifications offered
for the rule by the High Court and by legal scholars have been
deterrence of illegal activity by law enforcement officials and protection of individual privacy.[46] The Supreme Court has made clear
in its most recent cases on the subject that it currently regards
deterrence of improper searches and seizures as the primary rationale for the rule.[47] Yet six of the seven empirical studies of the
deterrent effectiveness of the rule conclude that it does not
generally deter,[48] and the author of the seventh study comes to no
definitive conclusion on the question.[49] Indeed, the staunchest de-
fender of the rule in the social science community has recently admitted that "the rule has not always or even often worked [to
deter police misconduct]."[50]

There are many reasons to doubt the deterrent effectiveness of the rule. First, its impact falls only indirectly on police. It does not discipline the errant officer; the brunt of the exclusionary rule's effect is actually borne by the prosecution, which generally has little or no power to punish police misconduct.[51] Second, officers whose illegal actions result in loss of convictions may receive the implicit or explicit approval of their superiors.[52] Third, trial judges do not often explain to officers why their evidence is excluded; clearly the impact of the rule is limited if the police are not informed of the nature and effect of their wrongdoing.[53] Fourth, the loss of convictions through exclusion of evidence is not as serious a matter for police as might be thought, since police effectiveness usually is judged by numbers of "collars" or arrests, not by the number of convictions. Fifth, there are strong indications that the rule even encourages certain forms of police misconduct such as perjury or illegal searches and seizures. Such searches and seizures are conducted for public relations reasons—the police know that their fruits are inadmissible in court.[54] Sixth, the operating scope of the rule is limited only to evidence presented at trial, yet the trial constitutes but a narrow stage in the criminal process. As one presidential commission pointed out, "A great majority of the situations in which policemen intervene are not . . . criminal situations in the sense that they call for arrest, with its possible consequences of prosecution, trial, and punishment."[55] Because the rule is trial-oriented, it provides little or no remedy for police practices aimed at harassment or seizure of contraband rather than at prosecution and conviction.

In the past, the Court has portrayed the exclusionary rule as a partial protection of the privacy of victims of illegal searches and seizures: it is said to guarantee that, should the state invade the privacy of individuals during the course of a search and seizure, the fruits of that invasion will prove useless to the state in its prosecution, i.e., cannot be used to convict the person from whom they were taken.[56] But this justification cannot be sustained. Since criminal activity is predominantly a public concern, it should follow that a location is not private if activities of great public interest—crimes—are committed or concealed there; when the police find evidence of such activity—by whatever means—it is not an invasion of the individual's privacy to use this evidence in a criminal proceeding. A policeman who discovers evidence of a murder, robbery, assault, or drug factory should not be said to have happened upon private matters; the legitimate public concern for criminal activity and, in short, the public nature of the contraband, render the search for and the seizure of the contraband (but that only) a necessary and justifiable police activity on behalf of the public.[57] One can state this argument against the privacy justification a bit differently: a person who uses his home to store dead bodies or as a drug factory forfeits what would ordinarily be his right to privacy. This argument for the admissibility of criminal evidence does not, of course, extend to the fruits of police actions that are unrelated to search and seizure.

The social costs of maintaining the rule are extremely high, as the following brief catalogue of its disadvantages makes clear:

1. A substantial number of otherwise convictable persons escape prosecution or conviction because of the operation of the rule. Indeed, Oaks' landmark study of defense motions at trial to exclude evidence in gambling, narcotics, and weapons cases in Chicago indicates that "in every single one of these cases in which a motion to [exclude evidence] was granted, the charges were then dismissed."[58] It is sometimes possible to try or retry a suspect on the basis of evidence other than that illegally obtained; often, however, it is not, and persons dangerous to society are released. The argument has been made that a relatively small number of persons escape prosecution as a result of the rule. By using data developed by INSLAW concerning the disposition of felony and serious misdemeanor cases in seven representative communities during one year (1977–78), we can estimate that in the nation as a whole, 45,000 to 55,000 felony and serious misdemeanor cases were dropped by prosecutors during this period because of exclusionary rule problems.[59] In any case, if the exclusionary rule is misguided, then the release of even one convictable person is one release too many.

    A recently released study prepared by the National Institute of Justice (NIJ) of the U.S. Department of Justice found that the exclusionary rule had a major impact on criminal prosecutions in California.[60]

A significant number of felony cases were rejected for prosecution in California because of search and seizure problems. Statewide, 4,130, or 4.8 percent of all felony arrests rejected for prosecution from 1976 through 1979, were rejected becausse of search and seizure problems. In large urban areas a higher proportion of felony cases rejected were rejected for search and seizure problems. In San Diego County, search and seizure problems accounted for 8.5 percent of such rejections in 1980. In two Los Angeles County offices, the rates were 11.7 and 14.6 percent.[61]

In California, the greatest impact of the exclusionary rule was on drug cases, and for these cases the effect on case attrition was substantial: "71.5 percent of the felony cases rejected for prosecution in California between 1976–1979 because of search and seizure problems involved drug charges."[62]

Finally, the NIJ study found that, for most defendants, the arrest that ended in release because of the exclusionary rule was only a single incident in a larger criminal career.

About half of those freed were rearrested during a two-year follow-up period; they averaged approximately three arrests each.

45.8 percent of the 2,141 defendants not prosecuted for felonies in 1976 and 1977 because of the exclusionary rule were rearrested within two years of their release. The 981 individuals who were rearrested accounted for 2,713 rearrests, 1,270 of which were for felony arrests.[63]

Thus, the exclusionary rule prevented prosecution of repeat offenders.

2. Another problem with the rule is that it often excludes the most credible, probative kinds of evidence—fingerprints, guns, narcotics, or dead bodies—and thereby impedes the truth-finding function of our courts.

3. The exclusionary rule benefits only the guilty; it offers nothing—no help, remedy, or protection, and no compensation—to the innocent. A fundamental purpose of criminal law is to help the innocent. As Judge Wilkey says, "The exclusionary remedy flunks the basic test of protecting society."[64]

4. The rule undermines public respect for the legal and judicial system. One complaint about the legal system is that too many truly guilty suspects are released on technicalities. In

fact, this complaint most often refers to the operation of the exclusionary rule.

5. Both the suppression hearings and the appellate litigation made necessary by the rule are a significant drain on the limited resources of the courts. The 1979 General Accounting Office (GAO) study of the impact of the exclusionary rule on criminal prosecution, which covered forty-two of the ninety-five U.S. Attorneys' offices in the country, stated that "thirty-three percent of the defendants who went to trial filed Fourth Amendment suppression motions."[65] According to that report, exclusion was the most important single issue arising most frequently in federal criminal trials.[66] At the appellate level in the years 1979–81, 22.1 percent of the criminal cases reaching the U.S. Court of Appeals of the District of Columbia required analysis of a suppression question and a decision as to whether evidence should be excluded.[67]

6. Judge Wilkey has written eloquently about the way in which the rule deprives the innocent of adequate due process:

> The American standard of "due process" elevates the demand on whatever system is financed. The result has been plea bargaining, ostensibly the only way to keep the whole system from bogging down. Many innocent defendants who might well have been vindicated at trial are coerced into settling for a conviction on a lesser charge. . . . It is against this background that we must measure the diversion of energy, talent and dollars from the central task of fairly determining the guilt or innocence of defendants into adjudicating whether the police have blundered. . . . The exclusionary rule thus literally buys what little Fourth Amendment protections it affords at the cost of fewer and less adequate trials for criminal defendants. Even if the rule did a good job of promoting Fourth Amendment values, this would at best be a questionable bargain.[68]

7. The rule encourages judges to condone dubious or illegal searches and seizures in order to admit evidence they are loath to exclude. Because judges think that they must interpret probable cause expansively in order to admit crucial evidence, the rule may have the perverse and unintended effect of limiting the scope of privacy contemplated by the Fourth Amendment.[69]

8. The rule does not distinguish between more and less serious

crimes;[70] the same rule releases both the pickpocket and the murderer.

9. The rule makes no distinction between willful, flagrant violations by an officer and "good faith" errors committed in difficult circumstances.[71]

10. Internal disciplinary efforts by law enforcement authorities are sabotaged by the rule. Law enforcement agencies will be discouraged from meting out internal discipline if their findings are used to suppress evidence at trial. Conversely, law enforcement agencies will lack incentive to discipline internally if a judge has already ruled that a search was proper.[72]

11. The rule intensifies plea bargaining because prosecutors who fear suppression of important evidence at trial may be willing to negotiate regarding the seriousness of the charge or sentencing recommendations rather than risk dismissal.[73] To the extent that the rule is misguided, it gives defense attorneys an illegitimate and often powerful bargaining chip in their negotiations with prosecutors.

Alternatives to the exclusionary rule. Discussion of alternatives to the rule must begin with the primary objectives to be achieved through their use. These are effective deterrence of police misbehavior, compensation of the victims of illegal searches and seizures, and conviction of the guilty. The first two objectives require separate proceedings, a disciplinary proceeding against the offending police officer to achieve deterrence and a separate action to award compensatory damages. With such mechanisms in place, improperly obtained evidence could be admitted at trial and the third objective, conviction of the guilty, could be achieved.

As to discipline of the offending officer, a hearing should be held (separately from the criminal trial of the victim of search and seizure) before an independent review board that would investigate the nature and severity of the officer's misconduct. The board would assess an appropriate punishment ranging from a fine to permanent severance from the police force. It could take into account the record of the offending official. Furthermore, evidence that the officer acted in "good faith" (i.e., without knowledge of wrongdoing) or that he used reasonable force would be considered.

How would such a hearing be initiated? If a trial judge believed that there were evidence of illegal official behavior (regardless of the outcome of the trial), he could order such a hearing to be held. Under such a system, it would be the judge's responsibility to identify possible illegal police behavior, since defense counsel would not have the incentive of a suppression motion to point it out. In addition to judicial referral of possible misconduct, a citizen who is an innocent victim of illegal search and seizure, but who is never brought to trial involving this search, would be able to report his complaint directly to the review board for investigation. Some jurisdictions might even wish to allow suspects, whether convicted or acquitted, to bring their own complaints directly to the board, although (because of anger at the police) this could lead to the filing of substantial numbers of less than meritorious complaints.

The functions set out above could well be accomplished by an independent review board made up of citizens, judges, law officers, and any other groups whose representation may be desirable.

With regard to the civil remedy, we suggest a statutory civil action against the law officer's jurisdiction with provision for the award of monetary compensation, the amount depending on the gravity of the misbehavior (but with a minimum sum to be awarded in the event that any violation is found). Such an action would allow innocent victims to recover a basic compensatory amount plus counsel's fees without any showing of specific damage to the victim or flagrant violation by the officer. This civil action should not be available to the guilty—those who are discovered by the police with incriminating evidence on the basis of which they are found guilty at trial—because, as argued previously, their privacy has not been invaded and, thus, they deserve no compensation. The only proof necessary in this civil action would be a showing that the victim's Fourth Amendment rights had been violated; the greater the invasion of Fourth Amendment rights, the higher the compensation. The seriousness of the invasion, and thus the amount of compensation, would be measured by the amount of mental or physical suffering and inconvenience that was caused, as well as the degree to which an officer violated clear rules governing proper searches and seizures. There are now in existence state common law causes of action under which victims may recover damages, but civil actions are rarely instituted (and even more rarely won) because it is necessary to show either substantial harm to the victim (for compensatory damages) or outrageous official misconduct (for punitive damages). Winning the proposed civil suit would be easier because no such showing would be necessary. In addition to creating a means for compensation, this plan would provide an economic incentive for victims and for lawyers to bring cases of official misconduct to public attention.[74]

There may be difficulties with this proposal. Like any system, it would not deal properly with all violations, but it is superior to the exclusionary rule because direct discipline of law enforcement officers seems to be a much more effective deterrent than the weak and indirect deterrence of the exclusionary rule, and because the civil tort remedy provides compensation for the victims of illegal searches and seizures—a result conspicuously lacking under the exclusionary rule. Last but not least, all probative evidence would be admitted, regardless of the means used to obtain it.

One alternative to the rule in its current form has been suggested by the 1981 Attorney General's Task Force on Violent Crime:[75] the rule should be applied only when the officer acted in bad faith—that is, when he knew that his search and seizure was in violation of the law. This "good faith" approach to the exclusionary rule reform is incorporated in President Reagan's most recent proposal to Congress on the subject of crime, the Comprehensive Crime Control Act of 1983. However, the idea of abolishing the rule, while creating an independent review board and a civil tort remedy, seems preferable for four reasons:

1. *Each* of the 11 costs of the rule (except #9) will be maintained, although to a smaller degree, if the "good faith" approach is adopted.

2. The task force recommendation provides little or no deterrence for violations deemed by the courts to be in good faith. This might encourage police to see what can be gotten away with before the courts draw the line on what is an intentional violation.

3. The task force recommendation virtually guarantees years of trial and appellate litigation on what constitute "good faith" and "bad faith" violations.

4. The task force report puts a substantial premium on the ignorance of law enforcement officers. In order to render legitimate a search or seizure under the task force's proposal, the officer need only convince the judge that he did not know or fully
understand the applicable legal requirements.

Before concluding the discussion of the exclusionary rule, we
should note a justification for the rule given some, although not
primary, attention by the Supreme Court and legal scholars: it is
said to protect the integrity of courts. The theory seems to be that,
were the courts to admit illegally obtained evidence, they would be
condoning the methods used to obtain it and would consequently
lose the respect of the public.[76] Yet, does a court not lose the
respect of citizens when it frees dangerous, violent offenders? In
addition, while the courts surely have a duty to support Fourth
Amendment rights, due process, and fair play, they also have a
duty to pursue the truth—to free the innocent and convict the
guilty. Under the exclusionary rule, they fulfill only the former.
Under the plan described above, the courts to a large extent fulfill
both: they express their commitment to the Fourth Amendment
by turning over cases of possible police misconduct to the independent review board, and they express their commitment to pursuing the truth by judging evidence solely on the basis of its
reliability.

In conclusion, proponents tell us that we must tolerate the
manifold costs of the exclusionary rule because of what it accomplishes for us. But we have shown that the public policy
justifications for the rule cannot be sustained. What, then, does it
accomplish for us? In any case, there are a number of alternatives
that are clearly superior to the exclusion remedy.

Before we turn to habeas corpus, we should note that space
limitations prevent us from discussing an extremely desirable
reform of courtroom criminal procedure: reversal of the Supreme
Court's decision in *Griffin* v. *California*,[77] which proscribes
prosecutorial and judicial comment on the silence of the accused
at his trial. Prosecutorial and judicial comment, along with
defense rebuttal, aids significantly in the search for truth and
guides the jury in administering justice. The author has discussed
this matter in detail elsewhere.[78]

Habeas Corpus Petitions

Habeas corpus procedures provide a means for convicted persons to attack the legal validity of their convictions after their appeals have been unsuccessful. Article III of the Constitution extends "the great writ of habeas corpus" to federal prisoners, and the Judiciary Act of 1789 gives the courts of the United States the power to issue habeas corpus writs for federal prisoners. Congress extended habeas corpus relief to state prisoners in 1867. Many states have habeas corpus provisions in their constitutions or have provided for collateral attacks by statute.[79]

In order to initiate a habeas corpus petition at the federal level, a prisoner who has exhausted all available appeals files a petition with the appropriate federal district court outlining the facts of his claim as well as the legal matters in dispute. The petition must include a claim that he has been unconstitutionally denied his liberty. The federal court reviews the claim, either granting or denying it, and the prisoner has the right to appeal if it is denied.

The drawbacks of present federal habeas corpus procedures have become increasingly apparent and debilitating because, as will become clear shortly, habeas petitions, which were intended to be unusual, have become simply another appeal routinely taken by prisoners. The most serious problem is the lack of finality engendered by habeas corpus litigation. Since habeas corpus petitions must be filed after all appeals and remedies are exhausted, both prisoners and the public see that the law allows a lengthy stream of attacks on convictions. This lack of finality damages prospects for rehabilitation, which requires of the convict a realization "that he is justly subject to sanction, that he stands in need of rehabilitation."[80] While collateral attacks are still pending, the prisoner often has little or no need to concede his legal or moral responsibility; in Justice Powell's words:

At some point the law must convey to those in custody that a wrong has been committed, that consequent punishment has been imposed, that one should no longer look back with the view to resurrecting every imaginable basis for further litigation but rather should look forward to rehabilitation and to becoming a constructive citizen.[81]

In addition, prospective criminals see that those convicted still have strong expectations of being freed. Therefore the deterrent effect of incarceration, which depends on the expectation that a violation of law will lead to swift and certain punishment, is diminished.

Second, current habeas proceedings generate unnecessary friction between state and federal courts. State courts decode 98.8 percent of all cases in the United States.[82] United States Supreme Court Associate Justice Sandra Day O'Connor praised their ability as follows: "State judges in assuming office take an oath to support the federal as well as the state constitution. State judges do in fact rise to the occasion when given the responsibility and opportunity to do so."[83] State judges resent the flood of habeas proceedings, which often relitigate at the lowest tier of the federal judiciary the same issues that have been fully briefed, argued, and decided on their merits by competent state courts, often the highest ones. This relitigation affects the morale of state judges, who feel that their competence is questioned unnecessarily by habeas review.[84] Such judges are discouraged from striving for the highest standards of decision-making because federal courts reconsider so many of their decisions.[85]

Third, the sizeable volume of habeas petitions drains judicial resources; in 1981, 7,790 petitions were filed.[86] One author argues that this amounts to only 13 petitions per federal judge.[87] This argument, however, fails to consider that some petitions are complex and demand lengthy review; in addition, due to population concentrations, judges in many areas of the country review a substantially higher number of petitions. Since habeas petitions involving state prisoners must be defended by a state attorney general, collateral review burdens the states. In Maryland, for example, three assistant attorneys general do nothing other than litigate habeas claims.[88] In addition, the vast majority of habeas petitions present frivolous claims: of the nearly 8,000 filed in 1980, only 3.2 percent resulted in relief.[89] Due to the large volume of petitions and the small number of meritorious claims, habeas cases are sometimes accorded only cursory review, with the result that truly worthy claims may not be recognized. Justice Jackson has said that "it must prejudice the occasional meritorious application to be buried in a flood of worthless ones. He who must search a haystack for a needle is likely to end up with the attitude that the needle is not worth the search."[90]

Fourth, retrial of cases in which habeas relief has been granted, which can take place a number of years after the crime, is often extremely difficult if not impossible. As time passes memories fade, evidence disappears, and witnesses move away or die. In short, new trials, if they can be held at all, unduly impede prosecution.

Fifth, all of these costs diminish public confidence in the criminal justice system, which is perceived as encouraging endless attacks on convictions. Donald Santarelli describes this cost as the "worst of the consequences of our present habeas system—for a judicial system cannot survive the loss of public confidence and respect."[91]

Reforming habeas proceedings. It is apparent from the foregoing discussion that the formerly extraordinary remedy of habeas litigation has become commonplace. Some federal review is certainly necessary, but the number of cases must be made manageable. As the Attorney General's Task Force on Violent Crime points out, "The overall purpose of [habeas reform] is not to diminish the 'great writ' but rather to promote respect for it, by limiting the writ to situations where it is truly needed."[92]

With respect to finality, Chief Justice Burger notes that "[a]t some point, there must be finality. Without finality, justice is a myth."[93] Yet under current law, there is in effect no time limit on filing for habeas relief.[94] The Department of Justice has proposed a statute of limitation requiring that federal habeas corpus petitions be filed within one year from the time that all state remedies (appeals and collateral attack) are exhausted.[95] This limitation period could be delayed if the legal basis for the claim were a new retroactive right or new evidence. The president has proposed a similar time limit for the federal system in the Comprehensive Crime Control Act of 1983. This reform seems salutary. Since state prisoners have previously presented their claims under state rules governing habeas petitions or collateral attack, it is reasonable to require them to reintroduce the same claims to federal courts within one year. The Attorney General's Task Force and Senate Resolution 653 propose a three-year limitation on the filing of all habeas petitions, which would commence from the point at which all appeals are exhausted.[96] While this constitutes a salutary reform when we are dealing with federal prisoners, it is inadequate for state prisoners: if state collateral remedies were not exhausted within the specified period, a petition for habeas in the federal courts would be barred before the prisoner had the opportunity to apply for it.

In addition to providing some measure of finality, a time limit on filing for habeas relief would be fairer to the prosecution (and the public) in those cases where a new trial is granted, for it would minimize the amount of time between trial and retrial and thus obviate some of the difficulties of new trials discussed earlier.

A second area where reform is needed is the situation in which the prisoner failed to raise an issue properly at his trial or appeal. Under current law, the effect of such a failure is governed by a number of cases,[97] including *Wainwright* v. *Sykes*.[98] In that case, the Supreme Court ruled that issues not raised in state courts may not be heard on habeas review unless the defendant shows "cause" to excuse his procedural default and proves actual "prejudice" to his case resulting from this failure (prejudice consists of an error that affects the result of a trial or an appeal). This "cause and prejudice" standard was most recently reaffirmed by the Supreme Court in April 1982 when it denied habeas relief in two cases.[99]

The opinion in *Wainwright,* however, failed to define what constitutes "cause" for default, and this failure has been a source of great uncertainty. My view is that only the following elements ought to constitute "cause" under that test: (1) the procedural default was the result of a state action in violation of a federal constitutional right;[100] (2) the legal basis for the claim involves a new retroactive right or new evidence; (3) exclusion of evidence from the petitioner prevented the claim from being raised at state proceedings; (4) state court procedures precluded the prisoner from asserting the right.[101] This proposed codification of "cause" would lessen the volume of frivolous petitions and decrease the burden on federal judicial resources. In addition, it would afford appropriate deference to lower court procedures. The definition of "cause" found in President Reagan's proposed Comprehensive Crime Control Act of 1983 is similar to that described above.

A third area where reform is needed consists of cases in which the prisoner raised an issue properly at his trial or appeal but is dissatisfied with the court's disposition of the issue. Under current rules governing federal habeas corpus review of state court convictions, only factual determinations must be left undisturbed; the federal court is required to review legal and mixed legal-factual questions. In connection with current consideration in the United States Senate of S 653, the Department of Justice has recommended that this standard be changed. Specifically, the department would require deference to the result of state adjudications that are "full and fair." According to the Department, a state adjudication would be full and fair if:

(1) the claim at issue was actually considered and decided on the merits in state proceedings; (2) the factual determination of the state court, and disposition resulting from its application of law to the facts, and its view of the applicable rule of federal law were reasonable; (3) the adjudication was consistent with the procedural requirements of federal law; and (4) there is no new evidence of substantial importance which could not reasonably have been produced at the time of the state adjudication and no subsequent change of law of substantial importance has occurred.[102]

This language was incorporated into the portion of the legislative history of the Comprehensive Crime Control Act of 1983 that deals with federal deference to the results of state criminal adjudications.

This proposed standard would produce at least two beneficial results. First, it would not share the demeaning character of the current rules, "which relegate the highest courts of the states to the status of fact-finding commissioners whose conclusions on purely factual questions will be trusted under certain circumstances, but whose interpretation and application of law is accorded at best persuasive effect."[103] Second, the proposed standard would further the interests of finality and judicial economy. As the Department of Justice has argued:

In practical terms, the present rules can produce results that border on the absurd, requiring reversal of judgments many years after the normal conclusion of state proceedings on grounds that the habeas court may regard as no more than reasonable differences of opinion concerning close or unsettled questions in which the federal courts themselves may well disagree. In addition to enhancing the finality of criminal judgments and avoiding the burden on the state of retrying the petitioner which may occur when a writ is presently granted in such a case, this reform is likely to make it possible to decide cases more easily and with less extensive litigation, whether or not the petitioner would ultimately obtain relief under the current rules.[104]

As noted earlier, many states have habeas corpus provisions in their state constitutions or provide for collateral attack by statute; these provisions vary greatly among themselves.[105] Since state habeas procedures involve all the substantial costs noted earlier except for no. 2, states that have not already done so ought to consider the reforms discussed here—a statute of limitations on habeas petitions or collateral attack, codification of cause for procedural default, as well as a denial of habeas relief when the petitioner's trial and appeals have been "full and fair" as defined earlier.

In short, much can be done to restrict habeas corpus procedures to meritorious cases without impinging on constitutional and statutory guarantees.

Implementation of the reforms discussed in this chapter would constitute an important step—perhaps the most important step—in improving our system of courtroom criminal procedure. Whether the reforms are implemented will probably depend not only on the cogency of the arguments made for them but also—at least as much—on the existence of intensively publicized cases that illustrate the deficiencies at which the reforms are directed and on the effectiveness of "rebellions," organized or not, by the victims of crime. Some of the reforms discussed here—pretrial release agencies, preventive detention, speedier trials, independent review boards, and civil actions to deal with search and seizure violations—will require new types of government expenditures; whether these reforms are implemented will depend on the public's willingness to pay for the kind of criminal justice it desires.

12

DANIEL GLASER

Supervising Offenders Outside of Prison

Imprisonment is one way to keep criminals from committing further offenses in the community. Yet no nation can afford to lock up more than a small fraction of its lawbreakers for many years. Besides, doing so would be considered an excessive penalty for most crimes. Therefore, in the United States today persons found guilty of offenses are more likely to be released immediately than to be locked up, and almost all of those incarcerated are also eventually released. However, most are let out only on condition that they behave properly for a specified period. They are supervised in the community by government employees charged with the tasks of assisting them in the attempt to live a crime-free life, of determining whether their conduct is acceptable, and if it is not, of asking the authorities to revoke the conditional release.

A court-ordered supervised release of a convicted person is called *probation* (juvenile courts often call it *supervision*). Conditional release for the last portion of a confinement term, usually ordered by a board that is part of the executive rather than the judicial branch of government, is called *parole* (except in some agencies, mostly for juveniles, where it is called *aftercare*). At the beginning of 1982 there were about 1.25 million persons on probation and 250,000 on parole, as compared with 500,000 incarcerated in prisons and jails.[1]

Supervision in the community is similar for probationers, parolees, and aftercare releasees, but there is much closer control in *halfway houses* (sometimes called *community correction* or *community treatment centers*). These are usually in urban areas, operated for the most part by state or federal prison systems and occasionally by county authorities. Some halfway houses—especially for juveniles—are private establishments under contract to government agencies. Residents generally depart daily to work, attend school, or engage in other outside activities. In *work release* or *work furlough* programs there is similar daily departure and return, but the housing is in a prison or jail. The proportion of prisoners making such daily departures is diverse, ranging from 0 to about 20 percent in various prison and jail systems.

The same issues arise in assessing all varieties of conditional freedom: Who should be released and when? What are the best ways to supervise them? How can current policies be improved?

Selection and Scheduling of Penalties

A common assumption behind the sentencing of lawbreakers is that prisoners learn from confinement, but there is much difference of opinion about precisely what they learn. Some observers emphasize that punishment is supposed to "teach the criminal a lesson," a principle that criminologists call "special deterrence"—that is, one teaches the convict to refrain from further crime by instilling a fear of punishment. Others contend that new offenders are criminalized by incarceration because penal institutions are "schools for crime." This is one major argument for the use of probation. Yet prisons claim to be rehabilitative because they provide academic and vocational education as well as counseling. The punishment of criminals is also supposed to teach nonoffenders to fear the consequences of lawbreaking, an effect that criminologists call "general deterrence." A general deterrent effect on nonoffenders is presumed whenever criminals are punished, although the strength of this effect has never been demonstrated. In addition to being instructive in these many ways, confinement is incapacitating: the community is usually safe from the criminal as long as he is locked up.

From these standpoints of special deterrence, general deterrence, rehabilitation, and incapacitation, when should a criminal be confined? And when released? In practice the answer depends on both the particular offense and the offender, but some elementary principles of psychology and sociology are most relevant to deciding on an optimum policy.

A basic law of behavioral psychology is that behavior that is rewarding tends to be repeated, especially in circumstances like those in which its consequences were favorable. Therefore, delinquency and crimes that gratify the offender tend to be repeated as long as punishment can be evaded or tolerated. Furthermore, any special deterrence effects of penalties are likely to be only temporary unless alternative noncriminal behavior proves gratifying.

It follows from these principles that the earlier and more often an offender commits crimes and has been habituated to criminal associates, the less he or she will be either deterred or further criminalized by an additional increment of incarceration. Conversely, a true first offender, especially one who has been unsuccessful in crime and has had rewarding involvement in a legitimate occupation, is most likely to be deterred by the smallest experience or even the mere threat of imprisonment. It is with such first offenders, especially those past juvenile age, that the success rate of probation is highest. For juvenile first offenders the probation failure rate is higher than for adults, but it is also for such offenders that confinement is likely to be the most criminalizing. However, confinement and release decisions are not guided closely by such considerations, and to some extent they cannot be.

In light of the educative goals of incarceration, it would seem that the penalty should be fixed by consideration of the entire behavior record of the person found guilty. However, the legal theory that punishment should be a "just desert" for the offense has always limited this possibility. The maximum penalty for someone who has been a persistent criminal cannot be greater than that warranted by the seriousness of the offense for which he is being sentenced. Many are persistent petty offenders. When someone commits a very serious crime, however, a minimum penalty is demanded for general deterrence purposes, or on the abstract moral grounds that evil must be requited by the offender's suffering pain proportional to that caused by the offense. Thus, murder and rape are punished quite severely even for first offenders.

A major limitation for any court that tries to be guided by the expected effects of incarceration in sentencing is that it usually cannot know most of the criminal history of the offenders it must sentence. Questionnaire and interview responses of prisoners, notably in the Rand studies reported by Jan and Marcia Chaiken at the beginning of this book, reveal that only a small fraction of the crimes they committed were known to officials. Their crime rates probably can be estimated most accurately not by looking at their official criminal record, but by the discrepancy between their cost of living—including such items as an expensive drug habit—and their legitimate income. Also, the first officially punished crimes of adult offenders are often unknown to criminal courts because the highly predictive juvenile court records are inaccessible to outside agencies.

In most courts today, especially in high-crime-rate urban areas, the case loads of probation officers, who advise the judge on sentencing and supervise releasees, are too large to permit much investigation before sentencing recommendations are made. Penalties therefore tend to be applied mechanically, with juveniles frequently being released without penalty or with only nominal, largely unsupervised probation. This is especially likely when crimes are committed in slum areas, where arrests are most concentrated and complaints are not very influential.

A period of confinement long enough to interrupt crime pursuits appreciably was shown by a Chicago study to have what researchers Charles Murray and Louis Cox called a "suppression effect"; such incarceration reduced markedly the rate of rearrest for high-crime-rate juveniles.[2] These youngsters had an average of eight prior arrests, so they had probably come to expect only a brief detention by the time of their 1974–76 arrests, which this study followed up. Although the overall findings were controversial, the authors marshaled convincing evidence that only penalties appreciably more severe than probation markedly altered criminal patterns that had already survived less punitive experiences.

A more adequate study would assess the effects of alternative penalties on contrasting types of lawbreakers. This was attempted by the Community Treatment Project, a long-term experiment with teenagers committed to the California Youth Authority in 1961–69 from the cities of Sacramento and Stockton. After screening out the 35 percent of the boys and 17 percent of the girls who were committed for the most violent offenses or other crimes for which it was thought the community would insist upon punishment, the Youth Authority randomly divided the rest into an experimental group whose members were paroled in about a month and a control group whose members were left in institutions, and for whom preparole confinement averaged about eight months. Before this random division, all the youths were classified according to various psychological and sociological criteria. The experimentals were intensively supervised by agents with case loads averaging only about ten youths primarily of one criminal type, while the controls were in regular Youth Authority parole case loads that averaged about seventy offenders of all types.

The California Community Treatment follow-up eventually covered not only the period of Youth Authority control, which lasted about three years, but also a four-year postparole period. Critics alleged that results during parole were spurious because the supervisors of experimentals were more willing to confine violators briefly, but less willing to revoke parole, than were the supervisors of control cases. However, differences in rearrest rates turned out to be similar during both parole and postparole periods.

About half of the parolees were classified initially as "neurotics." They were described as emotionally unstable and immature in interpersonal relationships, with feelings of inadequacy. The rearrest rates for neurotics both during and after parole were about half as great for the promptly paroled experimentals as for the longer-incarcerated controls.

In contrast, for about a fifth of the sample classified as "power-oriented," who were described as members of delinquent groups exhibiting pride in toughness or in their ability to manipulate others, there was a somewhat lower rearrest rate for the long-incarcerated controls than for the early-paroled experimentals. This is consistent with the "suppression effect" reported in the Chicago study with similar delinquents. The remainder of youths in the California study had about the same rearrest rates regardless of whether they were among the experimentals or the controls.[3]

The California study, along with various other assessments of probation for first offenders, suggests that immediate probation or early parole prevents the criminalizing effects of incarceration on young lawbreakers who have not been much involved in crime or criminal groups. Immediately releasing offenders who are progressing well in school or in employment is a means of preserving alternatives to crime that give them a stake in conformity, and that make the mere shame of being arrested a painful punishment. If such a person has been supporting a spouse or children, probation may also prevent the dependents from becoming welfare burdens on the state and avoid home disruptions that increase their prospects of becoming offenders.

The California and Chicago evidence of a "suppression effect" of incarceration on advanced delinquents suggests that once youth have been criminalized by rewarding experiences with crime, an appreciable penalty may have a special deterrent effect for which arrest or probation do not suffice—and this effect outweighs whatever additional criminalization the incarceration may produce. Research suggests that while some institution programs may also provide a rehabilitation effect, for most advanced offenders this prospect is not great.

During the 1970s, reflecting "law-and-order" and just-desert movements, courts began increasingly to impose a "split sentence" or "shock probation," which consists of a term of probation with the condition that the first several months or even year be served in the county jail. Both the learning theory and research evidence cited indicate that whether this has a predominantly criminalizing or suppression effect depends on the offenders' prior involvement in lawbreaking or legitimate pursuits. If the just-desert emphasis results in the mechanical application of a split sentence on the basis of the offense rather than the offender, it may cause as much or more crime in novice offenders as it can prevent in others.

Monitoring Releasees

The concept of parole comes from the age of chivalry, when it meant the release of prisoners of war if they gave their word of honor to depart without resuming combat. Probation evolved from suspension of sentence on condition that the offender pledge to commit no further crimes for a specified period. Parole and probation acquired their modern denotation by adding supervision staff, whose job is to control and assist the releasees. Control varies from negligible to appreciable, but it has been increasing lately, and some speculate that it will eventually become all-encompassing.

Most control in probation or parole consists of monitoring the releasee's conduct. Usually offenders who are given these forms of conditional liberty are required to report to their supervising officer weekly or biweekly at first, but only monthly after a few months of good behavior. Sometimes they are required to report only monthly right from the start. Often, especially if employed, the releasee is allowed to telephone or mail the report.

Probationers and parolees are supposed to adhere to a variety of rules requiring, in addition to their refraining from all illegal acts, that they work or seek work or attend school, live in an approved residence, not move without permission, avoid all known criminals or certain specified associates, and neither leave the county nor marry nor buy a car nor incur debts without their supervisor's approval. Probationers are often also required to make restitution payments to the victims of their crimes or to do community service work. Their reports are to specify their residence and employment, and to certify conformity to their release conditions. To check on the veracity of these reports, the supervising office may make scheduled or surprise visits to the releasee, as well as inquiries to his family or employer. Rule violations that are deemed serious may result in revocation of the release or in added restrictions on freedom.

In several states where roughly half the prisoners are denied parole, comparisons have been made between the recidivism rates of parolees and those of similar offenders released without supervision at expiration of sentence. Such studies generally show that rearrest and reconfinement rates for nonparoled releasees exceed those of parolees, except in states where a large proportion of parolees are reconfined for violation of the supervision rules rather than for new offenses.[4] One might argue that revocation of parole for rule violations protects the public from crimes these releasees would have committed had their parole not been revoked. However, a California experiment with what was called "Summary Parole," in which the frequency of supervisor contacts was halved for a randomly selected group of parolees, showed no significant differences in new crime rates from those of the regularly supervised control group—although the random separation into these two groups was undertaken only with a preselected 32 percent of all parolees who were presumed to be the safest risks.[5] In a Wisconsin quasi-experiment, probationers and parolees classified as of minimum risk or need were contacted by supervisors half as frequently as similar parolees in a comparison group, but those classified as of maximum risk or need were contacted twice as frequently as similar parolees. The results showed no difference in recidivism rates for the minimum cases, but significantly less recidivism with closer supervision for the maximum risk cases.[6] In Connecticut, where revocation of parole for rule violations was relatively rare, a comparison of recidivism for similar parolees and nonparolees found lower rates for the parolees while they were under supervision but similar rates in a postparole follow-up, which led the researchers to conclude that parole only delayed recidivism.[7] A more extensive and rigorous study in another Northeastern state (not specified by the authors), in which reconfinement for rule violation was more frequent, found significantly less recidivism for parolees than for comparable nonparolees both during and after the parole period.[8]

Offenders with a history of opiate addiction may often have the added control of medical tests for drug use several times per month, on both scheduled and surprise occasions. California in 1961 initiated a large-scale program in which drug addicts charged with serious felonies could, instead of being convicted, be civilly committed to a seven-year or longer period of government control. This period began with three years in a treatment institution that had previously been a prison and was still administered by the Department of Corrections. Release from it was conditional, with frequent —often surprise—testing for opiates. In 1962–63 about 300 addicts in this institution were released unconditionally by court order because the procedures used for their admission were declared in violation of their civil rights. In 1974–75, the late William McGlothlin directed a follow-up study of these releasees and of about the same number of similar addicts admitted under revised procedures in 1964 who went through the regular program with drug-testing. In postrelease periods of the same duration for all cases, those released by the court without supervision had significantly more crime, addiction, and deaths from drugs than those released under supervision with drug-testing.[9]

Testing releasees to determine whether they have been using any type of illegal drug was formerly a slow, expensive, and imprecise process, but in the 1970s portable electronic urinalysis equipment became available that provides an accurate diagnosis in minutes. A growing number of probation and parole agencies have such equipment, with trained operators; an agreement to cooperate in such testing is made a condition of the offender's release. In the federal and many state probation and parole systems, instead of the former practice of automatically imprisoning any releasee whose tests revealed drug usage, each such case is now intensively reviewed; if the drug user seems to be pursuing a law-abiding life in other respects, warnings and possibly new release conditions may be imposed. One widespread reaction to this new perspective is that many supervisors accept addiction as their clients' chronic ailment, and therefore allow them to enter methadone maintenance programs to receive synthetic opiates legally, as long as their other activities are law-abiding.

Rational control clearly requires some classification of clients according to the relative risk of their reverting to crime, and hence the closeness with which they should be monitored. Usually they are classified by the officers' subjective impressions of them, augmented by a few administrative rules, such as requiring that former drug users and violent offenders receive more frequent surveillance. Statistical risk-prediction and need-assessment guidelines for closeness of supervision of probationers and parolees were developed in Wisconsin, and are being adopted in many other areas.[10] In many jurisdictions, however, budget cuts have so reduced the number of supervision personnel that it is difficult to maintain close supervision for the cases presumed to need it. Lax supervision of probationers or parolees obviously reduces the credibility of the threat that rule violations will result in confinement.

Halfway Houses and Work Release

If released offenders revert to crime, the more often they are checked on in the community, the sooner their crime sprees are likely to be interrupted by rearrest. The prospect of such quick incapacitation, moreover, is much enhanced if the releasee must return daily to a residence where correctional officials are always present.

Halfway houses and work release are usually justified primarily as ways of helping prisoners become accustomed to community life before they are more completely free, but they also impose considerable control on offenders. These residency programs give releasees much more frequent contact with correctional staff than they would have with even intensive supervision on probation or parole. For this reason, some federal and other judges conceive of the residences as halfway into a prison, and impose sentences of a short term in them instead of in prison; this contrasts with the usual understanding that they are for persons halfway out of prison. In Massachusetts a variety of community homes for serious delinquents have entirely replaced state correctional institutions for juveniles, and this example is increasingly being followed elsewhere.

Overcrowding has forced most prison systems to expand their halfway houses, since they are more quickly and cheaply procured than prisons. The best-risk inmates are now placed in these residences not just for the last two or three months before parole, but for six months or longer. Also, types of inmates that previously would not have been released from prison before their parole or maximum confinement dates are now being placed there. These developments have become safer in California and elsewhere by reliance on statistical prediction systems rather than on case study methods of selection, and by closer monitoring.

Residents sign out whenever they leave a halfway home or go on work release from a prison or jail, and they must indicate the destination, purpose, and duration of their departure. Passes for family visits or other purposes not directly involving work, job search, or school attendance are now generally more restricted than formerly, and granted for briefer periods. "Drunkometers" to check for alcohol abuse and drug-testing are used when the residents return, and staff more frequently check by phone or visit to ascertain that releasees are where they are supposed to be. Residents who seriously misbehave are jailed. Thus, postprison supervision of offenders can be significantly incapacitating.

Electronic monitoring has been proposed to increase supervision control. Releasees would be required to wear radio microtransmitters in nonremovable wristbands. If the transmitter left a monitored area of the city or if it or the wristband were damaged, a central monitoring station would immediately alert the authorities.

Counseling Assistance

Advocates of increased probation and parole have emphasized that the supervising officers can help offenders achieve a crime-free life. The more affluent agencies try—a few successfully—to employ only supervisors who have a master's degree in social work or another "helping profession" such as clinical psychology. Counseling and successfully "relating to" clients are the types of assistance most valued by such supervisors, although their most frequent aid is referral to other agencies for diverse services, from psychotherapy or medical care to welfare payments.

A standard complaint among probation and parole supervisors is that their case loads are too large to permit them to develop close relationships with their clients. However, controlled experiments, in which probationers or parolees were randomly assigned to different-sized case loads, have usually shown no clear differences in outcome rates.[11] The findings of California's Community Treatment Project, already described, suggest that benefits from extra time given to "neurotics" may be offset by higher failure rates from a counseling-oriented approach to the more hardened criminals. Also, closer supervision may uncover serious rule violations that would otherwise be overlooked—so these higher failure rates, rather than resulting from the more intensive counseling orientation, may be simply an artifact of tighter controls.

Perhaps most pertinent to the fact that small case loads do not effectively reduce rearrest rates, especially with probation, is that officers prefer to use the time gained by smaller case loads to improve their paperwork—particularly their presentence reports—rather than their supervision. These reports are their most tangible products, and career advancement in supervision is likely to depend much more on quality of reports than on relationship to clients. In the Federal Probation Service a case load of fifty was sought and sometimes achieved, with preparation of one presentence investigation and report counted as equivalent to supervision of four cases for one month. A study showed, however, that the actual time used for such a presentence study exceeded that given to the supervision of twelve clients for a month.[12]

Actually, there is evidence that intensive counseling, especially in the community rather than in institutions, does reduce the violation rates of young probationers, who are the adjudicated offenders least likely to be highly criminalized. Such counseling is especially effective if it promotes personal bonds between counselor and client, deals with day-to-day problems rather than psychodynamics, and provides training in the behavioral habits and skills needed in conventional social relationships. Accordingly, follow-up studies also find that the counselors who successfully reduce recidivism rates have strong anti-crime attitudes, much empathy, low job-change rates, appropriate matching to clients, and enthusiasm for their work.[13]

One major limitation of counseling approaches is that staff are predominantly from middle-class backgrounds with advanced college educations, while correctional clients are usually from poor and relatively uneducated families and often have a history of alienation from school and from middle-class teachers. A second limitation is that the supervisors are authority figures who must sometimes impose penalties on their clients, a role in which it is difficult—although not impossible—to build close personal bonds. Some agencies divide staff into those who specialize in surveillance, carry a gun, and are primarily detectives, and those who are unarmed and primarily social workers. Perhaps the most important limitation is simply that clients need substantive abilities and knowledge—such as writing skills, mathematics, or work skills—that cannot be acquired by talk alone; diligent study and practice are necessary, although appropriate counseling can help.

A remedy for the class discrepancies between staff and clients is to replace or augment typical staff with employees from the social settings to which the clients are accustomed. "Paraprofessionals" employed in such roles are ex-offenders, ideally about ten years older than their clients, and from neighborhoods similar to those in which the offenders reside. Ohio pioneered in making parole officers out of ex-offenders. These paraprofessionals have proved about as successful in the supervision role as the regular officers, despite having less education and being assigned the highest-risk parolees.[14]

Paraprofessionals seem to be ideally suited to working in casework *teams* with traditional supervision staff, all of whom share a common case load. The paraprofessionals then concentrate on providing personal assistance and surveillance in the community, while the professionals deal with the bureaucracies, arrange welfare payments or other needed assistance, and communicate with higher authorities regarding the client. In the Los Angeles County Probation Department, a civil service position of "community worker" was created for such paraprofessionals. Many of those supervisors were women who had been welfare mothers and probationers themselves. Initially, in a quasi-experiment called the RODEO Project, their task in dealing with recidivist juvenile probationers was to try to assist the entire family, rather than the violators alone. Such a community treatment focus has been shown in this and other Los Angeles experiments to be at least as effective as institution programs for moderately advanced offenders, and much less costly.[15] Nevertheless, none of these programs has yet been firmly established, although paraprofessionals continue to be used in various roles requiring direct contact with difficult clients.

In Massachusetts, an assessment concluded that small local residences can effectively replace large state institutions for serious delinquents only if staff develop good relationships with their wards. Frequently the regimentation, lack of personal bonds with adults, and suppression of individual initiative that characterize inmate life in traditional penal institutions for juveniles persist in the small community homes. Such problems are especially likely in the growing number of such homes that are run for profit by large corporations. Recruiting well-trained young couples as houseparents to bring enthusiasm and personal rapport to youth is desirable but not always feasible, and even when it occurs, the stress and limited future in such work often foster staff "burnout" and turnover in a short amount of time.[16]

Employment and Economic Aid

Most felonies are committed for purposes of obtaining money or other property. Most offenders have little successful employment experience, limited job qualifications, and few economic resources. Furthermore, for juvenile offenders crime is often a means of expressing adult-like autonomy and independence in search of a self-conception that can actually become secure only when they are fully self-supporting in conventional adult work roles. Although vocational skills may be taught in institutions, it is only in the community that the training can be tested and its deficiencies corrected—deficiencies that are often more in the area of work habits and attitudes than in skills.

Large-scale efforts by New York City's Vera Foundation to provide jobs for ex-addicts and others with extensive criminal histories have had mixed results. The federal government's Job Corps has been evaluated favorably in follow-up studies, as have the Outward Bound programs, both of which provide hard physical labor for youthful offenders and other unemployed young people, mostly at remote forest and mountain locations on public lands. What seem to be important for resocialization so that typical offenders can become gainfully employed are (1) training in diligence, punctuality, respect for authority, and other habits and attitudes expected in adult work roles; (2) challenging but not overly frustrating tasks, rewarded by both money and recognition according to performance, with gradually increased standards after initial conduct and skill goals are attained; (3) mingling of ex-offenders with workers of more conventional background and of diverse age as much as possible, and dealing with ex-offenders individually rather than as a group.[17]

Halfway houses assist prisoners in reentering community life by providing shelter and food, as well as job placement aid and immediately available counseling, plus behavior control. They help provide a gradual transition to more complete freedom in these important ways, preventing sudden liberty from becoming unfettered license. In the federal prison system, release through these "community treatment centers" has been shown to be especially effective in reducing subsequent unemployment and recidivism rates for minority group members.[18]

Since parolees have high rates of unemployment immediately after leaving prison, but are ineligible for unemployment insurance because they had no jobs in the preceding year, several experimental programs have been set up to provide them with unemployment insurance. In the early 1970s projects in Maryland and California allotted parole officers funds to pay randomly selected groups of their clients up to $60 or $70 weekly when unemployed, with some of this amount paid even if they had a low income from work.[19]

Because these programs proved cost-effective in reducing recidivism and increasing parolee earnings, the U.S. Department of Labor funded the 1976 Transitional Aid Research Project (TARP). About 1,000 parolees in Georgia and the same number in Texas, as well as control groups, were randomly selected to receive unemployment assistance for one year after release. The $63 (in Texas) and $70 (in Georgia) weekly payments were provided through the state employment offices that administered compensation to other unemployed persons. Two 400-man treatment groups had a 100 percent tax on low earnings, as was customary in those states, in that any amount earned was deducted from unemployment compensation. A 200-man group was to have only one-fourth of earnings deducted, to be comparable to the Maryland and California experiments, but it turned out that the parolees and payment offices were often unaware of this provision. One of the larger groups was eligible for twenty-six weeks and all the others for thirteen weeks of unemployment compensation, all paid only during their first year out of prison. A fourth experimental group of 200 received no unemployment compensation but job placement services were made available, plus up to $100 for tools or work clothes.

There were no significant differences in arrest rates among any of the treatment or control groups in a one-year follow-up. Those compensated worked less, earned less, and were arrested more than those not paid in the first six months out of prison, but the reverse was true in the second half-year. Unemployment compensation was evidently an incentive not to take low-paying or temporary jobs but to hold out for better employment, which made the records of all groups about the same for the full year. Idleness apparently fostered crime. It seems probable that if the follow-up had continued for a second year, the compensated parolees would have earned more and perhaps been arrested less than those who received no unemployment pay.[20]

In 1978 California legislated a five-year program that gives its convicts credit for work in prison toward unemployment compensation in their first year of release (when almost all are automatically on parole, under California's 1977 determinate sentence law). Up to $25 earnings per week would not reduce the $45 weekly compensation, but a 100 percent tax of the compensation was applied on all earnings over $25, so that those earning $70 or more were not compensated. This program has been poorly administered, with most parolees being unemployed for a month or more before receiving payments. A sophisticated analysis of the records of those receiving payments and those ineligible for them, controlled for numerous background variables, concluded that the payments reduced recidivism by about 13 percent and saved the state about $2,000 per offender by cutting reimprisonment rates. Not included in the calculations was the public gain from fewer crimes by the parolees.[21]

These findings suggest that the optimum economic assistance for released offenders would be work relief rather than compensation payments, paid with a variable deduction rate for low earnings and administered in a manner that would not interfere with job-hunting. This probably would further reduce crime if available more generally, such as to all unemployed youth whether or not on probation or parole. It is also evident that more diverse and rigorous research is needed for firmer knowledge on the optimum forms of aid to the unemployed.

"Contract" parole and probation are developments of growing prominence. The contracts are documents that offenders and correctional officials negotiate individually. They usually emphasize the kind of assistance a parolee will receive, but they also alter control and even selection processes. Parole contracts stipulate that if the prisoner does not seriously misbehave and completes certain activities, such as attending counseling sessions or Alcoholics Anonymous, and perhaps also completes certain courses or passes the high school equivalency examination, he will be paroled on a specified date. Sometimes other special duties or conditions on parole are added.[22]

Probation contracts oblige the offender to accomplish certain things on a stipulated schedule over and above the usual probation conditions. Sometimes the defense counsel proposes such a contract as a means of persuading the judge to grant probation, and for such attorneys there is a small but growing new field of private presentence investigation and proposal preparation. This has led to suggestions that all supervision of probationers, and possibly parole or even correctional institutions, be operated by private entrepreneurs contracting with the government. This type of contracting is now common in some areas of juvenile justice, and will probably spread to adult corrections as well.

Organizational Constraints of Correctional Reforms

In most courts in the United States, 80 to 90 percent or more of those found guilty do not have trials. Instead, during pretrial negotiations—often prolonged—between prosecution and defense, the accused agrees to plead guilty in exchange for the dropping of charges or for the lessening of the probable penalty in some other way. The judge may have to approve this agreement, and may thereby become committed to granting probation in order to secure a guilty plea that saves the court the time, uncertainty, and cost of a trial.

By contrast, many parole boards have much more autonomy than judges in deciding on the severity of an offender's penalties. Furthermore, a prison official's routine decision, sometimes made alone but more often in consultation with a few others, suffices to transfer a prisoner to a halfway house for the last two to six months before parole or to permit an inmate's daily departure from prison to work or to attend classes in the community, perhaps for a year or more.

Parole boards, and to a lesser extent legislatures and judges, were most heavily criticized for their release decisions in the 1970s by proponents of the just-desert theory of legal sanctions— an eighteenth- and early nineteenth-century faith that enacting laws to "make the punishment fit the crime" would both reduce crime and increase justice. Its twentieth-century spokespersons called for legislatures to mandate a precise penalty for each type of offense, to reduce drastically the power of judges to modify these statutory sentences, and to abolish parole. Many states, from Maine to California, have enacted "determinate sentence laws" that partly reflect these objectives, but like most legislation they are usually compromises of new ideas with the traditional practices in their locales.

Among the delusions of many persons in this movement were the assumptions (1) that legislatures can precisely and confidently determine a uniformly just penalty for all cases of each type of crime; (2) that politicians would not escalate the enacted penalties at almost every legislative session; (3) that the offenses for which a person is convicted, rather than his or her total criminal record, can determine the penalty most appropriate for society's protection; (4) that the outcomes of plea negotiations in the courts would conform closely to the penalties prescribed in just-desert legislation; and (5) that the main sources of disparate punishments for the same offense have been parole boards rather than the courts.

Many allegations that parole decisions are arbitrary, inconsistent, or prejudiced may be justifiable. Nevertheless, the major achievement of most parole boards is to reduce the widespread and unfair disparity in penalties—which they are in a unique position to recognize—among prisoners sentenced by numerous separate courts, each with diverse patterns of judicial arbitrariness or inconsistency and of plea negotiation.

In the 1980s there has been growing use of statistical guidelines for sentencing and parole decisions. Such guidelines rank offenses by severity according to the average past duration of the terms of confinement imposed for them, and rank offenders into risk categories according to attributes (often called "salient factors") that research shows to be most predictive of postrelease recidivism. These attributes are primarily aspects of the prior criminal record, such as number of arrests, confinements, and probation or parole violations, as well as drug and alcohol use, all of which predict recidivism. Also considered are such factors as the extent to which the offender has been legitimately employed or the lateness of his start at crime, which predict nonrecidivism.

For each combination of offense severity and recidivism risk, sentencing guidelines indicate the predominant range of penalties imposed in the past, and parole guidelines indicate the predominant range of preparole confinement.

Judges or parole boards may deviate from the guideline range of penalties for some cases, if they perceive mitigating or aggravating factors, but they are asked to record their reasons for these deviations. Periodic statistical compilations are made of the frequency of such deviations and the reasons for them. At last report, Chicago, Philadelphia, and Denver were among the largest cities to have adopted sentencing guidelines, but recent studies question whether the guidelines have actually affected the preexisting structures for negotiating penalties in these cities. Parole guidelines are employed by a majority of states and the federal parole boards, and are believed to have had great impact, although some states have guidelines based on very inadequate research.[23]

When used as intended—which is now primarily among parole boards—guidelines can make penalties more consistent with both just-desert and risk considerations, and reduce the disparity of punishments. Much more adequate theory and research are needed to (1) develop guidelines that also take correctional effects into account so as to better protect the public with postrelease supervision, and (2) develop strategies for introducing sentencing guidelines that are compatible with the organization of the courts for plea negotiation, and hence more capable of affecting actual sentences.

Policy Lessons

Most offenders under government control are supervised in the community. Although much of the public probably disapproves of this, they are unlikely to be willing to pay for the much costlier incarceration of these lawbreakers. Research evidence, as well as widely validated principles of behavioral theory, indicate the following:

1. Probation or early parole reduces recidivism rates among new offenders by preventing the criminalizing effects of their incarceration.

2. An appreciable confinement period reduces recidivism by more hardened offenders—as compared to the effects of their early release—by special deterrence, and they are incapacitated from crime while kept off the streets; this has been called the "suppression effect."

3. There is quasi-experimental evidence that close monitoring in the community, including surprise drug tests for ex-addicts, reduces rearrest rates among advanced offenders.

4. A marked reduction in the frequency of contact with supervision staff does not increase the failure rates among those classified as of low risk or need.

5. Halfway houses and work release make supervision in the community quite effective despite their imposing much less restraint than prisons.

6. Actuarial prediction tables permit the placement of larger numbers of prisoners into such community living without increasing escape rates.

7. Halfway houses are most successful in reducing recidivism rates for young but hardened offenders when they provide much job retention counseling as well as other aid and close control.

8. Counseling, often stressed as the chief component of probation and parole assistance, seems to reduce recidivism rates only for unadvanced offenders, and only then if provided in an optimum manner.

9. Reducing supervision case loads seems mostly to enhance the time probation officers devote to paperwork and does not affect recidivism rates unless the officers' job structures are appropriately reformed.

10. Paraprofessional staff of sociocultural background similar to that of the clients seem to be effective, especially if the paraprofessionals work with professionals as casework teams dealing with the same clients, and if they are oriented toward all problems of a juvenile delinquent's family rather than toward helping only the offender.

11. Employment training for supervised offenders seems to be most effective if it is concerned mainly with work habits and attitudes.

12. Financial aid for offenders supervised in the community achieves most if provided in a manner that is not a disincentive to work (indeed, such aid might prove best as soundly-administered work relief for all young unemployed persons).

13. Guidelines can improve the consistent rationality of sentencing and parole decisions, but more research is needed. First, we need to make the guidelines reflect knowledge about contrasting effects of penalties on different types of offenders. Secondly, we need to develop and test strategies for increasing the impact of sentencing guidelines in the courts.

13

ALFRED BLUMSTEIN

Prisons: Population, Capacity, and Alternatives

The most critical administrative problem facing the United States criminal justice system through the 1980s will be that of crowded prisons. Pressure will continue to mount for more and harsher prison sentences, seriously straining the already limited capacity of penal institutions. And most of the difficulties will be experienced at the state level. In the states that face this issue responsibly, the basic choices will involve either a costly commitment to increase the capacity to accommodate the steady influx of prisoners, or a search for alternative ways of dealing with the surplus. Of course, many states will not face the issue at all, simply allowing inmates to pile up in prisons until the pressure they create is relieved either by a federal court order or by a riot that focuses public attention on the problem.

Demographic Effects on Prison Congestion

Oddly, the problem of prison congestion comes at a time when the prospects appear reasonably bright with respect to crime. Crime rates, which are extremely age-sensitive, can be expected to decline as the large birth cohorts of the postwar baby boom (those cohorts born in the period 1947 to 1962) pass out of their late teens (the years of most active criminality).[1] This demographic effect was projected in a study focusing on Pennsylvania.[2] The study estimated that crime rates would reach a peak in 1980 and then decline subsequently, based only on demographic considerations.[3] This predicted peak was actually confirmed in both Pennsylvania[4] and in the U.S. generally[5] by declines in reported index crimes in 1981 and 1982.

The same demographic shift that bodes well for crime rates bodes ill for prison crowding. The shifting age mix that should generate a lower crime rate over the 1980s can be expected to generate larger prison populations. This seeming paradox results from the difference between the peak crime ages and the peak imprisonment ages. The peak arrest rates occur from the ages of 16 to 18, whereas the peak imprisonment ages are the mid-twenties.[6] The difference results mainly from the fact that very few people under 18 are sent to prison. Also, those in the adult age ranges who are convicted of crimes are generally put on probation for their first—or first few—convictions. By the time they have accumulated a sufficient number of convictions to become serious candidates for prison, they are well into their twenties.

As a result, we can expect to see prison populations increasing over the decade as the postwar baby boom continues to file through the high-imprisonment ages. By about 1990, those cohorts should also be past the peak imprisonment ages, and prison populations can be expected to decline. This forecast has been made in detail only for Pennsylvania,[7] but most of the states of the Northeast and Midwest have a similar underlying demographic structure. Thus the basic phenomenon of declining crime rates and increasing prison populations can be expected to prevail in that region. (In the rapidly growing states of the South and the Southwest, on the other hand, the effect of in-migration, especially of the highly mobile and more crime-prone young males,

may overshadow the effects associated with the aging of the resident population. In other words, crime will probably not show the
same declines, though prison populations will still increase.)
Sometime well into the 1990s, just about when prison populations
begin to decrease, the children of baby boom parents—the so-
called "echo boom" of the 1980s—could then begin to turn the
crime rate curves up once again.

These demographic projections were based on data drawn from
the period 1970 to 1975. During those years, the crime rate was
rising at a seemingly inexorable rate, but prison populations were
fairly low, still in the early phases of the upturn that began in
about 1972. This in turn had followed a period in the 1960s of
fairly stable prison populations, which declined slightly from
213,000 in 1960 to 196,000 in 1970.[8] In 1981, the FBI's *Uniform
Crime Reports* recorded a 1.7 percent decrease in the index crime
rate.[9] In contrast, prison populations in 1981 were reported to
have reached 369,000—an increase of 12.1 percent over the
populations of federal and state prisons in 1980.[10] The decline in
crime was confirmed in the FBI reports for the first six months of
1982.[11] U.S. index crimes then declined by 5 percent. This drop
was bigger for property than for personal crimes, and larger in the
East and Midwest (where there is less in-migration than in the
South and the West). While these two years represent less than
total confirmation of a reversal of the upward trend in crime rates
of the previous two decades, the effects on prison populations and
crime rates are nonetheless strikingly consistent with the projections based on the demographic shifts. The magnitude of the
population shift in those critical ages, combined with the strong
age-sensitivity of both crime rates and imprisonment rates, suggests that demographic factors are likely to have an important,
and possibly even dominant, influence on the crime levels and
prison populations through the 1980s.

Shifts in Attitudes toward Imprisonment

The problem of growth in prison populations resulting from
demographic shifts is exacerbated by a growing toughness in sentencing practice. For most of the first two-thirds of the twentieth
century, the dominant perspective on imprisonment viewed it as a

vehicle for "correction" or "rehabilitation." The notion was that upon release, a prisoner should be less likely to commit crimes. Prison professionals would recommend an offender's release when he was judged to be "rehabilitated." But the faith in rehabilitation was severely challenged in the early and mid-1970s by a succession of experimental studies that evaluated a variety of alternative rehabilitative strategies.[12] The dominant finding of these studies was a "null effect," i.e., that no particular approach consistently works any better than any other in changing postrelease criminal behavior. The implication was that individual traits of offenders and of the environment to which they are returned after release may have far more influence on subsequent recidivism than exposure to any rehabilitative program.

There remains a controversy between those who contend that the punishment experienced in prison rehabilitates some criminals by virtue of its "special deterrent" effect (i.e., its unpleasantness discourages future criminality) and those who argue on the contrary that prison is harmful because it socializes prisoners, especially younger ones, into a hardened criminal culture. The null effect finding does not necessarily invalidate either of these positions, but it does suggest that the opposing effects cancel each other out. Some individuals emerge from prison with sufficient distaste for the experience—and sufficient control over their own subsequent behavior—to avoid the risk of subsequent imprisonment by desisting from crime. Other, weaker individuals very likely are socialized into a criminal culture and may then commit more and more serious crimes than they might otherwise have committed. If one had a sure means of distinguishing those who would benefit from prison from those who would be harmed by it, and if judges were willing to employ such means (with the inequitable results in terms of punishment), then there might be a significant rehabilitative effect from imprisonment. So far, however, criminal justice authorities have been saved from having to face the legal and ethical dilemmas involved in making such decisions by the failure to find any valid method of identifying the appropriate candidates for rehabilitation through imprisonment.

The loss of faith in rehabilitation has probably contributed significantly to the growth in prison populations. There has been a growing focus on the deterrence and incapacitation effects of prison as the only means left to the criminal justice system to achieve its objective of reducing crime.

The political environment has also changed. The liberal perspective that emphasized rehabilitation has given way to a new emphasis on punitiveness, reflecting a pressure for greater retribution and an increased desire for crime control. Judges, too, have felt the influence of the growing public hostility toward criminals and of increasing demands for severe punishment. The standards for what level of punishment constitutes "just deserts"[13] have thus been increasing.

Yet the structural arrangements for decision-making within the criminal justice system regarding sentencing policy are such that the costs associated with increased punitiveness (i.e., prison overcrowding, large corrections budgets) are almost never faced by those who act punitively (e.g., legislators, prosecutors, judges). Thus it is easy for these decision-makers to respond to the public's demands for harsher measures. In most states, this has led to an increase in the severity of sentences, compounding the effects associated with the demographic trends in increasing incarceration rates.

Table 1, for example, compares the incarceration rates of males in U.S. state prisons in 1974 and 1979, based on surveys conducted by the Bureau of the Census for the Bureau of Justice Statistics. The table displays the age- and race-specific incarceration rates of prisoners per 100,000 population within each of the age-race categories. Over the five-year period the aggregate incarceration rate increased by 40 percent, and this increase was generally reflected in each of the age-race groups. It is possible that some of the increase might be attributable to growth in criminality within demographic groups, but that explanation would be inconsistent with the generally slow growth in crime rates during the mid-1970s. Thus, it is more likely that much of it is associated with the increasing punitiveness of those who control prison populations—especially judges and parole boards.

Another striking observation from table 1 is the very high incarceration rate of black males in their twenties—more than one per thirty population. If federal prisons and local jails are counted, the rate exceeds one in twenty. This raises an issue of profound social concern, for it represents a rate that must be close to the

Table 1

Age-Specific "Incarceration Rates" (Prisoners per 100,000 Population) for U.S. Males, 1974 and 1979

Age	1974 Rates Total U.S.	Black	1979 Rates Total U.S.	Black	% Increase, 1974–1979 Total U.S.	Black
18–19	825	3,497	902	3,600	9	3
20	720	3,009	885	3,391	23	13
21	664	2,627	889	3,734	34	42
22	724	3,286	944	3,602	30	10
23	698	3,078	941	3,912	35	27
24	580	2,620	849	3,676	46	40
25–29	455	2,168	681	3,211	50	48
30–34	307	1,368	408	1,868	33	37
35–39	231	901	303	1,158	31	29
≥40	58	263	70	324	21	23
Total	182	771	254	1,062	40	38

Source: Incarceration rates calculated from surveys conducted in 1974 and 1979 by the U.S. Bureau of the Census for the Bureau of Justice Statistics; demographic composition of the U.S. population determined from the Census Bureau report *Estimates of the Population of the United States by Age, Race, and Sex: 1977–1979* (Report #870 of Series P-25, *Populations Estimates and Projections)*, January 1980.

limit that could be experienced by any single population group. The gross disproportionality of the figures raises the question of the degree to which the difference is attributable to discrimination within the criminal justice system. I have examined that issue elsewhere and estimate that 80 percent of the racial disproportionality is attributable to differential involvement in arrest.[14] For the most serious crimes of murder and robbery, which compose 40 percent of prison populations, the black fraction of the prison population closely matches the black fraction of arrestees.

Responses to Public Pressure

These two factors, then—the demographic shifts and the growth in punitiveness—are responsible for our current large prison populations, and the situation is almost certain to get worse until at least 1990. The problem comes at a time when state governments are under extreme fiscal stress: taxpayer revolts have been manifested in the passage of referenda like California's Proposition 13 and Massachusetts' Proposition 2½, and in voter rejection of initiatives to increase prison capacity, whether through bond issues (as New York voters did in 1981) or through tax increases (as Michigan voters did in 1980). The burdens imposed on the states by the federal reduction in expenditures for social programs strain local tax bases still further. In the face of these severe pressures, governors would very much like to find ways to respond to the prison congestion crisis.

Of course, one possible response is additional construction—but that is expensive. It costs approximately $50–$75,000 to construct a prison cell and about $10–$15,000 per year to maintain a prisoner in state prison. Moreover, new construction does not answer the immediate crisis of prison overcrowding. There is a long delay from the time the decision is made to construct additional capacity until it becomes available to house prisoners. The legislature must authorize it, a site must be chosen that the neighbors will accept, and the institution must be designed, the money appropriated, and the facility finally built. The process normally takes at least two years and can take up to seven years—and then only if no major snags develop. Thus, additional capacity mandated in 1983 would probably become available around 1990—just about the time that the population pressure will begin to diminish. In many states, new capacity would be helpful simply as a replacement for obsolete and archaic prisons, provided the governments wanted to replace them. In such cases, new construction is not totally wasteful. But state governments faced with severe fiscal stress tend not to put replacement of old prisons very high on their list of priorities.

There is, in short, a widespread desire among state governments to find means of accommodating the growth in prison population without the large capital and operating expenditures associated with construction of additional capacity. What are the choices available to state governments for that purpose?

Broadly speaking, there are five possible approaches that states may take to the overcrowding crisis:

- *a null strategy:* doing nothing, and letting prisons become increasingly congested;

- *a construction strategy:* providing additional capacity;

- *a selective-incapacitation strategy:* using the available prison capacity more effectively by targeting it on those individuals whose incarceration promises to achieve the most in terms of crime control;

- *a population-reduction strategy:* reducing prison populations through some "front-door" method of diverting offenders from prison into alternative treatment programs, or by shortening the time served for those who do go to prison ("back-door" diversion); or

- *a population-sensitive flow-control strategy:* developing "population-sensitive" approaches to incarceration that base sentencing policies (e.g., determinate sentences or sentencing guidelines) or release policies (e.g., parole guidelines) on the current population, and revising those policies in response to changing prison congestion.

Each of these strategies has costs, including political costs for the legislature or the administration that must implement them. The costs associated with the different strategies, however, would be borne by different individuals or groups in each case.

The various strategies also differ in the time required to implement them. Some could be put into place immediately, whereas others might require several years to develop institutional arrangements (e.g., the creation of a sentencing commission to develop sentencing guidelines) before they could contribute to the reduction of prison overcrowding. The longest time is associated with new construction (a minimum of two and, more likely, as many as seven or eight years). In the current situation, where there is an immediate congestion problem to be alleviated, and where demographic forecasts suggest that the problem may well be alleviated naturally within a decade, the short-range solutions obviously have a certain attractiveness.

The Null Strategy

The easiest strategy in the short run is to make no systematic changes. Prosecutors can feed political ambitions by demanding severe sentences; judges can avoid public criticism by responding to those demands; and wardens can demonstrate their managerial skill by receiving the prisoners, putting two or more in a cell, using hallways and recreational areas for residential purposes as necessary, and keeping the increasingly crowded prisons under control. Crowding inevitably involves diminished control of the prisons by authorities; control tends to be transferred to the inmates, and often to the most brutal group of inmates. This inevitably results in greater suffering by those inmates who are not members of the controlling group; but since prisoners' political influence is generally weak, their suffering is likely to be invisible to the general public. Unless it is forcibly brought to public attention by the press or through the legal process, it is likely to be overlooked and ignored in the general political environment. Overcrowding and its consequences have become so commonplace that they hardly make news anymore.

A further consequence of the shift in control is the deterioration in staff morale and the attendant increase in staff turnover, which in turn accelerates the transfer of control to the prison inmates. Yet these problems rarely come to public attention. Overcrowding prevails as long as the disruption stays short of riot and does not prompt court intervention.

Court intervention, when it occurs, usually follows suits brought under the Eighth Amendment's prohibition against cruel and unusual punishment. Many such actions have been initiated by the American Civil Liberties Union Prison Project, with some success. Prisons in twenty-eight states have come under court intervention because overcrowding produced conditions that the courts viewed as unacceptably severe.[15] In its decision in *Rhodes* v. *Chapman,* however, the Supreme Court ruled that double-celling per se was not unconstitutional, particularly if it was a temporary expedient to respond to overcrowding in a prison that was not otherwise cruel. Even though that decision was carefully drawn to apply to one particular institution, it did represent an important reversal of momentum in federal court interventions, and has undoubtedly inhibited to some degree further court intervention in overcrowding cases.

The one consequence of prison overcrowding that actually rattles the public is the prison riot. The most sensational recent riot was the New Mexico disturbance of February 1980, which forced a major restructuring of the New Mexico correctional system. The New Mexico example notwithstanding, techniques of riot control in prisons appear to have reached a level of effectiveness such that explosive prison riots seem relatively unlikely, even under very difficult circumstances. When a riot does occur, however, it creates an occasion for major public inquiry into prison conditions and operations, with considerable political risk attending.

In the end, the most likely consequence of overcrowding is the transfer of control of the institutions from the management to the most aggressive and hostile segment of the inmate population. This transfer of control inevitably results in brutalization of prisoners, demoralization of the staff, reduction of programs, and acceleration of the decline in control of the institution. Such developments increase the risk of court intervention or riot, but neither is certain to follow.

Consequently, it is relatively easy for a state to follow a "null strategy," to close its eyes to the serious and often inhumane impact of overcrowding and to hold its breath hoping that no disasters follow.

Yet to the extent that a state government wants to avert these consequences and reduce these risks, either legislative or executive leadership is needed to pursue one of the more active strategies for accommodating the imbalance between the growing populations and the limited capacity.

Pros and Cons of Construction

The traditional response to prison crowding has been the construction of additional prison capacity. At present, however, this is not an attractive option. First, state budgets are under extreme stress. Taxpayer resistance limits growth in revenues, and transfer to the states of welfare burdens discarded by the federal government increases their obligations for expenditures. In 1980, for example, Michigan voters rejected a five-year increase of just 0.1 percent in the state income tax to pay for additional prisons. This decision followed by one year a referendum in which voters in the same state overwhelmingly eliminated the "good-time" or early release for good behavior in prison.

Voters thus seem prepared to demand—but not necessarily to pay for—increased severity. Tougher prison sentences are, in fact, expensive. Prison construction costs vary by the level of security required and by the amenities provided, but most construction estimates are in the range of $50–$75,000 per cell. Similarly, the operating costs of prisons will depend on the services provided and prevailing salary scales for correctional personnel, but most state systems spend about $10–$15,000 per year per prisoner. It is rare for these costs to receive any attention in the debate over punishment policies. It is not clear to what extent attitudes toward punishment would change if all sentencing policy proposals had to be accompanied by a "prison impact statement" reflecting the expected change in the number of prisoners that would result and the expected costs to house and supervise them.

One striking exception to the general practice of separating sentencing policy from its costs was the mandatory minimum sentencing legislation submitted to the Pennsylvania legislature by Governor Dick Thornburgh in September 1981. His legislative proposal replaced a mandatory minimum bill that covered a broad range of offenses. A prison impact analysis indicated that the prison capacity needed to house the extra prisoners would be excessive. Using the impact analysis in negotiation with the previous bill's sponsors, he got them to join him in endorsing a legislative package that combined a call for five-year mandatory minimum sentences for a narrowly limited group of offenses with a request for a legislative authorization of a $134 million bond issue to provide 2,880 additional prison spaces to accommodate the anticipated increase in prison population; and the governor let it be known that approval of the sentencing legislation without the bond issue would lead to a veto. Both components were passed with virtually no opposition.

In some states, the problems posed by the costs of new construction are further complicated by the problems involved in the siting of new facilities. Very few people are willing to have prisons located in their community. This problem is particularly severe in the smaller, more densely populated states of the Northeast. One approach to the siting problem involves building the additional capacity on the same site as existing prison facilities. A community that has already become accustomed to having a prison institutions in its midst, and indeed has built its economy around the institution, may well be willing to accommodate an increase in capacity at that site. Standards of correctional practice, however, argue against institutions' holding more than about 1,000 prisoners. This difficulty can be mitigated by operating multiple prisons on a single site as separate institutions.

But even if a state is willing to pay for the additional prison capacity and can find sites on which to locate it, it cannot be made available immediately. Planning, appropriation, design, and construction take time, and in the meantime overcrowding may be relieved by other developments. Moreover, demographic trends suggest that many prison systems could face a situation somewhat like that confronted by numerous local school districts in the 1970s as they found their newly constructed schools suddenly empty—vacated by representatives of the same cohorts that should be emptying out of prisons by the 1990s.

On the other hand, it would be very desirable to create new facilities to replace the existing, obsolete institutions that constitute much of the prison stock in the U.S. There is no assurance, however, that new buildings would end up serving that purpose, or that the old institutions would be closed when the population pressure receded.

One of the arguments most frequently voiced against new prison construction rests on the presumption that the prison population would fill up added capacity by a kind of Parkinson's Law. There is certainly a reasonable intuitive basis for this presumption, and certainly many judges knowingly avoid sending convicted criminals to prison because of concern about prison crowding. On the other hand, during the 1960s when there was spare prison capacity in the U.S., there was also a definite reduction in prison population. One study attempted to test this hypothesized Parkinsonian link between prison population and capacity by examining the time-series relationship between state prison populations and corresponding changes in prison capacity.[16] The analysis claimed that each new prison cell would inevitably be filled in two years' time. The widespread attention and acceptance accorded that finding are indicative of both its intuitive appeal and the desire by many to use the concept to limit the construction of additional prison capacity in any but the most extreme circumstances. The study, however, was found to be severely flawed technically—the result primarily of a computational error.[17] While the possibility of a Parkinsonian relation between population and capacity still exists (the failure to confirm a hypothesis does not prove the contrary), it is clear that a much more elaborate model must be formulated that will take account, at a minimum, of such considerations as the number of persons convicted of the most serious crimes, budget constraints on creating additional capacity, the level of seriousness of offenders not being sent to prison, and court orders limiting prison populations.

Still, one can reasonably expect that for many states in the U.S. (the exceptions include those with rapid population growth due to in-migration), prison congestion problems will be automatically alleviated over time by the aging of the population. In these cases, the need for additional capacity is in significant measure a temporary concern. There are means of augmenting the existing capacity for the intermediate period. One possibility is the use of the state mental hospitals, many of which had drastic reductions in population as a result of the deinstitutionalization movement that dominated mental health practice through the 1960s and the 1970s. These hospitals are typically owned by the state and staffed by civil servants who cannot easily be furloughed. Many would be qualified by training and experience to serve in correctional institutions. Consolidation of the diminished mental health population in a few hospitals, and conversion of the others to minimum-security correctional institutions, is one means of providing that temporary capacity fairly quickly.

Selective Incapacitation

There are important reasons—principally those of cost and of time lags—why a state should not seek to address its current and impending congestion problems primarily through increasing its prison capacity. Yet the continuing public demand for more effective crime control in the face of the capacity constraint suggests a need for using available capacity more effectively. This requires a view of prison capacity as a scarce resource, and the issue becomes one of allocating that scarce resource more efficiently.

Since a state's prison system can accommodate only a certain number of prisoners at any time, it would best serve the interests of the community to identify those prisoners who would represent the greatest threat if they were set free: i.e., the offenders who would commit the most serious crimes, who would commit them at the highest rate, and who would tend to continue committing them for the longest time into the future. If, among those convicted persons eligible for incarceration, the most serious predators—so-called "career criminals"—could be identified and sent to prison, such a strategy of "selective incapacitation" would greatly enhance control of crime.

Any sentencing policy, even if it makes no systematic attempt to focus on high-risk offenders, achieves *some* incapacitation effect—i.e., offenders in jail are not committing crimes on the outside. The principle of selective incapacitation involves an attempt to increase this effect by identifying those individuals who can be predicted to commit the most serious offenses—and the greatest number of them—in the future.

This principle raises many serious legal and ethical problems. First of all, there is the basic legal objection that in a democracy no individual should be punished by imprisonment for crimes he might commit in the future. Carried to its logical extreme, selective incapacitation might involve prediction at an early age of an individual's potential criminality and incarceration of those judged to be a high risk. Such a procedure would clearly be unacceptable if selective incapacitation were to be applied to an individual who had not been convicted of any crime. The worry loses much of its force, however, when the candidates for selective incapacitation are restricted—as they must be—to those who have already been convicted of committing a crime. No prediction regarding innocent people is involved, and any procedure of selective incapacitation would necessarily focus only on those who have already been legally convicted and are therefore vulnerable to punishment. Furthermore, other legal constraints should preclude imposing a punishment any more severe than one normally warranted.

At issue here is a mixture of technical and ethical questions associated with the problem of predictability. If it were the case, for example, that an offender's race were a reliable predictor of future criminality, there would be widespread and wholly justifiable rejection of such a prediction on both legal and ethical grounds.[18]

The opposition to other predictive variables is likely to be less clear, but these can also raise difficult problems. The difficulty arises from the fact that there is a strong correlation between many socioeconomic variables and race, and this raises the concern that even if race is excluded, socioeconomic proxies for race will nevertheless have a racially discriminatory effect. It may well be the case, however, that when one focuses on convicted persons, these socioeconomic indicators lose much of their importance. They are well known as discriminators between criminals and noncriminals, but they may simply be unsatisfactory in distinguishing high-risk from low-risk offenders.

Research in recent years claims to have begun to identify bases for discriminating high-risk from low-risk offenders.[19] Even though these results are still very preliminary and tentative, and have no independent verification, there is a danger that they will see widespread application in coming years. Much more research is required to be able reliably to identify the high-risk population. Furthermore, it is important to be able to assess the degree of improvement in incapacitation effect possible through such a prediction when compared to the best results under current practices, in which any judge or prosecutor does try to make some prediction about individual criminality.

Inevitably such prediction will necessarily be constrained by concerns about "deserts" and proportionality. However likely it may be that a shoplifter will recidivate, it would be wrong to impose on him a sentence that exceeds that imposed on a robber who would not be likely to recidivate. But these concerns are probably less serious than they might first appear. Preliminary indications suggest that those individuals who repeatedly engage in the most serious street crimes also tend to be associated with the highest recidivism rates. Nonetheless, assumptions must be tested at each stage in the development of a prediction strategy.

Population Reduction

States that are facing severe prison congestion and would like to avoid the risks associated with the null strategy could find a variety of other means for reducing their prison populations. Such approaches have been typically characterized as "front-door" and "back-door" strategies. The front-door strategies involve diverting from prison to alternative sentences or programs the most marginal of the offenders who might otherwise be sent to prison. Probation, introduced at the beginning of the twentieth century, is the most common such avenue, and is now offered to the great majority of convicted offenders.

In most jurisdictions, judges are faced with a choice between probation and prison; these alternatives span a great range of severity. A judge confronted with a repeat burglary offender who has already been on probation may seek an intermediate response that represents an escalation in severity; for many such offenders, imprisonment is too severe a sanction. In recent years a rich array of such intermediate programs, including community service restitution centers and community-based group homes, have been developed and used as alternatives to prison.

These programs handle a mixture of offenders—some who would otherwise have gone to prison if the programs were not available, and others for whom prison would not have been likely and who would have been put on probation. Most evaluations have found that the programs handle mostly individuals who would have been on probation ("widening the net") rather than those who would have gone to prison.[20] More recent analyses of programs in Colorado, however, are uncovering possibilities for moving in the other direction.[21]

While front-door strategies operate to divert offenders from entering prison, back-door strategies are concerned with increasing the release rate by shortening the time served by those who do go to prison. In the presence of constraints on total prison capacity, one can choose between sending more people to prison for a shorter time or fewer people for a longer time. Considerations of both deterrence and incapacitation argue for the former.

Research has consistently supported the position that sentence "severity" (i.e., the time served) has less of a deterrent effect than sentence "certainty" (the probability of going to prison).[22] Thus, there is a preference for increasing certainty even at the expense of severity.

In addition, from the standpoint of incapacitation, the longer the time served, the more likely it is that the individual would have terminated his criminal activity even if he were not in prison. In this sense additional prison time is "wasted." Studies of the duration of criminal careers suggest that offenders "retire" from crime at a rate of 10 to 20 percent per year.[23] Furthermore, the null effect finding in rehabilitation research suggests that this dropout rate is not significantly affected by the imposition of prison sentences or by the length of imprisonment. In any given year one might expect about 10 percent of the individuals in prison to have terminated their criminal activity even if they were on the outside. The interest of incapacitation is best served by incarcerating individuals during the period when they are most likely to be criminally active, which turns out to be the period closest to the time of conviction. Thus, from the perspective of incapacitation as well as that of deterrence, shorter sentences are to be preferred to fewer longer ones.

These considerations do not negate the value of long sentences for retributive reasons, but it should be recognized that use of long sentences for punishment in the face of a capacity constraint may well involve a diminished efficiency in the reduction of crime.

Population-Sensitive Flow-Control Strategies

All the strategies considered so far can be implemented without taking direct account of the current population or the current degree of crowding in a state's prisons. But one can also link sentencing policies more directly to prison population. It is possible to devise strategies that explicitly tie a measure of crowding (e.g., the relationship between population and capacity) to sentencing practices.

We will consider here three somewhat different approaches to a population-sensitive incarceration strategy: (1) a planned policy that uses sentencing guidelines and links those guidelines to prison capacity; (2) a policy that employs a population-responsive "safety valve" to release prisoners when overcrowding becomes excessive; and (3) a strategy that allocates the limited number of prison spaces to each court and its judges or prosecutors, who must take their limited allocation into account in making their own decisions.

The best example of a planned population-sensitive incarceration policy is the sentencing guidelines matrix developed by the

Minnesota Sentencing Guidelines Commission. The commission's work followed from an explicit legislative mandate to "take account of prison capacity" in developing its sentencing guidelines, and used prison capacity as a specific constraint on the sentencing schedule that emerged. Thus if some commission member wanted to increase the mandated sentence for robbery, he had to identify the offenses for which he would like to *reduce* the sentences in exchange. Such a procedure requires a technology (such as some kind of simulation or estimation model) that enables the policy group to calculate for each possible sentencing schedule the prison capacity it would consume. This in turn requires information on the expected number of convicted offenders in each category within the sentencing schedule (based, in Minnesota's case, on an offense severity score and on the length of the offender's prior conviction record) in order to estimate the prison capacity that the schedule would consume.[24]

The existence of this prison-capacity constraint imposes a rare discipline on the policy debate. In most settings where sanction policies are debated, advocates of tougher sentences gain political benefits without having to consider the costs of their actions. The methods developed by the Minnesota Sentencing Guidelines Commission deserve much credit for the fact that in 1981, when the U.S. prison population as a whole increased 12.1 percent from 1980, Minnesota had one of the lowest rates of increase, only 1.1 percent. There remains the important question of whether the willingness of the Minnesota criminal justice system—and especially its judges—to accept the discipline of sentencing guidelines is likely to be replicated in other jurisdictions where the commitment to rational government is less strong.

The Minnesota system is rather elaborate; a greater number of jurisdictions might be more comfortable with the "safety valve" policy adopted by the Michigan legislature in 1981. Under that approach, a corrections commission is charged with monitoring the population of the state's prisons in relation to their capacity, and with reporting to the governor when the population of the prisons exceed their capacity for longer than thirty days. Upon receipt of such a report, the governor is then mandated to reduce the minimum sentences of every prisoner by up to ninety days, thereby increasing the population eligible for parole. This does not represent an automatic release of all these prisoners because they still have to appear before the parole board, which can still retain the dangerous convicts until their maximum sentences expire.

This strategy diffuses the political cost of accommodating prison population to capacity. The legislature enacts the law; the independent corrections commission declares the condition of overcrowding; the governor orders the reduction of minimum sentences; and the parole board orders the actual release. This approach provides all participants with a politically palatable means of acting responsibly to avoid the consequences of prison overcrowding.

Finally, a more radical approach has been proposed by John Manson, commissioner of corrections for Connecticut.[25] In this proposal, a "ration" of prison cells is allocated directly to the individual courts within the state, or possibly even to the prosecutors. Then, if a court has used up its allocation and wants to send an additional convicted offender to prison, the court is required to identify which cell from among its allocation should be vacated. The judge must then release a current occupant in order to obtain the needed space for the new one. This approach forces the judge (or the prosecutor before him) to assume concern for the political costs of facing up to the problem of prison crowding, and to take those costs into account in making sentencing decisions. Such a policy seems highly unlikely to be implemented, but it certainly forces a focus on the allocation issues of concern, and directs attention to the Michigan or Minnesota approaches.

All of the approaches to population-sensitive flow control require an explicit formulation of the excessively flexible concept of "prison capacity." As long as double- or triple-celling is a possibility, capacity remains a very poorly defined notion, and represents no constraint whatsoever on any of the policy- or decision-makers within the criminal justice system. When considerations such as reasonable limits on prisoner density or privacy become more explicit and are taken into account, then capacity does become a more meaningful limit, and explicit policy statements can be formulated to define it. This can be done by a commission, including representatives of the legislature, the judiciary, the correctional administration, and prosecutors.

A Reasonable Mixed Strategy

As a state formulates its strategy for dealing with its prison over-crowding problems, it must consider approaches that will work in the short run to alleviate the immediate congestion—a problem faced by virtually all states—and also must develop a long-run strategy. As a first step it is important for a state to develop a projection of its demography, including anticipated in- and out-migration. That projection should extend until at least the year 2000, when the baby boom generation will pass out of the high-imprisonment age brackets. For states whose demography is not dominated by migration, such a projection should be reasonably accurate, since all individuals of interest to an adult prison system in the year 2000 were born by 1982.

The demographic projection should be augmented by an analysis of trends in demographic-specific crime rates (particularly in the crimes of murder, robbery, and burglary, which account for a majority of the prison population) and of trends in the punitive responses of the state's criminal justice system. If there has been a strong trend resembling that reflected in table 1, then the state must face the hard decision of assuming whether those trends will continue or will reverse.

Within the United States as a whole, as well as within the individual states, incarceration rates (prisoners per capita) have remained reasonably stable over history. It is in fact possible to speak of "stability of punishment,"[26] and it may even be reasonable to anticipate that current rates, now about 40 percent higher than long-term averages, will fall to more normal levels. Demographic projections, in combination with judgments about future punitiveness, should provide a reasonable basis for estimating the size of the prison population for the remainder of the century.

Construction cannot solve the short-term congestion problem. The introduction of a "safety valve" on the Michigan model, however, appears to be entirely appropriate; it could be made politically acceptable, and it could be readily implemented. In the absence of such a safety valve, or of the legislative leadership necessary to create one, means such as good-time release that will permit reduction of the time served by prisoners should be considered as a back-door strategy.

For the intermediate term, many states may well find it desirable to provide temporary extra capacity for the next decade. This could be done by converting vacated state mental hospitals or other such state-owned residential facilities that are no longer used for the human services for which they were originally constructed.

In addition, states should establish a linkage between their sentencing policies and their prison capacities. They can do this first by establishing legislative, judicial, and executive commissions charged with establishing a formal prisoner capacity for each of the state's prisons. Once the aggregate prison capacity has been calculated, a sentencing commission can be established. The role of the sentencing commission is to examine current sentencing patterns and to reconsider sentencing practice in terms of appropriate norms. The commission should then establish a schedule of sentencing guidelines consistent with those norms in a relative sense and consistent with the available (or potential) capacity in an aggregate sense. The commission should also continually assess the relationship between prison capacity and sentencing policy and practice, and should be in a position to adjust sentences downward or to recommend the construction of additional facilities as population exceeds capacity.

Meanwhile, research should continue on improving the selection process in sentencing and on the overall prison planning process. Research on selective incapacitation should be pursued carefully through a sequence of prospective studies that test the usefulness of various kinds of predictors of high-frequency predatory offenders.

Research is also needed to enable a state or its sentencing commission to better estimate the impact of policies on prison populations. Such methods of prediction have proved particularly important in Minnesota in developing its sentencing guidelines and in Pennsylvania, where they helped shape a sentencing policy compatible with a reasonable level of new construction. There is a need for further development and dissemination of methodologies that are applicable to any state that wants to pursue its policies in a similarly responsible way.

The prison congestion problem will remain serious throughout the 1980s. There are a variety of ways to address the problem responsibly, without imposing inhumane conditions on prisoners or suffering the risks of disaster associated with doing nothing. Effective action, however, will require a level of political leadership that has rarely been mobilized to address prison problems. Those who manage and live in the prisons, and who alone suffer from the effects of overcrowding, control none of the levers that can provide resolution. There is consequently a huge need for coordination across the criminal justice system—just the sort that the old Law Enforcement Assistance Administration (LEAA) was created to provide. After a decade of "criminal justice planning," however, such coordination is still not readily achieved, and it is of some concern that with the demise of the LEAA and the criminal justice planning process it was intended to support, this critical opportunity for cross-system planning will be missed in many states.

14

PETER W. GREENWOOD

Controlling the Crime Rate through Imprisonment

With respect to the use of imprisonment, the American criminal justice system is at an important crossroads. At the same time that a dissatisfied public is pressing vociferously for greater protection against violent crime and prisons are overflowing with new inmates, the concepts on which we formerly based our decisions about the sentencing and release of offenders have undergone a major revision. Most of the existing sentencing laws in the U.S. were written at a time when a principal goal of imprisonment was thought to be rehabilitation. In recent years, however, a growing body of research has questioned the efficacy of rehabilitation programs and called attention to the inequities produced by sentencing policies based on this goal. As a result, the emphasis on rehabilitation has been largely set aside, and the latest revisions in sentencing policy have begun to stress the role of imprisonment in simply punishing offenders and keeping them off the streets.

The most conspicuous consequence of this shift has been the unprecedented growth of the number of offenders going to prison.

Yet the question remains: given the limited resources of the system, how can we best use imprisonment to contribute to the control of crime? The research reviewed here suggests that a more selective approach to sentencing—the use of so-called "selective incapacitation"—offers one potentially effective method of crime reduction. Modern research on criminal careers has shown that fewer than half of all active criminals are continually engaged in serious criminal behavior at rates high enough that their incarceration could lead to significant reductions in crime. In addition, researchers have been able to show a strong correlation between career criminality and certain conspicuous traits—prior convictions for serious crime, involvement in serious crime as a juvenile, drug use, etc. In combination, these findings suggest that by sentencing the predicted high-rate offenders to longer prison terms, while reducing the terms of low-rate offenders, we could secure a significant reduction in serious crime without any increase in the overall level of incarceration.

This chapter reviews the relevant research findings and discusses the potential advantages—and hazards—of a selective incapacitation policy.

The Impact of Incarceration on Crime Rates

There are three basic means through which incarceration can affect future crime rates: (1) the incarceration experience can change the propensity of those incarcerated to engage in crime when they are released; (2) the threat of incarceration can deter potential offenders from engaging in crime; and (3) incarceration prevents those crimes that would have been committed by inmates during their period of incarceration.

Rehabilitation. Prison may reduce the tendency of an offender to commit further crimes through either rehabilitation or what is termed "special deterrence." It is also possible that criminal propensities of some offenders will be intensified by prison experiences, either because inmates, having been labeled as criminals, will come to behave as such; because prisons are "schools for crime"; or because long periods of incarceration may inhibit an in-mate from learning to function in an open society. Whatever the cause, the basic measure of the outcome is the recidivism rate.

For most of the past century, the criminal justice system at-tempted to control the crime problem through efforts at re-habilitation. Research and experimental programs were focused on developing improved methods for diagnosing the underlying problems that led to an offender's criminal behavior and develop-ing programs that could respond to those problems. Probation, presentence investigation reports, reception clinics in prison, in-determinate sentences, and parole services are all legacies of this faith in the rehabilitation ideal.

By the 1970s, the picture had changed considerably. None of the numerous approaches to rehabilitation tested during the preced-ing decade was found to produce consistently significant reduc-tions in recidivism rates, particularly for the more serious offend-ers. The view that "nothing works" has since become the conven-tional wisdom among most corrections practitioners and re-searchers.[1] It is now universally recognized that a substantial number of inmates will not recidivate after their release, but there is little faith that the size of this fraction can be increased by rehabilitation programs. Whatever residual hope remains for rehabilitation is focused on juveniles and the least sophisticated adult criminals.[2]

The same research tends to contradict the claim that prisons in-tensify criminal behavior. There is no compelling evidence that in-carceration either extends the length of the criminal career or leads to increases in crime severity. In all likelihood, imprison-ment has a positive effect on some inmates and a negative impact on others, with the two effects canceling each other out. Until a way is found of predicting in which category any given offender falls, a prediction that many practitioners continually attempt to make—apparently in most cases unsuccessfully—neither reha-bilitation nor special deterrence effects can provide a useful basis for sentencing decisions.

Research on deterrence. Although general deterrence has historically been recognized as a major objective of the criminal justice system, it is only in the past twenty years that researchers have begun to explore its effect in detail. At its simplest level, deterrence theory holds that criminal behavior is influenced by the same types of cost/benefit incentives as any other type of economic activity. As the costs or risks associated with a particular type of crime are increased, the attractiveness of that type of crime to potential offenders should decrease. As a matter of public policy, the cost of engaging in crime can be increased by increasing the probability of apprehension, conviction, and incarceration, or by increasing the length of terms.

There is little disagreement that the criminal justice system does deter many would-be offenders. Debates about the impact of deterrence are concerned with the effects of marginal changes in sentencing patterns on particular types of offenders.[3] For instance, there is considerable disagreement about the ways in which risks are communicated to offenders. Do they respond to the language of a statute or to the ways in which it is applied? If a law is passed requiring a prison term for every defendant who is convicted of residential burglary, does it matter whether the law is strictly applied or whether a number of defendants are allowed to plead guilty to lesser counts? There is considerable debate about the relationship between the severity of sanctions and the certainty with which they are applied. Will longer sentences for robbery deter potential offenders if fewer than 5 out of 100 robberies result in conviction? Should more offenders be sentenced to prison for shorter periods of time? There is also debate about how sanctions may affect offenders differentially, at different points in their career. Some would argue that young, unsophisticated offenders, who are not yet fully committed to a criminal way of life, are the ones who are most easily deterred by sanctions. Yet this view directly contradicts those who argue that criminal processing only reinforces the criminal identity of these marginal offenders by labeling them as criminal, and that they should be diverted out of the criminal justice system to be treated by community-based programs.

Unfortunately, empirical studies have done little to resolve most of these disputes. Quasi-experimental studies, which attempt to measure the impact of changes in sanction severity over time, and cross-sectional studies, which compare crime rates across jurisdictions that differ in their sanction severity, are both plagued by a number of methodological difficulties. A recent review of these studies by a panel established by the National Academy of Sciences concluded that while the findings of the research are generally consistent with the deterrence hypothesis—i.e., jurisdictions with high sanctions generally have lower rates of crime—the data do not prove the existence of deterrence effects or indicate their magnitude.[4]

Of course, criminal justice officials do not have the luxury of postponing sentencing decisions until the final evidence on deterrence questions is in. Officials must establish or support sentencing policies that, in effect, conform to or depart from deterrence theory. For instance, deterrence studies suggest that the marginal impact of changes in certainty is more important than the effect of changes in severity. If a jurisdiction convicts, on the average, about 1,000 robbery defendants per year, this finding would argue that sending 1,000 defendants to prison for one year would deter more crimes than sending only 500 to prison for two years—the kind of policy now followed in most jurisdictions. Thus deterrence theory turns out to produce policy guidance that is in direct conflict with theories of rehabilitation or incapacitation, both of which would focus resources on those offenders thought to represent the greatest risk to society.

Incapacitation and crime rates. The third method through which incarceration can affect crime rates is called incapacitation. For any offenders who would have continued to commit crimes after their conviction, incarceration prevents the crimes they would have committed during their period of confinement. The amount of crime prevented by incapacitation is obviously directly related to the rate at which inmates would have committed crimes if they were free. The higher the crime rates of individual inmates, the greater the incapacitation effects of any given period of imprisonment.

But this general observation must be qualified. Incapacitation effects will occur only if the period of incarceration is subtracted from the total length of a criminal's career. If a one-year sentence simply extends an offender's career by one year, then the incapacitation effects are zero; his crimes are merely postponed. Similarly, if the incarceration of one robber leads his partners to recruit another offender to take his place, then the incapacitation effect of his sentence will be offset by the crimes attributable to his replacement.

Just as is the case with deterrence theory, there is currently no practical way of measuring the aggregate incapacitation effects of a sentencing policy, or of marginal changes in it. Crime rates are affected by a number of other social, economic, and demographic factors that are difficult to measure, and whose precise relationship to crime is unknown. Even the amount of crime occurring in any specific time period is subject to considerable measurement error. In reponse to these quandaries, researchers attempting to study how prison sentences might affect crime rates have turned increasingly to analysis of individual offenders.

Research on Criminal Careers

Information about the characteristics of criminal careers comes from a variety of sources. Between 1930 and 1950, when the emphasis of criminal justice research fell on prevention and rehabilitation, a number of studies collected extensive information on family backgrounds and social environments of young offenders, but did not focus explicitly on criminal activities.[5] Other studies from this period used extensive interviews to describe the activities of particular adult offenders, but did not try to draw a representative picture of adult criminality.[6]

Recent research on criminal careers has been more responsive to current sentencing issues and has followed three different approaches. The first is the cohort study, an approach pioneered by Marvin Wolfgang and his colleagues at the University of Pennsylvania in 1972[7] and replicated by Lyle Shannon and David Farrington.[8] Researchers in these studies assembled criminal justice and social (school, employment, etc.) records for all youths born in a given year in a given geographic area who continued to reside there through a given age (usually 18). The Philadelphia cohort studies by Wolfgang consisted of all males born in 1945 who resided in the city from ages 10 to 18. This form of study is the most accurate means of determining the prevalence and distribution of criminal activity, as reflected in official records, across the general population. It also provides a useful means to examine such issues as the age of onset of criminality and the age of desistance as a function of socioeconomic and other behavioral characteristics.

The second method of studying criminal careers involves collecting self-reported information from a sample of known offenders, usually while they are incarcerated. This method of research was pioneered at the Rand Corporation in a 1977 study of 49 incarcerated robbers,[9] a 1981 study of 624 California prison inmates, and a 1982 study that involved 2,190 male jail and prison inmates from California, Texas, and Michigan.[10] These self-report studies have the advantage of providing a picture of an offender's criminal activities that is more complete than one drawn exclusively from facts known to the police.[11]

It has been shown that while there is considerable variation between self-reports and official records (i.e., police contacts or convictions), there is no systematic bias toward either over- or underreporting across different types of offenders, as categorized by age, race, or conviction offense.[12] The primary problem with self-reported studies of incarcerated populations is the sample bias inevitably introduced by criminal justice processing decisions.

The third approach to criminal career studies involves the analysis of longitudinal data on criminals' contact with the justice system (arrests, indictments, convictions) for a sample of known offenders in a given geographic area. This form of research has recently been pursued in a 1979 study at the Institute for Law and Social Research (INSLAW) and in an analysis by researchers at Carnegie-Mellon University. The use of arrest histories has the advantage of avoiding the expensive data collection required for self-report studies (all of the studies to date have used computerized files) and also avoids the problems of respondent veracity (although criminal justice records have their own reliability problems). The disadvantage of this approach is that criminal justice data provide information on only a fraction of each individual's crimes and usually say nothing about his social background.

In general, of the three approaches, cohort studies provide the most complete picture of criminal career development. But when data collection costs are limited, studies based on self-reporting and official records provide a clearer picture of the most serious types of offenders, who are rarely encountered in cohort studies.

A number of models have been proposed for estimating the incapacitation effects of imprisonment on individuals.[13] The most generally accepted model[14] was developed by Shinnar and Shinnar.[15] They assumed that there is only one type of crime and that all offenders commit crimes at random intervals at the same average rate (λ). They further assumed that all offenders are subject to the same probability of arrest and conviction (q) for any one crime and have the same probability of being incarcerated upon conviction (J). It was assumed that the sentences served by the various offenders have an average duration of S, with the sentences ranging exponentially around this mean.

With this model, the average or expected time served for any one crime is qJS—i.e., the probability of arrest and conviction multiplied by the probability of incarceration and by the average term. The fraction of time that an offender will be free to commit crime is:

$$\eta = \frac{1}{1 + \lambda q J S}$$

This formula also represents the amount of crime that will occur under sentencing policy q, J, S, measured as a fraction of the crime that would occur if no offenders were incarcerated.

The difficulty with this model lies in estimating the offense rate of individual offenders—λ. At the time the model was developed, estimates of λ, which were either assumed or inferred from aggregate data, ranged from less than one index crime per year[16] to ten crimes per year.[17] Within this range of estimates, the predicted crime reduction effect from incapacitation could range from less than 10 percent to more than 30 percent of the violent crimes that would occur if no offenders were incarcerated.[18]

The first serious attempts to estimate individual crime rates were undertaken by Mark Peterson and Harriet Braiker in 1981,[19] who based their estimates on self-reports by prison inmates, and by Alfred Blumstein and Jacqueline Cohen in 1979, who based their estimates on arrest history files.[20] These two studies produced remarkably similar estimates of individual offense rates for several specific crime types: between 2 and 3.5 offenses per year for robbery; 6 or 7 offenses per year for burglary; and 3 to 3.5 offenses per year for auto theft.

In addition to providing estimates of individual offense rates for specific crime types, these two studies also produced several other findings that bear directly on the measurement of incapacitation effects. First, it turns out that most offenders are largely unspecialized, engaging in several different types of crime during any one time period; second, the distribution of individual offense rates is highly skewed toward the high end, with most offenders committing crimes at fairly low rates. The first observation implies that the sentences given to convicted burglars, in addition to reducing burglary rates through incapacitation, will reduce other crime rates as well. The second suggests that the average offense rate for any given group of offenders is heavily influenced by the offense rates of the few high-rate offenders out in the right tail of the distribution. This second finding raises the possibility of focusing the use of imprisonment on the high-rate offenders as a means of increasing the incapacitation effects of imprisonment—if such criminals can be identified.

There are two basic methods for attempting to identify dangerous or high-rate offenders. One is subjective and relies on expert evaluations of an offender's background, behavior, and psychological characteristics. The other relies on actuarial data. The subjective approach has been the traditional method used in sentencing. A convicted defendant may be referred to a panel of court-appointed psychologists or psychiatrists or to a reception clinic within the correctional system. The evaluations of the panel or clinic are then considered by the court in determining the sentence. If a defendant is sentenced to an indeterminate term, periodic evaluations will be made to determine when he is suitable for release. Recent evaluations of these procedures have shown that they have very little predictive accuracy.[21]

The second method of prediction, based on actuarial data, has been used most frequently in the form of parole experience tables to guide release decisions.[22] These tables, which use a variety of factors to predict an offender's chances of success on parole, have been shown to be more accurate than diagnostic studies.

The most recent Rand survey of nearly 2,200 jail and prison inmates in California, Michigan, and Texas provided an opportunity to determine how accurately high-rate offenders could be identified using the actuarial approach.[23] For the convicted robbers and burglars in this sample, a seven-item scale was developed using variables that could conceivably be obtained from official records and that might be appropriate for selective sentencing purposes.[24] The seven binary variables selected were:

1. Incarceration for more than half of the two-year period preceding the most recent arrest.

2. Prior conviction for the crime type that is being predicted.

3. Juvenile conviction prior to age 16.

4. Commitment to a state or federal juvenile facility.

5. Heroin or barbiturate use in the two-year period preceding the current arrest.

6. Heroin or barbiturate use as a juvenile.

7. Employment for less than half of the two-year period preceding the current arrest.

An affirmative answer to any of these seven questions adds one point to an offender's score. The total scale can range from 0 to 7.

In order to simplify later analysis, this scale was used to distinguish between low-, medium-, and high-rate burglars or robbers. Offenders who scored 0 to 1 on this scale were predicted to be low-rate; those who scored 2 or 3, medium-rate; and those who scored 4 or more, high-rate. The distribution and mean offense rates for each group, in each of the three sample states, are shown in table 1. In most instances, the average λ for the predicted high-rate offenders exceeds that of the predicted low-rate group by a factor of 4 or more.

Of course, average or mean offense rates are not the only measure of the accuracy of this scale. While the mean rates are useful in practice, there is a methodological problem: as simple averages, the figures are greatly affected by the extremely high offense rates reported by the small fraction of high-rate offenders. But there are two other tests that tend to confirm the effectiveness of this scale. First, comparison of *medians*—which are not sensitive to the offense rates reported by high-rate offenders—shows a similar relationship: in every case, the median offense rate reported by the predicted high-rate group is at least five times greater than the median rate reported by the predicted low-rate

Table 1
Distribution and Mean Offense Rates for Offenders in the Three Sample States

State	Predicted offense rate	Robbery N	Robbery λ	Burglary N	Burglary λ
California	Low	36	2.2	37	12.6
	Medium	58	11.0	69	87.6
	High	84	30.9	54	156.3
Michigan	Low	52	6.1	25	71.6
	Medium	72	11.7	65	34.0
	High	26	20.6	34	101.4
Texas	Low	49	1.4	70	6.0
	Medium	49	5.4	92	20.5
	High	19	7.7	41	51.1

Source: Peter W. Greewood with Allan Abrahamse, *Selective Incapacitation*, The Rand Corporation, R–2815–NIJ, August 1982.

group. Second, when one compares the accuracy with which offenders are classified by this scale with the accuracy of the predictions of their criminality implicit in the sentences imposed on them, one finds that the scale correctly classified 51 percent of the sample while their sentences were an accurate reflection of their offense rates for only 42 percent.

The analysis of these offenders was retrospective (i.e., focused on past behavior), and it relied on self-reported rather than official record data. Consequently, it does not provide a completely accurate method of determining how well high-rate offenders might be identified in the future on the basis of their official records. Nevertheless, the results that it achieved support the general supposition that it may be possible to distinguish among low-rate and high-rate offenders using actuarial prediction methods.

Selective Incapacitation

Suppose that the policymakers in some jurisdiction decided they would like to reduce the amount of some specific type of crime, say robbery, by changing their sentencing policy. In the past, this has been done either by increasing the proportion of convicted offenders who are sent to prison or by increasing the length of prison terms. Both approaches will lead to an increase in the prison population; both approaches will theoretically result in increased deterrence and incapacitation effects; and both approaches ignore any information about differences among offenders' individual crime rates.

The alternative would be to adopt a selective incapacitation policy—a policy explicitly aimed at ensuring that predicted high-rate offenders serve the longest terms.[25] In most jurisdictions it offers a means of increasing incapacitation effects without increasing the level of incarceration. In order to adopt a formal selective incapacitation strategy, a jurisdiction would follow a three-step procedure:

• Determine which of the many characteristics that have been shown to be correlated with individual rates of offending constitute acceptable criteria on which to base sentencing decisions.

• Using arrest histories for a large sample of offenders, estimate the distribution of individual offense rates and determine their correlation with the predictor variables.

• With the information developed and statistical information on current sentencing practices, estimate the effect of various selective sentencing policies on crime rates and on the size of prison populations.

The selective incapacitation approach described above also provides a means of determining how sentencing policies can be changed to *reduce* prison population levels with a minimal loss in incapacitation effects. This is particularly useful for jurisdictions faced with severe prison-crowding problems.

The key to any selective incapacitation policy is the ability to identify high-rate offenders. Yet in addition to the technical problems raised by this process, there are legal and moral issues. The concept of selective incapacitation is controversial, both because it conflicts with other theories of sentencing and also because it makes explicit issues that remain hidden by traditional sentencing practices. Traditionally the decision to incarcerate, the place of incarceration, and the length of confinement have all been predicated on an offender's "amenability to treatment" and his perceived response to treatment programs. Recent research findings notwithstanding, many practitioners continue to believe that an offender's susceptibility to rehabilitation should be reflected in sentencing practices.

To the degree that the theory of rehabilitation has lost ground in recent years, it has generally given way to sentencing based on the notion of "just deserts." Adherents of this view hold that the severity of punishment should primarily reflect the seriousness of the criminal act for which an offender is being punished.[26] The obvious problem with this approach, aside from the difficulty of determining how severity should vary among different types of offenses,[27] is that it ignores the potential impact that sentencing practices have on crime rates.

But perhaps the greatest theoretical barrier to the adoption of a policy of selective incapacitation is the idea that sentencing offenders to prevent crimes that they might commit in the future is on its face unjust. But of course courts and parole boards have always in practice considered future dangerousness in sentencing and release decisions, whether explicitly or not. Selective incapacitation does not alter this practice; it merely seeks to base predictions on objective evidence. All of the factors involved in the prediction scale described previously are routinely included in presentence or diagnostic reports, along with many more subjective assessments of an offender's current life-style and future risk. Moreover, to the degree that we use sentencing policies to deter crime, we are always thinking about the future; it is certainly no more just to impose sanctions on offenders in order to prevent crimes that *others* may commit than to prevent crimes they may commit themselves.

Selective incapacitation does raise the specific issue of which of the many potential predictive factors available will be allowed for selective sentencing purposes. The more restricted the set of allowable predictors, the less accurate the predictions will be. For most people, the use of prior adult convictions raises the fewest objections. When we move to include juvenile record, drug use, or employment history, more objections are raised, while most people would agree that such personal characteristics as race, social class, or education level should be excluded. It is not our point here to argue which of these factors should be allowed and which should not. Rather, we raise the issue to point out that they involve fundamental trade-offs in the effectiveness of sentencing practices that every jurisdiction must make, whether as a matter of conscious policy or on a case-by-case basis.

Potential Applications

Research on the prediction of individual crime rates could be used in a number of different ways. At the most informal level, it could be used by practitioners throughout the criminal justice system simply to focus their efforts on the most serious offenders. Police investigators could use it as a guide in deciding which cases or suspects should receive the most thorough investigation, since it is the quality of this investigation that largely determines the likelihood of successful prosecution. Prosecutors could use the information in case management decisions or in setting plea negotiation policies to ensure that high-rate offenders are convicted of appropriate charges, as many prosecutors already do with so-called "career criminal" cases today; selective incapacitation principles provide a basis for determining who should be targeted by career criminal prosecution units. Judges and parole boards could use the information in determining sentences on a case-by-case basis.

The information could also be used more formally to develop sentencing and parole guidelines or determinate sentencing laws that explicitly recognize the predictive factors as a basis for enhancing or reducing terms. It might be expected that the more formally these factors are embodied in specific statutes or guidelines, the greater the chance that they will be based on objective data and reflect informed decisions on the questions of judgment that this paper touched upon previously.

Any decision to adopt selective incapacitation principles as a formal basis for sentencing policies must begin with a clear idea of what these principles are designed to achieve and how they will interact with other policy concerns. For what types of crime are they to be applied? Are they to be used to limit the prison population, to reduce crime rates by some specific percentage, or to achieve some balance between these two competing goals? What other principles will be used to guide sentencing?

As a method of crime control, selective incapacitation will vary in effectiveness depending on the crime. For certain violent crimes—homicide, rape, and assault—selective incapacitation may have little effect. These crimes often involve people who know each other; moreover, arrest rates suggest that the commission of violent crime is so infrequent for any one offender that the overall rate cannot be influenced much by incapacitation policies. For these offenses, sentences will continue to be based primarily on the concept of just deserts, since the punishment deserved for any one crime will normally override any concerns about future offenses.

For the least serious property crimes such as larceny, fraud, or auto theft, very few offenders are now incarcerated. Therefore, any attempt to use selective incapacitation principles to reduce these crimes would place an additional burden on already overcrowded prison facilities.

The crimes for which selective incapacitation principles appear to offer best prospects are burglary and robbery. These are high-volume predatory offenses of which the public is most fearful. They are also the offenses in which career criminals predominate, and they are the crimes for which a substantial number of convicted defendants are currently incarcerated.

The 1982 Rand study previously cited used the survey data from convicted robbers in California, and the seven-item prediction scale, to estimate the incapacitation effects that would result from a number of different sentencing policy changes that differed in their degree of selectivity. Among the policy changes they investigated were four defined as follows:

1. *Nonselective increases in the prison commitment rate.* Under the sentencing policy in effect at the time of the study, 86 percent of all convicted robbers were incarcerated: 61 percent were sentenced to short jail terms (less than one year) and 25 percent were given longer state prison terms (an average of 52 months). Increasing the prison commitment rate would result in fewer short jail terms and a greater number of longer prison terms for all types of offenders. This is the least selective method of increasing the incarcerated population, since low-rate offenders are currently more likely to be sentenced to the shorter jail terms.

2. *Nonselective increases in prison term length.* Under this policy, the probability of being sentenced to jail or prison remained unchanged for all three types of offenders—i.e., those predicted to be low-, medium-, or high-rate. The only change was that the length of time served by those committed to *prison* became longer. This policy is somewhat more selective than policy 1 in that high-rate offenders are currently more likely to be committed to prison than low-rate offenders, who tend to serve jail terms.

3. *Selective increases in prison term length.* Under this policy, which is more selective than the previous two, only the terms of predicted *high-rate* prison inmates were increased; the probability of being sentenced to jail or prison remained unchanged.

4. *Imprisonment for only high-rate offenders.* This was the most selective policy tested. The fraction of defendants incarcerated in either jail or prison remained unchanged. However, all predicted low- and medium-rate offenders were sentenced to jail terms of one year and all predicted high-rate offenders were sentenced to prison terms.

The predicted impacts of these four different policies on robbery rates and incarceration levels are shown in figure 1.

Each line in the figure represents a specific policy and shows the expected adult robbery rate (vertical axis) that will result for a range of incarceration levels (horizontal axis). Both the robbery rate and prison population levels are expressed as a percentage of their current estimated value.

As figure 1 shows, the more selective sentencing policies result in lower crime rates for any given level of incarceration. Under policy 1, it would require a 15 percent increase in the number of offenders incarcerated to bring about a 10 percent reduction of the robbery rate. But by using the most selective policy (policy 4), it is possible to achieve a 20 percent reduction in the robbery rate with no increase in the overall number of offenders incarcerated. Note that in none of the policies would the terms of the predicted high-rate offenders be increased by more than a factor of two.

Figure 1

**Crime Rate/Incarceration Level Trade-Offs
under Alternative Selective Incapacitation Policies
(California Robbers)**

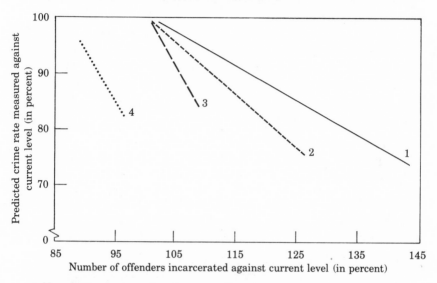

1 Nonselective increases in prison commitment rate
2 Nonselective increases in prison term length
3 Selective increases in prison term length
4 Imprisonment for only high-rate offenders

Source: Peter W. Greenwood with Allan Abrahamse, *Selective Incapacitation,* The
Rand Corporation, R–2815–NIJ, August 1982.

Implementation

Any state that decided to use selective incapacitation in determining its sentencing policies would have to take a number of actions.
It would have to begin by determining the distribution of individual offense rates among its offenders and identifying those
factors that predict high offense rates. This could be done by using
either arrest histories[28] or self-reports.[29]

It would also be necessary to estimate sentencing patterns for
each different type of offender in order to estimate the total number of offenders and to provide a base for comparing alternative
policies. Finally, one would have to evaluate the various alternative sentencing strategies.

Regardless of the policy adopted, it is unlikely that incapacitation will ever be the sole consideration in setting terms. Punishment and deterrence undoubtedly will play a role, even if their effects cannot be quantified. Some additional steps thus need to be taken.

First, the state must project both its future crime rates and its incarceration capacity on the basis of its current crime rates and incarceration levels (for both jails and prisons). (At this point, it would probably be best to ignore the effect of incarceration on crime rates, since incapacitation is unlikely to have much effect on such crimes as homicide, rape, and assault, which make up a sizeable proportion of the total incarcerated population.)

Second, the state must develop a pattern of minimum sentences based on just deserts and deterrence considerations alone, ignoring incapacitation. For instance, despite the fact that their recidivism rate is usually quite low, offenders convicted of manslaughter might be required to serve terms of six years, based on concerns of punishment alone. Similarly, the terms for unarmed and armed robbery might be set at eighteen months and three years, with an additional two years added for seriously injuring a victim.

Finally, in light of this pattern of minimum sentences and the expected crime rate, it will be possible to estimate the incarcerated population that would be generated by these terms. The difference between the population to be generated by the minimum terms and the predicted capacity is the amount of space available for selective incapacitation. In California, for instance, the projected population to be generated for minimum terms might be 30,000, while the available capacity might be 32,000. If it were decided to use all of this excess capacity to reduce robberies, and the projected minimum robbery population were 8,000, there would be room for a 25 percent increase in the incarcerated robbery population. Depending upon the sentencing policy chosen, one could obtain reductions in the robbery rate ranging from 12 to more than 30 percent. Of course, after one such cycle of estimates, it would be possible to go back and revise the minimum terms in order to provide more or less for incapacitation.

In undertaking these reforms, policymakers need to proceed with caution. One of the major lessons from experience with policy initiatives in criminal justice over the past twenty years is that nothing is simple. The system is complex and responds to change in ways that are difficult to anticipate. There is much that we do not know about how specific types of offenders will respond to different types of sanctions. Any jurisdiction that decides to implement more selective sentencing policies should therefore proceed gradually, continuously monitoring the impact of its policies on the disposition of cases and the subsequent behavior of offenders. Any less systematic approach will in all likelihood miss the mark.

V

Conclusion

15

JAMES Q. WILSON

Crime and Public Policy

If this book had appeared fifteen years ago, its contents would
have been very different. Depending on the political inclinations
and professional affiliations of its authors, it would have either
drawn attention to the possibility of improving human nature and
man's social arrangements or vigorously condemned the changed
legal context within which crime control objectives were being
pursued. In the first case, we would have been treated to skepticism that crime was increasing, a demand for the redirection of
police efforts toward "community relations," a belief that crime
would go down automatically if social progress were accelerated, a
call for greater resources to be spent on proven methods of
rehabilitating offenders, and a reminder that imprisonment
causes crime and therefore should be used as rarely as possible. In
the second case, we would have been told that crime has gone up
rapidly and in large measure because the courts had handcuffed
the police, and we would have been urged to remedy this by ap-
pointing new judges and a better attorney general; beyond that,
bringing back capital punishment would help put an end to increasing levels of violence.

The book you have just read does not explicitly reject all these views so much as it exposes them to far more thoughtful and scientifically informed opinion than would have been possible in the 1960s or earlier. Because it can draw on the accumulated research of the authors of this book as well as on the work of scores of others acknowledged in the footnotes, it can present an account of crime and a set of policies directed at its control that are far more sophisticated (and thus, inevitably, far more complex) and, alas, much more modest than anything that could have been written before. Readers looking for arguments on behalf of bold, decisive solutions to the problem of high crime rates have already been disappointed; we offer no "magic bullet" that will produce safe streets or decent people. But neither do we think that nothing can be done. What needs to be done is difficult, complex, and costly, and the gains will be deferred and moderate. But they may be all the more lasting because they have been achieved by linking scientific knowledge and practical wisdom to the interests of both citizens and public officials. Though we cannot find a magic bullet, neither do we counsel despair or mere cosmetic surgery.

There is little here about police-community relations of the kind discussed in the 1960s, not because the matter is unimportant, but because the best such community relations begin with public order and safety. Thus, how the police manage crime and disorder, alone and in association with community groups, must be the first priority. There is no essay here devoted to the wonders of rehabilitation, but neither is there any essay based on the supposition that jails and prisons are the only, or even the major, institutions by which we try to control offenders. As Daniel Glaser points out, like it or not we must supervise far more offenders in the community than can ever be supervised inside institutions. We may not be optimistic about rehabilitating them all, but we cannot ignore them lest we fail to help those who can be helped and encourage to further criminality those who mistake our indifference for weakness.

Social progress is not an unmixed blessing. There is evidence in the chapter by Jan and Marcia Chaiken that a widespread belief in the desirability of bringing babies into this world, coupled with the inflation that so often accompanies economic growth, can increase crime rates. And the spread of personal freedom may have contributed to changes in family life that, as Travis Hirschi notes, lead to higher levels of misconduct.

For decades, prison has been the dirty secret of criminal justice, condemned by reformers for allegedly corrupting those sent there and ignored by others except when a prison riot occurs or a federal judge takes control. Yet as both Peter Greenwood and Alfred Blumstein point out, prison is an essential component of the criminal justice system, a vital resource that we must learn to manage more rationally and efficiently if it is to serve any of the objectives—retribution, deterrence, or incapacitation—we may have for it. We have treated an important part of an orderly society the way Victorians treated sex, and with approximately similar results—a combination of degradation and hypocrisy.

Concern over court-fashioned rules that constrain the police and prosecutors remains a legitimate matter, if not for reasons of crime control then in order to serve the equally important objectives of insuring fairness and finality in the processing of accused persons. Steven Schlesinger and Brian Forst both agree that the proportion of crimes that go unpunished because of the exclusionary rule is relatively modest (and far smaller than the number that go unpunished because the police bring in untainted but weak evidence) but that even a modest proportion of the total (there may be as many as 50,000 felonies and serious misdemeanors rejected a year) can deeply offend victims and society. Both agree that our society has not managed to devise a set of rules governing bail, evidence, and appellate review that adequately reconciles the partially competing needs of crime control and due process.

If in the 1960s some people thought we should "unleash" the police, we must now ask, on the basis of evidence summarized by Lawrence Sherman, "unleashed to do what?" Respond more rapidly to calls for help? But rapid response times seem to make little difference in protecting citizens or securing arrests. Patrol more visibly, or more frequently? But feasible changes in the frequency of preventive patrol seem to have little effect on either crime or the fear of crime. More important than how fast, how visibly, or how numerously the police patrol is what they do when they are on patrol. There is reason to believe that foot patrol, at least in certain kinds of neighborhoods, helps promote community order and a sense of personal well-being; there is also reason to believe that aggressive patrol, involving frequent street checks, especially of suspicious juveniles, can help reduce the rate of certain kinds of crime in certain cities.

There was no discussion here of the death penalty, not because it is an unimportant topic but because I, at least, think that it has little to do with controlling the most common and worrisome crimes. For reasons I have set forth elsewhere,[1] I believe that the evidence purporting to show the deterrent effect of executions on the murder rate is inconclusive, and will remain so, and the evidence that might link executions to reduction of other kinds of crimes—for example, rape and armed robbery—is nonexistent, and will remain so.

All of the authors of these chapters share at least one view, and that is of the importance of careful research and evaluated experiments in designing a crime control strategy. We share it not because we ourselves are researchers, eager for more grants and richer data, but because we have seen how often things that "everybody knew" to be true proved to be untrue, or at least questionable. At one time everybody knew that if we tried with sufficient money and good will, we could rehabilitate criminals. Glaser, who has always been sympathetic to that impulse but, unlike others, hardheaded about acting on the basis of it, shows how selective and limited must be our efforts in that direction, how important it is to link control with therapy if the latter is to have much effect at all, and how much more we have to learn about what works. Sherman has devoted a large part of his professional life to finding out what police strategies work, and as a result has cleared away much of the underbrush of conventional wisdom that has obscured a true understanding of the problem; but his essay vividly highlights how much more we have to learn. Charles Murray reviews all the studies trying to prove the commonsense (and perhaps correct) belief that the physical design of our neighborhoods and the sense of community that we may bring to them will materially affect the crime rate. He finds some promising leads, but little that can as yet constitute a blueprint for action. Richard Freeman carefully examines the many efforts made to show that unemployment causes crime and finds, contrary to what many politicians like to assert, that the evidence gives, at best, only weak and heavily qualified support to that view. Some analyses, notably those that compare crime rates in areas with differing levels of unemployment (the "cross-sectional" studies), come to no significant conclusions at all and others, especially those that are based on evaluations of experimental efforts to reduce crime by giving jobs or other tangible benefits to offenders, suggest that in most cases (but not all), job-training and financial aid programs have no effect on individual crime rates. None of this should be surprising to a nation that has seen crime rise sharply during the 1960s, when adult unemployment rates were falling, and level off in many parts of the country during the late 1970s, when unemployment was rising. Freeman does not claim that there is no relationship between unemployment (or poverty) and crime, but only that the relationship is complex, hard to detect, and even harder to address. Because of this, persons who try to reduce crime by job creation programs ought to be prepared for some disappointments.

If the reader learns nothing else from this book, he or she should have learned that the acquisition of sound knowledge about the effects of crime control policies, while expensive, is a good deal less costly than the prolonged commitment to error.

The authors have not simply described our ignorance, however. They have also showed us how much we have learned and suggested ways by which that knowledge can be put to good use. We have learned more than some persons may realize about the characteristics of serious offenders. The Chaikens describe the typical "violent predator" as he emerges from their analysis of interviews with thousands of prisoners in three states. They draw his portrait on the basis of things that might be learned about him from a complete criminal justice record (a record that, in many jurisdictions, is woefully inadequate), and suggest how this information might be used to identify him when it comes time to pass sentence. Richard Herrnstein summarizes the psychological literature describing the same person—the high-crime-rate delinquent—and indicates the extent to which certain temperamental and constitutional traits recur among such persons and how early in life these traits first appear. Greenwood takes up on this theme and explores in detail the implications for crime and prison populations of concentrating our attention on this type of offender. Herrnstein's account, based on psychological and other

278 JAMES Q. WILSON

tests rather than on official records, sets the stage for Glaser's explanation of the ways in which different kinds of offenders might profitably be handled in the community—an explanation that depends importantly on improving our ability to distinguish between those persons who are and who are not amenable to treatment. As Glaser notes, giving counseling to persons who are not amenable to it—who are the chronic offenders—might actually increase their crime rates by persuading them that they can manipulate the system.

This discussion of types of offenders underscores the need for a suitable information system to guide the decisions of police, prosecutors, and judges. We have already seen improvements in this regard with the advent of "career criminal" programs based on computerized criminal justice records that permit prosecutors to identify serious and high-rate offenders from among those brought to their attention by the police, so that these especially dangerous persons can receive high-priority investigation and processing. Forst, who has been among the leaders in the effort to develop the information basis for these programs, points out how much further we have to go before their full potential can be realized. Prosecutors now give high-priority attention to persons who commit very serious crimes and to those who have prior felony convictions. But to judge from the evidence supplied by Greenwood, the Chaikens, and Forst himself, the prior convictions of an arrestee are probably not a very reliable indicator of whether he commits many crimes or few crimes while free on the street. Indeed, many of the most serious offenders are young adults who have no prior felony convictions at all and whose juvenile records may be either unavailable or incomplete. The best research indicates that the high-rate offenders and "violent predators" are, compared to low-rate offenders, younger, drug-using persons who began their criminal activities at an early age, who have a number of arrests (but not necessarily a number of convictions), and who are involved in robbery and burglary.

These findings imply that the most effective (in terms of crime reduction) career criminal programs would be ones that routinely examine the juvenile as well as the adult arrest record of arrestees, that routinely conduct urinalyses of arrestees in order to identify drug users, and that worry more about young adults who are at or near the peak of their criminal activity than about older adults who, though they may have by now accumulated some prior felony convictions, are perhaps nearing the end of their criminal careers.

The need both to reduce crime and to conserve scarce financial resources suggests that we should be concerned about how to make the most rational and efficient use of prosecutorial energies and prison space. Blumstein reminds us of the acute problem of prison crowding and suggests a variety of ways by which it can be addressed—building more space (which is expensive and takes a long time), diversion (which, unless carefully done, may put dangerous persons back on the street faster than we wish), and selective incapacitation (which reserves the most spaces and longest terms for those offenders who commit the most crimes while free on the street). The data supplied by the Chaikens and by Greenwood can help identify these persons; Glaser shows how similar data are being used with some success in Wisconsin and elsewhere for managing probation and parole programs. Greenwood provides a preliminary estimate of the effect on the crime rate and the size of the prison population of using one variant of these guidelines, and concludes that for some states, such as California, a carefully managed policy of selective incapacitation could reduce the rate of certain crimes, such as robbery, without further increasing the number of persons in prison. There are a number of difficult issues that must be resolved to make such a policy both effective and fair, but they are no more difficult than the issues that had to be confronted in designing a fair parole release policy. It is not enough to say, in opposition to selective incapacitation, that it involves predicting behavior, as if that were intolerable and never done. The entire criminal justice system is shot through at every stage (bail, probation, sentencing, and parole) with efforts at prediction, and necessarily so; if we did not try to predict, we would release on bail or on probation either many more or many fewer persons, and make some sentences either much longer or much shorter.

Even with the most rational sentencing system, we would still need more prison space to relieve overcrowding and facilitate the humane management of inmates, and we would still have to supervise in the community two or three times as many persons as are in prison. There are many useful purposes that might be served by such supervision—restitution to victims, service to the community, counseling and job assistance for the offenders—but almost all of these require at least two things: a sensible way of classifying offenders so we know who is appropriate for what program, and an effective means of control to insure that they actually stay in that program. Glaser reviews the options. He notes that offenders who have been successful in crime might best be handled by a short, sharp shock of imprisonment to persuade them that society means business and takes its rules seriously. The study by Charles Murray and Louis Cox, to which Glaser refers, on the effect of varying degrees of control—ranging from probation to incarceration—on the crime rates of juveniles in Chicago, suggests that doing nothing to repeat offenders accomplishes little save inculcating the belief that being arrested is no cause for concern. And the study of juveniles in California who were unsuccessful in crime (and often in other things as well) suggests, as Glaser notes, that counseling may make a useful difference. In between are those programs, such as restitution, halfway houses, and treatment for drug abuse, that depend for their value on the willingness of probation officers to control their charges and of judges to revoke probation and send miscreants to jail when the latter flout the terms of their release. It may come as a surprise to readers to learn that often probation officers do not report (and sometimes do not know) the misbehavior of their charges and frequently judges do not respond to these reports by enforcing the law. Dealing seriously with these "small-time" offenders seems unimportant to busy, harassed officials; yet the failure to attach unpleasant consequences to minor transgressions is a sure way of reinforcing the belief that such transgressions are costless and worth repeating. This is especially the case when the transgression represents a violation of an explicit contract with society.

Society watches not only how we deal with those who violate the terms of probation, but also, and more importantly, how we deal with serious offenders who are candidates for prison. Whatever the effect on the crime rate of the exclusionary rule, liberalized bail provisions, and the opportunity for seemingly endless appeals, the effect on the police and the public seems clear. The former are confused, the latter outraged. Excluding evidence from a trial because it was improperly gathered was largely intended, as Schlesinger shows, to be a way of controlling police misconduct; but there is very little evidence that it has done so. What it has done is to create a baffling and constantly changing set of constraints on police activity that in many cases serves neither to protect the innocent nor to improve the police. Schlesinger calls for abolishing the exclusionary rule and substituting for it a disciplinary proceeding, initiated by either a judge or a citizen, against any police officer engaging in misconduct combined with an opportunity to recover civil damages from the misbehaving officer's jurisdiction. With these measures in place, judges could then allow, as they do now in countries such as Canada and Great Britain, any material evidence into a criminal trial regardless of how it was obtained. Schlesinger's proposal is one of many now being considered to redress the imbalance operating in the courts. Though all are controversial, taken together they represent an expression of the growing dissatisfaction among judges and lawyers, as well as the public, with the inadequacy of the present system—a dissatisfaction that ought to lead to some constructive changes. A similar desire for change exists with respect to the ability now afforded offenders to appeal their convictions, not simply through the state courts but through the state *and* federal courts, and not once but in many cases several times.

Schlesinger's suggestions for changing the bail rules are equally forthright and fundamental. He combines two ideas usually thought to be incompatible—greater reliance on releasing on their own recognizance (ROR) arrested persons who are not dangerous and who have a high probability of appearing for trial, and detaining, regardless of their ability to post bail, persons who are dangerous or who are likely to flee. The present system of requiring cash bail to be posted by a large number of offenders imposes financial hardships on persons who are not a risk and fails to protect the community from those who are.

All the changes so far discussed—in policing, prosecutorial strategies, incarceration policies, and court procedures—are directed at what the criminal justice system should do. But to leave matters there would be misleading; indeed, even the title of this book, by calling attention to crime and *public* policy, is misleading. If we are to deal adequately with crime, we must bear in mind that the chief restraints on misconduct are the bite of conscience, the fear of disrepute, and the watchfulness of neighbors. Police forces and penitentiaries are, for the most part, inventions of the nineteenth century; they were not sufficient then, and they are woefully inadequate now, to serve as the principle force insuring public order and human decency. We have delegated crime control to large and expensive public bureaucracies and it is only natural that we should turn first to them when we want crime better controlled, but in doing so we forget how limited their role can be. A thorough discussion of crime requires a consideration of the setting in which it occurs, the commodities that affect its rate, and the private efforts required for its reduction.

Hirschi reminds us, forcefully, of the supreme importance of the family, and in so doing may succeed in getting family studies back on the criminological agenda from which they were expunged in the 1960s during a wave of faddish concern for how "the system"—i.e., capitalism, representative government, and middle-class values— was actually to blame for crime. We already know that the physical and social structure of our neighborhoods may affect how often we are victimized, but Charles Murray points out that, ironically, criminals seem to be more knowledgeable about these effects than innocent citizens. We all are aware, of course, of the importance of locking our doors and looking over our shoulders, and we suppose that brightly lighted streets are safer than dark ones. Some of us have been persuaded to join "Operation Crime Watch" or "Operation Identification." A few of us have become members of citizen patrols in our housing projects and neighborhoods. What may come as a surprise to all of us is how weak or uncertain the evidence is linking any of these techniques to crime reduction. This may be because such methods have no effect, but it is far more likely that it is because we have not looked closely enough at what kinds of activities in what kinds of neighborhoods under what circumstances will make a difference. Murray suggests that worrying about street lighting and "defensible space" in a neighborhood where crime rates are already high as a result of the predatory activities of persons living in the neighborhood may be wasted effort: only vigorous police activity can, under these circumstances, make much of a difference. More profitable is to worry about these matters in neighborhoods that are at the tipping point, hovering precariously on the edge of disorder and victimization but still populated by persons who are prepared to reassert public control of the streets against threatening outsiders. Citizen patrols and better urban design seem to work chiefly in those areas with an intact and confident social structure; they are less likely to make a difference in areas with high levels of public disorder, a weak social structure, and a pervasive fear of retaliation. Where a great effort was made, by rerouting traffic and otherwise improving the physical features of the area, to reduce crime in a high-crime neighborhood in Hartford, Connecticut, there was some reduction in the fear of crime but no reduction in crime itself. Perhaps the first order of business for police and citizens alike is to identify the threatened but salvageable neighborhoods and to begin the attack on crime with an attack on offenses against public order— loitering drunks, public drug-dealing, aggressive panhandling, extensive littering, and graffiti. These activities are not criminal in any serious sense, but they breed a fear of public places that can, if unchecked, reduce the extent to which citizens will feel confident about asserting their right to be left in peace.[2]

One setting for crime that is especially important because it is both pervasive and under public control is the school. Jackson Toby reminds us that not only are many public schools dangerous places, but schooling itself may contribute to crime by forcing the institution to keep under its (weak) control a captive audience of uninterested, restless, and aggressive persons. Unteachable youths, or at least youths who are unteachable given the realities of most public school systems, are kept in school by a combination of compulsory attendance laws, welfare regulations, and minimum wage laws. We require children to stay in school today for periods far longer than we once did and far longer than do many other nations. Indeed, in the 1950s and 1960s we worried about the problem of the dropout and designed programs to minimize the number of boys and girls who left before graduating from high school. At the same time, we raised the minimum wage and did other things, such as allowing some unions to place sharp restrictions on who could enter apprenticeship programs, that reduced the chances of young persons' finding employment. These changes may help explain the paradoxical fact, noted by Freeman, that crime rose in the 1960s despite a drop in the adult unemployment rate and a rise in real family income. We had changed the structure of that part of the labor market that young persons might enter (we had also changed, I suspect, youthful attitudes toward work); as a result, the unemployment rate of young persons went up while the unemployment rate of adults went down. Our effort to reduce the number of school dropouts was based on the supposition that if children dropped out of school they would turn to crime, unless, of course, they had first been equipped with a high school diploma, in which case they would quickly enter college or the labor force. The supposition was false. Various studies cited by Toby show that delinquency rates rise just *before* children leave school; after leaving, they often drop or at worst remain constant.

If we allowed persons to leave school at age 15 and took steps to facilitate their entry into the labor force, the schools would be relieved of an immense disciplinary burden that now makes learning difficult for students who want to learn and impossible for students who do not. Toby's proposals are only some of several that might be offered (for example, parents might be given more choice over where to send their children if something akin to educational vouchers or tuition tax credits were generally available), but they are especially important because, no matter how much choice exists or how schools are organized, there will always be many public schools that must contend with youth who find schooling irrelevant or, worse, an invitation to predation. Allowing such persons to do something else may be better both for them and for the schools.

Crime rates respond not only to the setting in which people find themselves but also to the commodities to which they have access. Mark Moore shows how three commodities—heroin, alcohol, and handguns—affect crime rates, and offers an insightful new way of thinking about what our policy should be toward them. Conventional opinion tends to be so deeply and inconsistently divided on these matters as to make fresh thought particularly valuable. There are two opposed views: allow generally free access to these commodities, or prohibit their free distribution. Unfortunately, people who are prohibitionists with respect to one thing (such as guns) tend to be libertarians with respect to another (such as alcohol or heroin), and vice versa. Moore shows that the real prob-

lem is not to prohibit access to guns or alcohol (such efforts are politically impossible and practically unworkable) but to increase
the cost of abusing them. Our policies should be aimed, that is, at
making it much riskier to carry concealed handguns in public
places, not at reducing the total inventory of guns in private
possession. Policymakers should recall the lessons to be learned
from studies of alcohol consumption—that its usage goes down as
the price goes up—and rethink the drift toward ending police
responsibility for public drunkenness. The wave of new laws
aimed at drunk driving may be a sign that we are once again taking seriously the abuse of the substance that contributes more to
violent death, including murder, than any other. Policymakers
should also bear in mind that the true purpose of our anti-heroin
laws is to reduce the recruitment of new heroin addicts (by making the drug expensive and hard to find) and to encourage the
movement of confirmed drug users into treatment programs (by
keeping the cost of the drug high and by making treatment readily
available). A price we pay for this policy is to cause the crime rate
of confirmed addicts not interested in treatment to be much higher than it would otherwise be, as they rob and steal to support expensive habits. Society's judgment about this difficult trade-off,
and Moore's as well, is that we are willing to accept a higher rate
of crime by confirmed addicts in order to discourage the recruitment of new addicts. When we make this judgment explicitly, we
realize that in this respect, as in so many others, we do not wish to
reduce crime to the exclusion of all other considerations.

Nowhere is this trade-off clearer than in our attitude toward the
family. There can be little question that a disposition toward crime
is affected by family experiences. An especially poignant fact is
that those families whose children are constitutionally most likely
to display behavior problems (for all the reasons that Herrnstein
suggests) are often the very same families that, to Hirschi, are
least well-equipped to prevent or manage those problems. It is not
hard to design better families or to imagine ways of supplying
some alternative to the incompetent family, but we do not, for very
good reasons, look very kindly on governmental intrusion into
familial affairs.

All of the recommendations made by the authors of this book
have in common the fact that they call for complex, difficult

changes in how citizens, police officers, prosecutors, and judges behave. No author thinks that by merely passing a law, great gains—or perhaps any gain—will ensue. Even those proposals most clearly involving the modification of legal rules, such as Schlesinger's suggestions regarding bail, appeals, and the exclusionary rule, will require judges in various jurisdictions to modify the standards by which they evaluate evidence, legislators to devise and judges to administer new methods for holding police officers accountable, and court officers to create and finance procedures for discriminating between those eligible for release on their own recognizance and those who ought to be detained awaiting trial. Persons even moderately familiar with how complex, decentralized organizations work (or fail to work) will know how difficult it is to coordinate the behavior of so many people to achieve the capacity for routinely making such subtle distinctions.

Every other change will be at least as difficult. At the risk of distorting or oversimplifying the suggestions of my colleagues, let me offer this summary statement of what I take to be the primary implications of much of this book. Citizens, in cooperation with the police and perhaps also with private security services, would work to control misconduct in public places and to report suspicious behavior. Neighborhood groups would press the city to help them define and protect neighborhood boundaries by, for example, changes in traffic patterns, and they would press the school system to reserve schooling for those persons beyond a certain relatively young age who wanted to learn. Police departments would experiment with using patrol officers to encourage and sustain citizen involvement in community protection and with directing investigators toward the task of identifying and arresting high-rate offenders, even when the latter had in a given instance committed only a relatively minor offense. Prosecutors would screen all arrested persons on the basis of complete criminal history files, juvenile as well as adult, and give priority both to those who had committed a serious crime and to those who, whatever their crime, were predicted to be high-rate offenders. The decision to release on bail would take into account the offender's likely behavior while free on the street as well as his prospects for appearing for trial; to minimize the detention of those who could not safely be released, delays in going to trial (or to a plea bargain)

would be sharply cut. Judges would be loath to grant continuances for convenience of counsel. Should the accused go to trial,
all relevant and material evidence would be admitted, with separate proceedings to punish officers who gathered such evidence
improperly and to determine the compensation, if any, to which
innocent citizens whose rights were violated would be entitled. If
found guilty, the offender's sentence would be shaped both by the
magnitude of the offense (which would set the upper and lower
limits of the penalty) and by an informed judgment as to whether
he committed crimes at a high or low rate when free on the street.
The criminal history information necessary to make this judgment would contain certain juvenile as well as adult arrest data
and entries regarding drug use verified, where possible, by
urinalysis. Persons who were neither high-rate nor especially
serious offenders would be ordered to participate in supervised
community programs appropriate to their personality and behavior; and a failure to abide by the terms of supervised release
would lead to the swift imposition of a jail sentence. Drug treatment and alcohol detoxification programs would be readily available for arrestees who had not committed a serious crime, and the
police would not hesitate to arrest persons who were illegally using
drugs or who were intoxicated in public places as a way both of
protecting the quality of life in neighborhoods and of inducting
troubled persons into treatment programs they might not otherwise use. Scarce prison space would be conserved by keeping the
terms of low-rate offenders very short and by reserving the longer
terms for the minority of "violent predators."

Some persons, including perhaps some of the authors of this
book, will disagree with one or more elements of this set of proposals, but I suspect that most citizens will find these ideas plausible and some will even be astonished that scholars have to work
so hard to come up with suggestions so commonplace. And every
jurisdiction in the country does some of these things now and a
few may do many of them. Yet in general, this package of ideas is
resisted in practice while applauded in theory. The blunt fact is
that citizens, school administrators, legislators, police officers,
prosecutors, and judges do not behave as I have suggested they
ought to behave.

Neighborhood and citizen patrols are resisted by police who fear

losing their monopoly of power, by individual officers who fear losing their jobs, and by citizens who quickly become bored with such
volunteer work. School administrators are loath to lose more
ground to competing private schools and they resist the admission
of failure implied by any lowering of the minimum school-leaving
age. Improving the identity and defensibility of neighborhoods
ranks low on the list of priorities of municipal officials who
struggle to find the money to support routine city services. Assigning more police officers to maintain order, perhaps on foot, is
difficult for police chiefs who have undergone reductions in personnel and may be resisted by citizens who value (wrongly,
perhaps) speed of police response to their calls over police supervision of rowdy juveniles and panhandling drunks. Assigning more
investigative efforts to persons thought to be high-rate offenders
may be unappealing to prosecutors who find it more rewarding to
concentrate on major crimes or offenses that lead to easy convictions (even when they involve low-rate offenders). Speedy trials
are easier to conceive than to arrange. The offices of prosecutors
and defense attorneys are often so thinly staffed as to make court
continuances essential or at least very useful. Postponing cases is
for prosecutors a way of evening out workloads and for defense attorneys a way of making evidence turn cold and witnesses lose interest. Supervised release programs exist almost everywhere, but
many offenders assigned to them discover that they can ignore
their requirements with impunity because busy probation officers
and judges may not be inclined to enforce such requirements with
a credible sanction. Sentencing guidelines that might direct judges
to use offense-rate predictors are often resisted by those judges
either because they do not believe in prediction (though they practice it every day) or because they regard any guidelines as an unwarranted intrusion on their freedom to tailor sentences to individual personalities and circumstances. Some thoughtful legislators will support socially useful guidelines. Yet inevitably there
will be other, less thoughtful legislators who base their anti-crime
programs on calls for very severe (and infrequently imposed) sentences with little regard for whether they will affect crime rates
more than will less severe but more frequently and swiftly imposed sanctions. Taxpayers overwhelmingly want the criminal
justice system to crack down on crime, but they regularly vote

down bond issues to finance new or better prison facilities and generally oppose having any new prisons located in their neighborhoods.

In short, the entire criminal justice system, from citizen to judge, is governed by perverse incentives. Though most of its members are in broad agreement as to what they want to achieve and many agree as to how best to achieve it, individually they face incentives that lead them to act in ways inconsistent with those views. In my opinion, which I think is shared by many of my colleagues, the principal problem facing policymakers concerned about crime is how to rearrange those incentives to facilitate shared ends and to further systematic efforts to discover and implement new knowledge about how best to attain those ends. It is not impossible. Police departments are far more inclined to experiment today than in the past, though tight budgets and shrinking personnel make experimentation far most costly than was once the case. Citizens have on their own initiative created thousands of anti-crime organizations, but interest in the more arduous of these, such as citizen patrols, has proved difficult to sustain. Prosecutors, by using computerized information systems and rearranging their staffs, have directed much more effort toward "career criminals," but it is not clear that they have yet focused on the optimal candidates for such intensive efforts. Legislatures in many states have revised their sentencing laws to reduce unjustified disparities, and judges in many jurisdictions, by their decisions or their language, have indicated a willingness to rethink the current status of the exclusionary rule. New prisons are being built, but whether building programs alone, apart from more efficient use of the penal sanction, will be sufficient is far from clear. Meaningful ways of supervising nondangerous offenders in the community seem to exist, but evaluations as to their real effect are few and serious efforts to control the offenders in these programs (by insuring, for example, that they remain in them) are almost as rare.

It should be apparent from everything that has been said so far that the lessons of this book, few and qualified as they are, are directed chiefly at state and local officials, and at private citizens. The federal government has a role to play, but this role is primarily to develop, test, and disseminate useful information about what works, to implement in its own criminal justice system the best lessons of that information, and constantly to improve its ability to cope effectively with those criminal conspiracies (such as drug trafficking) that cut across state and national boundaries. Presidents cannot be police chiefs or prison wardens, and Congress is not a state legislature. The federal role in dealing with crime may involve matters outside the criminal justice system as much as matters that belong to it. The institutions that have the greatest effect on crime, chiefly the family, may not be easily reached by any governmental program; but they are influenced, over the long term, by the moral and material environment in which they exist, and that environment in turn may be affected (at least at the margin) by the moral leadership of public officials who take seriously the character-forming features of human society and the need to maintain an appropriate balance between responsibilities and rights.

Notes

Contributors

Index

NOTES

1. James Q. Wilson: "Introduction"

1. These criteria for federal action are taken from the introduction to the *Final Report* of the Attorney General's Task Force on Violent Crime (Washington, D.C.: U.S. Department of Justice, August 1981), pp. 1–2. I was a member of that task force and had some hand in developing these criteria.

2. Jan M. Chaiken and Marcia R. Chaiken: "Crime Rates and the Active Criminal"

1. Jim Galvin and Kenneth Polk, "Any Truth You Want: The Use and Abuse of Crime and Criminal Statistics," *Journal of Research in Crime and Delinquency*, vol. 19, no. 1 (1982): 135ff.

2. Stephen E. Fienberg and Albert J. Reiss, Jr., eds., *Indicators of Crime and Criminal Justice: Quantitative Studies* (Washington, D.C.: Bureau of Justice Statistics, NCJ–62349, June 1980).

3. William H. Webster, *Crime in the United States 1981,* U.S. Department of Justice (Washington, D.C.: U.S. Govt. Printing Office, 1982).

4. Murder, nonnegligent manslaughter, forcible rape, robbery, and aggravated assault.

5. Alfred Blumstein and Daniel Nagin, "On the Optimum Use of Incarceration for Crime Control," *Operations Research* 26 (1978): 381–405.

6. People from outside the jurisdiction who commit crimes inside are ignored in this simplified formula. However, the formula is easily modified to include them. National and other large-area crime rates are not much influenced by this consideration.

7. Richard Block and Carolyn Rebecca Block, *Decisions and Data: The Transformation of Robbery Incidents into Official Robbery Statistics* (Chicago: Illinois Law Enforcement Commission, July 1980).

8. In addition, pilot and bounding surveys were conducted in 1970–72.

9. James Garofalo and Michael J. Hindelang, *An Introduction to the National Crime Survey* (Rockville, Md.: U.S. Department of Justice Reference Service, SD–VAD 4, 1977).

10. John Ernest Eck and Lucius J. Riccio, "Relationship between Reported Crime Rates and Victimization Survey Results: An Empirical and Analytical Study," *Journal of Criminal Justice,* vol. 7, no. 4 (Winter 1979): 293–308.

11. Ted Robert Gurr, "On the History of Violent Crime in Europe and America," in *Violence in America,* ed. Hugh Davis Graham and Ted Robert Gurr (Beverly Hills, Calif.: Sage, 1979), ch. 13.

12. President's Commission on Law Enforcement and Administration of Justice, *Task Force Report: Crime and Its Impact—An Assessment* (Washington, D.C.: U.S. Govt. Printing Office, 1967).

13. Gurr.

14. Dane Archer and Rosemary Gartner, "Homicide in 110 Nations," in *Criminological Review Yearbook,* ed. Egon Bittner and Sheldon Messinger (Beverly Hills, Calif.: Sage, 1980), ch. 20.

15. William H. Webster, *Crime in the United States 1980,* U.S. Department of Justice (Washington, D.C.: U.S. Govt. Printing Office, 1981).

16. Judith A. Wilks, "Ecological Correlates of Crime and Delinquency," in President's Commission on Law Enforcement and Administration of Justice, op. cit., Appendix A.

17. Archer and Gartner.

18. Ibid.

19. Wesley G. Skogan, "Crime in Contemporary America," in *Violence in America,* ed. Hugh Graham and Ted Robert Gurr (Beverly Hills, Calif.: Sage, 1979), ch. 14.

20. William P. Butz, Kevin P. McCarthy, Peter Morrison, and Mary E. Vaiana, *Demographic Challenges in America's Future* (Santa Monica, Calif.: The Rand Corporation, R–2911–RC, May 1982).

21. President's Commission on Law Enforcement and Administration of Justice, op. cit., Appendix D.

22. Marvin Wolfgang and Bernard Cohen, *Crime and Race* (New York: Institute of Human Relations Press, 1970).

23. Ibid., p. 31.

24. Skogan.

25. James Alan Fox, *Forecasting Crime* (Lexington, Mass.: Lexington Books, 1978).

26. Scott H. Decker and Carol W. Kohfeld, "Fox Reexamined: A Research Note Examining the Perils of Quantification," *Journal of Research in Crime and Delinquency,* vol. 19, no. 1 (1982): 111–21; see also the response, in the same volume, of James Alan Fox, "Reexamining Some Perils of Quantification in the Econometric Study of Crime: A Reply to Decker and Kohfeld," *Journal of Research in Crime and Delinquency,* vol. 19, no. 1 (1982): 122–31; and their reply, "Reply to Fox," pp. 132–34.

27. Alfred Blumstein, Jacqueline Cohen, and Harold Miller, "Demographically Disaggregated Projections of Prison Populations," *Journal of Criminal Justice,* vol. 8, no. 1 (1980): 1–26.

28. Webster, 1982.

29. Lawrence E. Cohen, "Modeling Crime Trends: Criminal Opportunity Perspective," *Journal of Research in Crime and Delinquency,* vol. 18, no. 1 (January 1981): 138–64.

30. Robert Bales, "Attitudes toward Drinking in the Irish Culture," in *Society, Culture, and Drinking Patterns,* ed. David Pittman and Charles R. Snyder (New York: Wiley, 1962), ch. 10.

31. Peter A. Lee, "Normal Ages of Pubertal Events among American Males and Females," *Journal of Adolescent Health Care,* vol. 1, no. 1 (September 1980): 26–29.

32. Lyle W. Shannon, *Assessing the Relationship of Juvenile Careers to Adult Criminal Careers* (Iowa City: University of Iowa Urban Community Research Center, 1980).

33. Jan Chaiken and Marcia Chaiken, *Varieties of Criminal Behavior* (Santa Monica, Calif.: Rand Corporation, R–2814–NIJ, August 1982); Marvin E. Wolfgang and Paul E. Tracy, *The 1945 and 1958 Birth Cohorts: A Comparison of the Prevalence, Incidence and Severity of Delinquent Behavior* (Philadelphia: University of Pennsylvania Center for Studies in Criminology and Criminal Law, 1982).

34. Dan A. Lewis and Michael Maxfield, "Fear in the Neighborhoods: An Investigation of the Impact of Crime," *Journal of Research in Crime and Delinquency,* vol. 17, no. 2 (July 1980): 160–89.

35. Dan A. Lewis and Greta Salem, "Community Crime Prevention: An Analysis of a Developing Strategy," *Crime and Delinquency,* vol. 27, no. 3 (July 1981): 405–21.

36. Don C. Gibbons and Joseph F. Jones, *The Study of Deviance: Perspectives and Problems* (Englewood Cliffs, N.J.: Prentice-Hall, 1975).

37. Daniel Glaser, "The Classification of Offenses and Offenders," in *Handbook of Criminology,* ed. Daniel Glaser (Chicago: Rand McNally, 1974), ch. 2.

38. Don C. Gibbons, "Offender Typologies—Two Decades Later," *British Journal of Criminology,* vol. 15, no. 2 (1975): 140—56.

39. John Irwin, *The Felon* (Englewood Cliffs, N.J.: Prentice-Hall, 1970).

40. Ibid.

41. Chaiken and Chaiken; Don C. Gibbons, *Society, Crime and Criminal Careers* (Englewood Cliffs, N.J.: Prentice-Hall, 1968); Daniel Glaser, *Adult Crime and Social Policy* (Englewood Cliffs, N.J.: Prentice-Hall, 1972); Julian B. Roebuck, *Criminal Typology* (Springfield, Ill.: Charles C. Thomas, 1967).

42. Ten percent commit crimes at rates over the 90th percentile.

43. Oakley Ray, *Drugs, Society and Human Behavior* (Saint Louis, Mo.: The C.V. Moseby Company, 1978).

44. M. Joan McDermott and Michael J. Hindelang, *Analysis of National Crime Victimization Survey Data to Study Serious Delinquent Behavior* (Albany, N.Y.: Criminal Justice Research Center, 1981).

45. Charles P. Smith and Paul S. Alexander, *A National Assessment of Serious Juvenile Crime and the Juvenile Justice System: The Need for a Rational Response,* U.S. Department of Justice (Washington, D.C.: U.S. Govt. Printing Office, 1980).

46. McDermott and Hindelang.

47. Lloyd D. Johnston, Jerald G. Bachman, and Patrick M. O'Malley, *Student Drug Use in America 1975—1981* (Rockville, Md.: National Institute of Drug Abuse, 1982).

48. Ira M. Schwartz, *Juvenile Justice: Before and After the Onset of Delinquency,* U.S. Department of Justice (Washington, D.C.: U.S. Govt. Printing Office, 1980).

3. Richard J. Herrnstein: "Some Criminogenic Traits of Offenders"

1. Sheldon and Eleanor Glueck, *Unraveling Juvenile Delinquency* (New York: Commonwealth Fund, 1950); idem, *Delinquents and Nondelinquents in Perspective* (Cambridge, Mass.: Harvard University Press, 1968).

2. Sheldon and Eleanor Glueck, *Physique and Delinquency* (New York: Harper, 1956).

3. W. H. Sheldon (with S. S. Stevens and W. B. Tucker), *The Varieties of Human Physique* (New York: Harper, 1940).

4. Glueck and Glueck, *Unraveling Juvenile Delinquency,* p. 196.

5. W. H. Sheldon (with E. M. Hartl and E. McDermott), *Varieties of Delinquent Youth* (New York: Harper, 1949).

6. See, for example, J. B. Cortes and F. M. Gatti, *Delinquency and Crime* (New York: Seminar Press, 1972) and T. C. N. Gibbens, *Psychiatric Studies of Borstal Boys* (London: Oxford University Press, 1963).

7. Glueck and Glueck, *Delinquents and Nondelinquents in Perspective.*

8. See A. J. Reiss, Jr., "*Unraveling Juvenile Delinquency,* II: An Appraisal of the Research Methods," *American Journal of Sociology* 57 (1951): 115—20; S. Rubin, "*Unraveling Juvenile Delinquency,* I: Illusions in a Research Project Using Method Pairs," *American Journal of Sociology* 57 (1951): 107—14.

9. Sheldon Glueck, "Ten Years of *Unraveling Juvenile Delinquency:* An Examination of Criticisms," *Journal of Criminal Law, Criminology and Police Science* 51 (1960): 283—308.

10. S. D. Porteus, *The Maze Test and Mental Differences* (Vineland, N.J.: Smith, 1933); idem, "Q Scores, Temperament, and Delinquency," *Journal of Social Psychology* 21 (1945): 81—103; idem, "Maze Test Qualitative Aspects," *British Journal of Medical Psychology* 27 (1954): 72—79.

11. For a summary see M. Riddle and A. H. Roberts, "Delinquency, Delay of Gratification, Recidivism, and the Porteus Maze Tests," *Psychological Bulletin* 84 (1977): 417—25.

12. Porteus, "Q Scores, Temperament, and Delinquency," p. 85.

13. Ibid., p. 88.

14. Cited in Riddle and Roberts.

15. S. B. G. Eysenck and H. J. Eysenck, "Crime and Personality: An Empirical Study of the Three-Factor Theory," *British Journal of Criminology* 10 (1970): 225–39; summarized in H. J. Eysenck, *Crime and Personality* (London: Routledge and Kegan Paul, 1977).

16. M. P. Feldman, *Criminal Behavior: A Psychological Analysis* (London: Wiley, 1977).

17. H. J. Eysenck, "Crime and Personality Reconsidered," *Bulletin of the British Psychological Society* 27 (1974); Eysenck, *Crime and Personality*.

18. E. I. Megargee and M. J. Bohn, Jr. (with J. Meyer, Jr., and F. Sink), *Classifying Criminal Offenders* (Beverly Hills, Calif.: Sage, 1979).

19. S. R. Hathaway and E. D. Monachesi, *Analyzing and Predicting Juvenile Delinquency with the MMPI* (Minneapolis, Minn.: University of Minnesota, 1953); E. D. Monachesi and S. R. Hathaway, "The Personality of Delinquents," in *MMPI: Research Developments and Clinical Applications* (New York: McGraw-Hill, 1969).

20. Megargee and Bohn, Jr., pp. 77ff.

21. Other samples include ibid. and J. D. Edinger, D. Reuterfors, and P. E. Logue, "Cross-Validation of the Megargee MMPI Typology: A Study of Specialized Inmate Populations," *Criminal Justice and Behavior* 9 (1982): 184–203.

22. D. J. West and D. P. Farrington, *The Delinquent Way of Life* (New York: Crane Russak, 1977).

23. Ibid., p. 1.

24. Ibid., p. 158.

25. S. Dinitz, "Chronically Antisocial Offenders," in *In Fear of Each Other,* ed. J. P. Conrad and S. Dinitz (Lexington, Mass.: Lexington Books, 1977); M. E. Wolfgang and N. A. Weiner (with W. D. Pointer), *Criminal Violence: Psychological Correlates and Determinants* (Washington, D.C.: U. S. Department of Justice, National Institute of Justice, 1981).

26. West and Farrington, p. 158.

27. Cortes and Gatti; W. H. Sheldon (with the collaboration of S. S. Stevens), *The Varieties of Temperament* (New York: Harper, 1942).

28. L. J. Eaves and H. J. Eysenck, "The Nature of Extroversion: A Genetical Analysis," *Journal of Personality and Social Psychology* 32 (1975): 102–12; L. Eaves and P. A. Young, "Genetical Theory and Personality Differences," in *Dimensions of Personality: Papers in Honor of H. J. Eysenck,* ed. R. Lynn (Oxford: Pergamon, 1981); B. Floredus-Myrehed, N. Pedersen, and I. Rasmuson, "Assessment of Heritability for Personality, Based on a Short-Form of the Eysenck Personality Inventory: A Study of 12,898 Twin Pairs," *Behavior Genetics* 10 (1980): 153–62; J. C. Loehlin and R. C. Nichols, *Heredity, Environment and Personality: A Study of 850 Sets of Twins* (Austin, Tex.: University of Texas, 1976); A. B. Zonderman, "Differential Heritability and Consistency: A Reanalysis of the National Merit Scholarship Qualifying Test (NMSQT) California Psychological Inventory (CPI) Data," *Behavior Genetics* 12 (1982): 193–208.

29. See, for example, S. A. Mednick and K. O. Christiansen, eds., *Biosocial Bases of Criminal Behavior* (New York: Gardner, 1977).

30. See, for example, R. D. Hare, "Temporal Gradient of Fear Arousal in Psychopaths," *Journal of Abnormal Psychology* 70 (1965): 442–45; R. D. Hare, "Psychopathy and Physiological Responses to Adrenalin," *Journal of Abnormal Psychology* 79 (1972): 138–47; R. D. Weiner (Beverly Hills, Calif.: Sage, 1982); R. D. Hare and D. Craigen, "Psychopathy and Physiological Activity in a Mixed-Motive Game Situation," *Psychophysiology* 11 (1974): 197–206; J. W. Hinton and M. T. O'Neill, "Pilot Research on Psychophysiological Response Profiles of Maximum Security Hospital Patients," *British Journal of Social and Clinical Psychology* 17 (1978): 103;

W. W. Lippert, Jr., and R. J. Senter, "Electrodermal Responses in the Sociopath," *Psychonomic Science* 4 (1966): 25–26; D. T. Lykken, "A Study of Anxiety in the Sociopathic Personality," *Journal of Abnormal and Social Psychology* 55 (1957): 6–10; P. B. Sutker, "Vicarious Conditioning and Sociopathy," *Journal of Abnormal Psychology* 76 (1980): 380–86; E. Ziskind, K. Syndulko, and I. Maltzman, "Aversive Conditioning in the Sociopath," *Pavlovian Journal of Biological Science* 13 (1978): 199–205.

31. R. D. Hare, "Psychophysiological Studies of Psychopathy," in *Criminal Violence,* ed. M. E. Wolfgang and N. A. Weiner (Beverly Hills, Calif.: Sage, 1982).

32. H. H. Goddard, *Feeble-Mindedness: Its Causes and Consequences* (New York: Macmillan, 1914).

33. E. H. Sutherland, "Mental Deficiency and Crime," in *Social Attitudes,* ed. K. Young (New York: Holt, Rinehart and Winston, 1931).

34. Reviewed in N. S. Caplan, "Intellectual Functioning," in *Juvenile Delinquency,* ed. H. C. Quay (New York: Von Nostrand, 1965); R. A. Gordon, "Crime and Cognition: An Evolutionary Perspective," Proceedings of the II International Symposium on Criminology (São Paulo, Brazil: International Center for Biological and Medico-Forensic Criminology, 1975); R. A. Gordon, "Prevalence: The Rare Datum in Delinquency Measurement and Its Implications for the Theory of Delinquency," in *The Juvenile Justice System,* ed. M. W. Klein (Beverly Hills, Calif.: Sage, 1976); T. Hirschi and M. J. Hindelang, "Intelligence and Delinquency: A Revisionist Review," *American Sociological Review* 42 (1977): 571–87.

35. Ibid.; D. J. West, *Who Becomes Delinquent?* (London: Heinemann, 1973).

36. Discussed by Hirschi and Hindelang, and Gordon, "Prevalance: The Rare Datum in Delinquency Measurement and Its Implications for the Theory of Delinquency."

37. dV. Fox, "Intelligence, Race, and Age as Selective Factors in Crime," *Journal of Criminal Law and Criminology* 37 (1946): 141–52.

38. A. B. Heilbrun, Jr., "Psychopathy and Violent Crime," *Journal of Consulting and Clinical Psychology* 47 (1979): 509–16.

39. For a tally of the world's data on intrafamilial correlations, see T. J. Bouchard, Jr., and M. McGue, "Familial Studies of Intelligence: A Review," *Science* 212 (1981): 1055–59.

40. C. Jencks, *Who Gets Ahead?* (New York: Basic Books, 1979).

4. Travis Hirschi: "Crime and the Family"

1. My discussion of the Oregon Social Learning Center work is based on G. R. Patterson, "Children Who Steal," in *Understanding Crime,* ed. Travis Hirschi and Michael Gottfredson (Beverly Hills, Calif.: Sage, 1980), pp. 73–90. As Patterson notes, the conclusion that punishment is necessary derives from "a series of studies" in the social learning tradition. These studies have found that *successful* teaching of social behavior does not reduce antisocial behavior. As a result, it appears the teacher must focus directly on the behavior he or she wishes to reduce. Since one cannot hope to reduce unwanted behavior by rewarding it, the "lack of transfer" finding has profound implications for the entire social learning tradition. To the everlasting credit of scholars in this tradition, they are a major source of the evidence against their original point of view.

2. An excellent, extended discussion of the theory and practice of socialization may be found in Werner Stark, *The Social Bond* (New York: Fordham University Press, 1978). Stark's thesis, directly opposed to what he calls "the unconscious metaphysic of the age," is that "the principles of civilized and cultured conduct must be pressed on the developing individual, not merely presented to him."

3. Patterson, pp. 88–89. Patterson's list of "parenting skills" contains seven items: "(a) notice what the child is doing; (b) monitor it over long periods; (c) model social skill behavior; (d) clearly state house rules; (e) consistently provide sane punishments . . . ; (f) provide rein-

forcement for conformity; and (g) negotiate disagreements so that conflicts . . . do not escalate" (p. 81). I have reduced and modified this list in a manner consistent with Patterson's discussion and, I believe, consistent with the results of research on the family correlates of delinquency. Thus, for example, the strongest family correlates identified by the Gluecks were *affection* of the parents for the child, *supervision* of the child by the parents, and *discipline* of the child by the parents. Another factor emphasized by the Gluecks' data, cohesiveness of the family ("pride" in family), I interpret as equivalent to "affection," as another source of the willingness to supervise (monitor) and discipline (punish) the child. See Sheldon Glueck and Eleanor Glueck, *Unraveling Juvenile Delinquency* (Cambridge, Mass.: Harvard University Press, 1950). In short, most of the components of this simplified model find support in research beyond that conducted by Patterson and his colleagues. As mentioned in the text, I see the "parenting skills" not included in the model as dealing with "fine-tuning" issues not directly relevant to delinquency, or even as potentially misleading bits of advice. For example, I doubt that it does that much good for the parent to "model" appropriate behavior. (This view gives some of the fun back to adults, but its origins are not solely in class- or self-interest. See note 2, and Travis Hirschi, *Causes of Delinquency* [Berkeley, Calif.: University of California Press, 1969], pp. 94–97, 145–52.)

   4. According to Gary Jensen, one of the *best* predictors of drug use in a large suburban high school was the size of the student's weekly allowance.

   5. The relation between weak families and high criminality holds across cultures. Jackson Toby has shown that measures of family control differentiate offenders from nonoffenders in such diverse settings as Philadelphia, Stockholm, Tokyo, and Ghana. See his "Delinquency in Cross-Cultural Perspective" in *Juvenile Justice: The Progressive Legacy and Current Reforms*, ed. Lamar T. Empey (Charlottesville, Va.: University Press of Virginia, 1979), pp. 104–49. For a summary of the literature on this topic, see Gwynn Nettler, *Explaining Crime* (New York: McGraw-Hill, 1978).

   6. D. J. West and D. P. Farrington, *The Delinquent Way of Life* (London: Heinemann, 1977).

   7. Much research has examined the relation between the socioeconomic status of the family and the criminality of the child. The "results" of this research are controversial. Some see a relation in the data; others see little or no relation. Even if we accept the idea that an inverse relation between socioeconomic status of the family and the criminality of the child has been established, we do not have to conclude that this relation reflects the impact of "poverty" on crime. Poverty suggests deprivation or need. As such, the term itself embodies a theory of crime that sees the offender as being forced into crime by honest needs that cannot be otherwise satisfied. Since, as mentioned, offenders do not appear to be deprived of food, drink, sex, drugs, jobs, excitement, or freedom, some other interpretation of the relation (e.g., less effective child-rearing) would seem to be required.

   8. This statement should probably read: criminality in adolescence predicts socioeconomic status in adulthood better than parental socioeconomic status predicts criminality (at whatever age such criminality occurs). But it would also be true were it to read: criminality predicts *employment* better than employment predicts criminality. In other words, if we (temporarily) control employment, we continue to have differences in delinquency, and we eventually have predictable differences in employment as well. For example, the bulk of the Gluecks' large sample of delinquents and nondelinquents, identified before World War II, eventually ended up in the armed forces. (For psychiatric and moral reasons, the delinquents were less likely to be eligible for such employment.) Differences in delinquency persisted: the delinquents were much more likely to be "brought up on charges"—two-thirds as opposed to one-fifth; the delinquents did not advance in rank as far as the nondelinquents; and the delinquents were more likely to be dishonorably discharged. See Sheldon Glueck and Eleanor

Glueck, *Delinquents and Nondelinquents in Perspective* (Cambridge, Mass.: Harvard University Press, 1968), chapter XIII. In contrast, if we "control" delinquency and employ some and not others, we find (1) no effect on subsequent delinquency; (2) a very small effect in the "right" direction; (3) a small effect in the "wrong" direction. (The latter finding is the rule in nonexperimental studies comparing employed adolescents with "other" adolescents of the same age. See West and Farrington; Glueck and Glueck, *Delinquents and Nondelinquents in Perspective*, p. 191; and Hirschi, p. 188.) For an experimental study of the effects of employment, see Richard A. Berk, Kenneth J. Lenihan, and Peter H. Rossi, "Crime and Poverty: Some Experimental Evidence from Ex-Offenders," *American Sociological Review* 45 (1980): 766–86.

9. West and Farrington, p. 109.

10. Marvin Wolfgang et al., *Delinquency in a Birth Cohort* (Chicago: University of Chicago Press, 1972).

11. West and Farrington, p. 116.

12. Draft registration resister Benjamin Sasway, quoted by the *Arizona Daily Star,* 1 September 1982. In standard contradiction, Sasway also says that the "only difference" between people in prison and those on the outside "is that these people have got caught." Although I am willing to grant that, in some contexts and with respect to some forms of behavior, offenders may be relatively tolerant, I realize that in most respects they are unusually intolerant.

13. Robert L. Burgess, "Family Violence," in Hirschi and Gottfredson, eds., pp. 91–101. Burgess discusses a good many of the correlates of child abuse beyond the two mentioned here, and I am indebted to his article beyond the extent suggested by this and subsequent references to it.

14. Glueck and Glueck, *Unraveling Juvenile Delinquency.*

15. See Hirschi, pp. 237–39, and F. Ivan Nye, *Family Relationships and Delinquent Behavior* (New York: Wiley, 1958).

16. Lawrence E. Cohen and David Cantor, "Residential Burglary in the United States," *Journal of Research in Crime and Delinquency* 18 (1981): 113–27. Cohen and Cantor show that "less occupied households" are more likely to be burglarized. "More occupied" households were those in which at least one person did not go to school or work for more than fifteen hours a week.

17. Burgess, p. 98.

18. West and Farrington, pp. 154–55.

19. Gwynn Nettler, *Explaining Crime* (New York: McGraw-Hill, 1978), p. 341.

20. Edward Shorter, *The Making of the Modern Family* (New York: Basic Books, 1977).

5. Jackson Toby: "Crime in the Schools"

1. Jackson Toby, "Orientation to Education as a Factor in the School Maladjustment of Lower-Class Children," *Social Forces* 35 (March 1957): 259–66.

2. U.S. Department of Health, Education, and Welfare, *Violent Schools—Safe Schools: The Safe School Study Report to the Congress* (Washington, D.C.: U.S. Govt. Printing Office, 1978); Gary D. Gottfredson and Denise Daiger, "Disruption in Six Hundred Schools: The Social Ecology of Victimization in the Nation's Public Schools" (Center for Social Organization of Schools, Johns Hopkins University, Baltimore, Md., 1977, Mimeographed).

3. Fox Butterfield, "Peking Is Troubled about Youth Crime," *New York Times,* 11 March 1980.

4. Frank M. Hewett and Philip C. Watson, "Classroom Management and the Exceptional Learner," in *Classroom Management,* ed. Daniel L. Duke (Chicago: University of Chicago Press, 1979).

5. Jackson Toby, "Crime in American Public Schools," *The Public Interest* 58 (Winter 1980): 29–32.

6. Ibid.

7. Jackson Toby, "Violence in School," in *Crime and Justice: An Annual Review of Research,* ed. Michael H. Tonry and Norval Morris, vol. IV (Chicago: University of Chicago Press, 1983), pp. 1–47.

8. Since training and continuity are very important to a good security program, CETA-funded guards were not ideal. After the elimination of CETA-funded guards, New York City hired guards out of the regular city budget, trained them, and reduced school crime in 1981–82 over the rates in 1980–81 (*New York Times,* 8 August 1982).

9. Edward Muir, "Annual Report of the School Safety Committee for the 1978–1979 Academic Year" (United Federation of Teachers, New York, 1979, Mimeographed).

10. Vance W. Grant and C. George Lind, *Digest of Education Statistics* (Washington, D.C.: U.S. Govt. Printing Office, 1979), p. 43.

11. Richard L. Rapson, *Fairly Lucky You Live in Hawaii!: Cultural Pluralism in the Fiftieth State* (Lanham, Md.: University Press of America, 1980); U.S. Bureau of the Census, *Statistical Abstract of the United States: 1981* (Washington, D.C.: U.S. Govt. Printing Office, 1981), p. 138.

12. Hawaii Crime Commission, *Violence and Vandalism in the Public Schools of Hawaii* (Honolulu: Hawaii Crime Commission, 1980).

13. Toby, "Crime in American Public Schools."

14. James S. Coleman, Thomas Hoffer, and Sally Kilgore, *Public and Private Schools* (Washington, D.C.: Educational Resources Information Clearinghouse, 1981).

15. *Goss* v. *Lopez,* 491 U.S. 565, U.S. Supreme Court (1975).

16. Toby, "Violence in School."

17. U.S. Department of Health, Education, and Welfare, p. B–6.

18. Sanford M. Dornbusch, "To Try or Not to Try," *The Stanford Magazine* 2 (Fall/Winter 1974): 51–54.

19. Thomas Sowell, "Black Excellence: The Case of Dunbar High School," *The Public Interest,* no. 35 (1974): 1–21. When Dunbar stopped being selective in 1955, it developed all of the academic and behavior problems of neighborhood schools in the inner city.

20. Jackson Toby, "Educational Maladjustment as a Predisposing Factor in Criminal Careers: A Comparative Study of Ethnic Groups" (unpublished Ph.D. diss., Harvard University, 1950); Walter E. Schafer and Kenneth Polk, "Delinquency and the Schools," in *Juvenile Delinquency and Youth Crime,* The President's Commission on Law Enforcement and Administration of Justice (Washington, D.C.: U.S. Govt. Printing Office, 1967).

21. Jerald G. Bachman, Swayzer Green, and Ilona D. Wirtanen, *Youth in Transition, Vol. III: Dropping Out—Problem or Symptom?* (Ann Arbor, Mich.: Survey Research Center, 1971); Delbert S. Elliott and Harwin L. Voss, *Delinquency and Dropout* (Lexington, Mass.: Lexington, 1974).

22. U.S. Department of Health and Human Services, *1977 Recipient Characteristics Study: Aid to Families with Dependent Children* (Washington, D.C.: U.S. Govt. Printing Office, 1980). p. 37.

23. U.S. Bureau of the Census, *Statistical Abstract of the United States: 1982* (Washington, D.C.: U.S. Govt. Printing Office, 1982), p. 139.

24. If the child has withdrawn from school, AFDC benefits are still possible over the age of 16, but only if the child is registered for work under the Work Incentive Program (WIN).

25. U.S. General Accounting Office, *Labor Market Problems of Teenagers Result Largely from Doing Poorly in School* (Washington, D.C.: U.S. Govt. Printing Office, 1982).

26. Ibid., pp. 9–10.

27. Walter E. Williams, *Youth and Minority Unemployment* (Stanford, Calif.: Hoover Institu-

tion Press, 1978); Thomas Sowell, *Knowledge and Decisions* (New York: Basic Books, 1980), p. 175.

28. Nathan Glazer, "A Sociologist's View of Poverty," in *Poverty in America,* ed. Margaret S. Gordon (San Francisco, Calif.: Chandler, 1965), p. 18.

29. Thomas Albrecht of the National Institute of Justice suggested in a personal conversation raising the minimum wage either with increasing age or with increasing education.

30. Beatrice F. Berman and Gary Natriello, "Perspective on Absenteeism in High Schools: Multiple Explanations for an Epidemic," in *School Crime and Violence,* ed. Robert Rubel (Lexington, Mass.: Lexington, 1980).

31. Jackson Toby and Marcia L. Toby, "Low School Status as a Predisposing Factor in Subcultural Delinquency" (Rutgers University, New Brunswick, N.J., 1961, Mimeographed).

32. U.S. Department of Health, Education, and Welfare, Appendix B, p. 28.

33. Jackson Toby, "The Socialization and Control of Deviant Motivation," in *Handbook of Criminology,* ed. Daniel Glaser (Chicago: Rand McNally, 1974).

34. Jackson Toby, "Hoodlum or Businessman: An American Dilemma," in *The Jews: Social Patterns of an American Group,* ed. Marshall Sklare (Glencoe, Ill.: The Free Press, 1958).

6. Richard B. Freeman: "Crime and Unemployment"

1. R. W. Gillespie, *Economic Factors in Crime and Delinquency: A Critical Review of the Empirical Evidence,* final report submitted to the National Institute for Law Enforcement and Criminal Justice, Washington, D.C., 1975; Sharon Long and Ann Witte, "Current Economic Trends: Implications for Crime and Criminal Justice" and "Executive Summary of Some Thoughts Concerning the Effects of Recession on the Level of Illegal Activity" (Chapel Hill, N.C.: University of North Carolina, 1980); Thomas Orsagh and Ann Witte, "Economic Status and Crime: Implications for Offender Rehabilitation" (Chapel Hill, N.C.: University of North Carolina, 1980).

2. See National Academy of Sciences—National Research Council, *Deterrence and Incapacitation: Estimating the Effects of Criminal Sanctions on Crime Rates* (Washington, D.C.: NAS, 1978); Philip J. Cook, "Research in Criminal Deterrence: Laying the Groundwork for the Second Decade," in *Crime and Justice: An Annual Review of Research,* vol. 2, ed. Norval Morris and Michael Tonry (Chicago and London: University of Chicago Press, 1982).

3. This work was pioneered by G. S. Becker, Isaac Ehrlich, and B. M. Fleisher.

4. Unemployment aid after release, for instance, reduces the need to engage in crime to make money but also may keep a person unemployed for a longer period of time, increasing the likelihood of criminal activity if unemployment leads to crime. See P. H. Rossi, R. A. Berk, and K. Lenihan, *Money, Work and Crime* (New York: Academic Press, 1980).

5. Perhaps the most serious criticism of studies is that they rarely include a full set of variables to explain crime rates. The earliest study (by B. M. Fleisher) can be faulted for its poor dependent variable; the lack of deterrence variables in most of the others is a major problem.

6. The specific regression result was estimated with a correction for serial correlation as

$$\text{crime} = +.05 \text{ unemployment} + .13 \text{ time}$$
$$(1.55) \qquad\qquad (9.02)$$
$$R^2 = .75 \quad p = .84 \quad \# \text{ of years} = 24$$

where the numbers in parentheses are t-statistics, R^2 is the proportion of variance explained, and p is the first-order serial correlation parameter.

7. When a variable is poorly measured, estimates of its impact are biased toward zero. That labor market variables are probably more poorly measured than deterrence variables does not mean the deterrence variables are themselves well measured. There are no good data on non-prison sanctions. Some data on commitments by state show more persons committed for more

than one year than are committed with no restrictions on sentence length; see National Academy of Sciences–National Research Council, p. 238. Because of the data problems, the NAS–NRC panel stated in its report that "[t]here is a fundamental need for various standard data items" (p. 14).

8. National Academy of Sciences–National Research Council, p. 7.

9. Orsagh and Witte, p. 8.

10. For a criticism of Rossi's work by Hans Zeisal, a response, and a rejoinder, see "Disagreement over the Evaluation of a Controlled Experiment," *American Journal of Sociology* 88 (September 1982): 378–96.

7.   Charles A. Murray: "The Physical Environment and Community Control of Crime"

1. Oscar Newman, *Defensible Space: Crime Prevention through Urban Design* (New York: Macmillan, 1972).

2. Jane Jacobs, *The Death and Life of the American City* (New York: Vantage, 1961).

3. "Territoriality," "natural surveillance," and "image and milieu" were the constructs used by Newman. Others since have used different phrases and rhetoric, but I know of no rationale for a "defensible space" design innovation that cannot be recast in terms of these three constructs. There have been remarkably few improvements on Newman's original discussion of the logic behind designs for defensible space.

4. Robert Ardey, *The Territorial Imperative* (New York: Atheneum, 1966).

5. Ralph B. Taylor, Stephen D. Gottfredson, and Sidney Brower, "The Defensibility of Defensible Space: A Critical Review and a Synthetic Framework for Future Research," in *Understanding Crime,* ed. Travis Hirschi and Michael Gottfredson (Beverly Hills, Calif.: Sage, 1980), pp. 64–65.

6. Herb Rubenstein, Charles A. Murray, Tetsuro Motoyama, and W. V. Rouse, *The Link between Crime and the Built Environment: The Current State of Knowledge,* vol. 1 (Washington, D.C.: U.S. Govt. Printing Office, 1980), p. 63.

7. Oscar Newman, *Architectural Design for Crime Prevention* (Washington, D.C.: U.S. Govt. Printing Office, 1973), p. xii.

8. For example, see L. Hand, "Cincinnati Housing Authority Builds Safety into Project," *HUD Challenge,* March 1977.

9. I. Kohn, Karen A. Franck, and S. A. Fox, *Defensible Space Modifications in Row House Communities,* unpublished report prepared for the National Science Foundation by the Institute for Community Design Analysis, 1975.

10. James M. Tien et al., *Street Lighting Projects: National Evaluation Program, Phase I Final Report* (Cambridge, Mass.: Public Systems Evaluation, Inc., July 1977).

11. There have been other "combined strategies" demonstrations, but they were not fair tests of defensible space theory. The leading example is the Cabrini-Green project in Chicago, where the physical changes consisted of target-hardening and increased *formal* control measures—i.e., security guards—rather than changes based on defensible space theory. Other attempts at combined strategies, notably the demonstration projects undertaken in the Crime Prevention through Environmental Design (CPTED) program sponsored by LEAA, did not produce new knowledge about the crime-reducing potential of defensible space theory except in the negative sense that no major changes were observed. Scheduling and implementation problems plagued each of the demonstration sites. In any event, the projects did not reduce crime. See Westinghouse National Issues Center, Arlington, Virginia, for the three unpublished reports: *CPTED Commercial Demonstration Evaluation Report* (1979); *Final Report on Schools Demonstration, Broward County, Florida* (1978); and *Final Report on Schools Demonstration, Minneapolis, Minnesota* (1978).

12. Floyd J. Fowler, Jr., Mary Ellen McCalla, and Thomas W. Mangione, *Reducing Residential Crime and Fear: The Hartford Neighborhood Prevention Program* (Washington, D.C.: U.S. Department of Justice, 1979); and Floyd J. Fowler and Thomas W. Mangione, *Neighborhood Crime, Fear and Social Control: A Second Look at the Hartford Program* (Washington, D.C.: U.S. Department of Justice, 1982).

13. Fowler and Mangione, p. 31.

14. Ibid., p. v.

15. Ibid., p. 123.

16. See Wesley G. Skogan, "Public Policy and Fear of Crime in Large American Cities," in *Public Law and Public Policy*, ed. John A. Gardiner (New York: Praeger, 1977), pp. 1–18.

17. Fowler and Mangione, p. 123.

18. For comment on the "expected value" assumption, see Ralph B. Taylor, "Neighborhood Physical Environment and Stress," in *Environmental Stress*, ed. G. W. Evans (New York: Cambridge University Press, 1982), pp. 295ff.

19. Tien et al., exhibit 4.4.

20. Kohn et al., discussed in Rubenstein et al., p. 58.

21. I refer to design changes related to defensible space theory, ignoring in this context reductions in fear that follow from purely target-hardening strategies (fences, locks, etc.). Such measures obviously can have a direct effect on fear.

22. Rubenstein et al., p. 64. Emphasis in the original.

23. Taylor et al.; and Rubenstein et al.

24. Described in Sally Engle Merry, *Urban Danger: Life in a Neighborhood of Strangers* (Philadelphia: Temple University Press, 1981); and Sally E. Merry, "Defensible Space Undefended: Social Factors in Crime Control through Environmental Design," *Urban Affairs Quarterly*, vol. 16, no. 4 (June 1981): 397–422. See also Thomas A. Repetto, *Residential Crime* (Cambridge, Mass.: Ballinger, 1974).

25. Merry, "Defensible Space Undefended: Social Factors in Crime Control through Environmental Design," p. 418.

26. C. Bevis and J. B. Nutter, *Changing Street Layouts to Reduce Residential Burglary* (St. Paul, Minn.: Governor's Commission on Crime Prevention and Control, 1977); Barbara Dietrick, "The Environment and Burglary Victimization in a Metropolitan Suburb," paper presented to American Society of Criminology, Atlanta, Ga., November 1977; Oscar Newman and F. Wayne, *The Private Street System in St. Louis*, unpublished report to the National Science Foundation by the Institute for Community Design Analysis, 1974; and Stephanie W. Greenberg, William M. Rohe, and Jay R. Williams, "Safety in Urban Neighborhoods: A Comparison of Physical Characteristics and Informal Territorial Control in High and Low Crime Neighborhoods," *Population and Environment*, vol. 5, no. 3 (1982).

27. See Richard A. Gardiner, *Design for Safe Neighborhoods* (Washington, D.C.: LEAA, September 1978).

28. Greenberg et al., p. 23. Quotations and page numbers are taken from the typescript for the article by permission of the authors.

29. Ibid., p. 22. Subsequently, Greenberg et al. undertook a comprehensive review of the informal social control literature for the National Institute of Justice and drew broader conclusions favoring the natural surveillance explanation over territoriality. See Stephanie W. Greenberg, William M. Rohe, and Jay R. Williams, *Informal Social Control and Crime Prevention at the Neighborhood Level: Synthesis and Assessment of the Research* (Denver, Colo.: Denver Research Institute, August 1982).

30. Oscar Newman and Karen Franck. *Community and Instability* (Washington, D.C.: U.S. Govt. Printing Office, 1980).

31. Ralph B. Taylor, Stephen D. Gottfredson, and Sidney N. Brower, *Informal Control in the Urban Residential Environment*, draft manuscript, cited with permission of the authors.

32. Ibid., p. 52.

33. Ibid., pp. 28–38, passim; and Taylor, personal communication, 1982.

34. See Rubenstein et al., vol. 2, pp. C104–133 for a discussion of both the content and methodological cautions associated with the Newman and Franck study.

35. Merry, "Defensible Space Undefended: Social Factors in Crime Control through Environmental Design," p. 404.

36. Ibid., p. 410.

37. Ibid., p. 419.

8. Mark H. Moore: "Controlling Criminogenic Commodities: Drugs, Guns, and Alcohol

1. I believe I am the first to coin the phrase "criminogenic commodities" and apply it to drugs, guns, and alcohol. It is interesting that while each of these commodities has, at various times and with varying degrees of intensity, attracted public interest, no one has treated them as a coherent unit of analysis. The reason may be that like many other issues in criminal justice policy, the analysis of criminogenic commodities has also been ideologically split. Liberals have always encouraged tighter regulation of guns and more liberal regulation of drugs. Conservatives, predictably, have urged the opposite. In effect, each side had their favorite commodity to control, and the one they chose to control symbolized the "bad" values of the other side: to liberals, guns signified the "machismo" values of conservatives; to conservatives, drugs signified the license and irresponsibility of liberals. For an analysis of the same terrain but with different conclusions, see A. Etzioni and R. Kemp, *Technological Shortcuts to Social Change* (New York: Russell Sage, 1973).

2. For an argument that crime should be controlled through restructuring society, see Charles Silberman, *Criminal Violence, Criminal Justice* (New York: Random House, 1978). For analyses of the possibilities of controlling or rehabilitating offenders, see Robert A. Martinson, "What Works?: Questions and Answers about Prison Reform," *The Public Interest,* no. 35 (Spring 1974); and Peter W. Greenwood (with Allan Abrahmse), *Selective Incapacitation* (Rand Corporation, Santa Monica, Calif., 1982, Mimeographed).

3. William C. Eckerman, et al., *Drug Usage and Arrest Charges* (Washington, D.C.: Bureau of Narcotics and Dangerous Drugs, 1971); Panel on Drug Use and Criminal Behavior, *Drug Use and Crime* (Washington, D.C.: NIDA, 1976), p. 64; and Eric D. Wish et al., *An Analysis of Drugs and Crime among Arrestees in the District of Columbia* (Washington, D.C.: INSLAW, 1981).

4. Bruce D. Johnson, "The Drug-Crime Nexus: Research on the Drug-Crime Relationship, with Emphasis upon Heroin Users/Injectors as Criminal Recidivists" (Interdisciplinary Research Center, New York, N.Y., December 1981, Mimeographed), pp. 10, 36. See also Wish et al.

5. John C. Ball et al., "The Criminality of Heroin Addicts When Addicted and When Off Opiates," in *Sage Annual Reviews of Drug and Alcohol Abuse,* vol. 5, ed. James A. Inciardi (Beverly Hills, Calif.: Sage, 1981).

6. Johnson, pp. 37–39.

7. William H. Webster, *Crime in the United States* (Washington, D.C.: Federal Bureau of Investigation, 1981), p. 191, table 24.

8. Franklin Zimring, "The Medium Is the Message: Firearm Calibre as a Determinant of Death from Assault," *Journal of Legal Studies* I (January 1972): 97–124.

9. Philip J. Cook, "The Effect of Gun Availability on Robbery and Robbery Murder: A Cross-Section Study of Fifty Cities," in *Policy Studies Review Annual: Vol. 3,* ed. Robert H. Havemann and B. Bruce Zellner (Beverly Hills, Calif.: Sage, 1979). See also Philip J. Cook, "The Effects of Gun Availability on Violent Crime Patterns," *Annals* 455 (May 1981).

10. For a review of the literature on alcohol involvement in criminal episodes, see Kai Per-

nanen, "Alcohol and Crimes of Violence," in *The Biology of Alcoholism: Vol. 4, Social Aspects of Alcoholism* (New York: Plenum, 1976), p. 358. Specific studies supporting this conclusion are: Marvin E. Wolfgang, *Patterns in Criminal Homicide* (New York: Wiley, 1958); L. M. Shupe, "Alcohol and Crime," *Journal of Criminal Law, Criminology, and Police Science* 44 (1954); D. J. Pittman and W. Handy, "Patterns in Criminal Aggravated Assault," *Journal of Criminal Law, Criminology, and Police Science* 55 (1964); and H. L. Voss and J. R. Hepburn, "Patterns of Criminal Homicide in Chicago," *Journal of Criminal Law, Criminology, and Police Science* 59 (1968). Moreover, these findings tend to be replicated in studies carried out in foreign countries. See, for example: T. Aho, "Alkoholi Ja Aggressiinen Kayttaytyminen," *Alkoholipolitiika* 32 (1967); and W. D. Connor, "Criminal Homicide, USSR/USA: Reflections on Soviet Data in a Comparative Framework," *Journal of Criminal Law, Criminology, and Police Science* 64 (1973).

11. Wolfgang.

12. Police Executive Research Forum, "Victimization Rate by Event Category for Various Types of Commercial Premises," *Summary Report of the Crime Classification Systems in the City of Peoria, Illinois* (Washington, D.C.: Police Executive Research Forum, 1981). Similar findings are reported for Colorado Springs.

13. Jared R. Tinklenberg, "Drug Involvement in Criminal Assaults by Adolescents," *Archives of General Psychiatry* 30 (1974).

14. Eckerman et al., Panel on Drug Abuse and Criminal Behavior, p. 76; and Nicholas J. Kozel and Robert DuPont, *Criminal Charges and Drug Use Patterns of Arrestees in the District of Columbia* (Rockville, Md.: National Institute of Drug Abuse, 1977).

15. James V. DeLong, "The Drugs and Their Effects," in *Dealing with Drug Abuse*, Drug Abuse Survey Project (New York: Praeger, 1972).

16. Ibid.

17. Wish et al.

18. For a more complete discussion of the relationship between heroin use and crime, see Mark H. Moore, *Policy towards Heroin Use in New York City* (Ph.D. diss., Harvard University, 1973), ch. 2.

19. When I was conducting research on addiction in New York, an addict and I were approached by a derelict who asked for a quarter. The addict remarked with contempt, "Look at that guy! He can take care of his habit for pennies." I am, perhaps, overly impressed by his analysis.

20. The concentration of heroin use in poor communities is well established. See Isidor H. Chein, et al., *The Road to H* (New York: Basic Books, 1964), for a classic analysis. Why this concentration should exist is a little less clear. I suspect it is a function of both *demand* factors (e.g., social deprivation creates greater motivation for drug use) and *supply* factors (e.g., weaker policing and less public support for police efforts allow heroin to be distributed more freely).

21. Howard Cappell and C. Peter Herman, "Alcohol and Tension Reduction: A Review," *Quarterly Journal of Studies on Alcohol* 33 (1972).

22. C. MacAndrew and R. B. Edgerton, *Drunken Comportment* (Chicago: Aldine, 1969).

23. Claire Jo Hamilton and James J. Collins, Jr., "The Role of Alcohol in Wife Beating and Child Abuse: A Review of the Literature," in *Drinking and Crime: Perspectives on the Relationship between Alcohol Consumption and Criminal Behavior*, ed. James J. Collins (New York: Guilford, 1981), p. 261. They relied on R. J. Gelles and M. A. Strauss, "Violence in the American Family," *Journal of Social Issues* 35 (1979).

24. Pernanen.

25. Cook, "The Effect of Gun Availability on Violent Crime Patterns," pp. 65–71.

26. Ibid.

27. Zimring; Cook, "The Effect of Gun Availability on Robbery and Robbery Murder."

28. Cook, "The Effect of Gun Availability on Violent Crime Patterns."

29. For a fuller development of this argument, see Mark H. Moore, "Drug Abuse and Crime: A Policy Perspective," in Panel on Drug Abuse and Criminal Behavior, *Report of the Panel on Drug Abuse and Criminal Behavior Appendix* (Washington, D.C.: National Institute on Drug Abuse, 1976), pp. 511–34.

30. Leonard Berkowitz, "Impulse, Aggression and the Gun," *Psychology Today* 2 (September 1968); and Leonard Berkowitz, "How Guns Control Us," *Psychology Today* 15 (June 1981).

31. Mark H. Moore, *Buy and Bust: The Effective Regulation of an Illegal Market in Heroin* (Lexington, Mass.: Heath, 1977).

32. For empirical evidence on this, see Arthur J. Swersey and Elizabeth Enloe, *Homicide in Harlem* (New York: New York City Rand Institute, 1975). This study found that increases in homicides in New York City were closely related to increases in murders among people dealing narcotics.

33. For a presentation of federal policy towards drugs, see Strategy Council, *Federal Strategy for Drug Abuse and Drug Trafficking Prevention: 1979* (Washington, D.C.: U.S. Govt. Printing Office, 1979).

34. At one time, the position described here *was* federal policy. See *White Paper on Drug Abuse* (Washington, D.C.: U.S. Govt. Printing Office, 1974). For a sharp contrast, see *Federal Strategy for Prevention of Drug Abuse and Drug Trafficking: 1982* (Washington, D.C.: U.S. Govt. Printing Office, 1982).

35. Ibid.

36. Johnson.

37. George Nash, "Impact of Drug Abuse Treatment upon Criminality—A Look at 19 Programs" (Montclair St. College, New Jersey, 1973, Mimeographed); Dale K. Sechrest and Paul R. Cirel, "Criminal Behavior of ARTC Drug Program Patients—Final Report" (Harvard University Law School, Cambridge, Mass., 1974, Mimeographed); D. Levine, et al., "Public Drug Treatment and Addict Crime," *Journal of Legal Studies* 5 (June 1976); Paula H. Kleinman and Irving Lukoff, "Methadone Maintenance: Modest Help for a Few" (New York: University Institute of Justice, 1975); George Nash, "Analysis of Twelve Studies of the Impact of Drug Abuse Treatment upon Criminality," in *Drug Use and Crime: Report of the Panel on Drug Use and Criminal Behavior* (Washington, D.C.: NIDA, 1976).

38. N. Waggner, "Directory of Pre-Trial Services—TASC, 1979–80 Supplement" (Washington, D.C.: Pre-Trial Services Resource Center, 1980).

39. For a more detailed extension argument, see Mark H. Moore, *Policy towards Heroin Use in New York City,* ch. 2.

40. 18 United States Code, ch. 44.

41. For an organizational description of ATF, see Mark H. Moore, "Gun Control (B): The Bureau of Alcohol, Tobacco, and Firearms," Kennedy School of Government, Case #C95–81–404, Cambridge, Mass., 1982.

42. Philip J. Cook and James Blose, "Statement Programs for Screening Handgun Buyers," *Annals* 455 (May 1981).

43. Mark H. Moore, "The Police and Weapons Offenses," *Annals* 452 (November 1980).

44. In 1974, Baltimore, Md., experimented with a buy-back program. They spent nearly $700,000 to acquire 13,000 guns before halting the program eight months after it began.

45. For a brief history of federal legislative proposals, see Mark H. Moore, "Gun Control (A): The Legislative History," Kennedy School of Government, Case #C95–81–403, Cambridge, Mass., 1982.

46. For an argument in favor of policies of this kind, see Philip J. Cook, "Making Handguns Harder to Hide," *Christian Science Monitor,* 29 May 1981.

47. Moore, "Gun Control (A): The Legislative History."

48. For a more complete analysis of the supply system for handguns, see Mark H. Moore, "The Supply of Handguns" (Harvard University, Cambridge, Mass., 1979, Mimeographed).

49. The reason is that the profit margins in selling illegal handguns will be small due to the availability of alternative sources of supply, and the market will be composed almost entirely of nonrepeat customers. These facts, taken together, suggest that firms would have to be large to make much money, but that large firms will be exceedingly vulnerable to informants or undercover operations. The implication, then, is that the business will be an occasional side-line for criminals rather than a mainline business. For a more complete exposition of this point, see Moore, "The Supply of Handguns."

50. Mark H. Moore, "Keeping Handguns from Criminal Offenders," *Annals* 455 (May 1981).

51. Ibid.

52. For a preliminary analysis, see Moore, "The Police and Weapons Offenses."

53. Webster.

54. Norman H. Clark, *Deliver Us from Evil: An Interpretation of American Prohibition* (New York: Norton, 1976).

55. Philip J. Cook, "The Effect of Liquor Taxes on Drinking, Cirrhosis, and Auto Accidents," in *Alcohol and Public Policy,* ed. Mark H. Moore and Dean R. Gerstein (Washington, D.C.: National Academy of Sciences, 1981).

56. Medicine in the Public Interest, *The Effects of Alcohol Beverage Control Laws* (Washington, D.C.: Medicine in the Public Interest, 1979).

57. "Report of the Panel," Moore and Gerstein, pp. 83–89.

58. Medicine in the Public Interest.

59. P. J. Giffen and S. Lambert, "Decriminalization of Public Drunkenness," in *Research Advances in Alcohol and Drug Problems, Vol. 4,* ed. Yedi Israel et al. (New York: Plenum, 1978).

60. David E. Aaronson, C. Thomas Dienes, and Michael C. Musheno, *Decriminalization of Public Drunkenness: Tracing the Implementation of Public Policy* (Washington, D.C.: National Institute of Justice, 1982).

9.   Lawrence W. Sherman: "Patrol Strategies for Police"

1. Data from U.S. Bureau of the Census, *Census of Selected Service Industries: 1972,* vol. 1, and *1977,* U.S. Summary SC 77–A–52, as compiled in table 1489 of U.S. Department of Commerce, Bureau of the Census, *Statistical Abstract of the United States: 1981,* 102d. ed. (Washington, D.C.: U.S. Govt. Printing Office, 1981).

2. George L. Kelling, et al., *The Kansas City Preventive Patrol Experiment* (Washington, D.C.: The Police Foundation, 1974).

3. Tony Pate, et al., *Three Strategies for Criminal Apprehension* (Washington, D.C.: The Police Foundation, 1976).

4. Kansas City Police Department, *Response Time Analysis* (Washington, D.C.: National Institute of Justice, 1977).

5. John E. Boydstun, *San Diego Field Interrogation: Final Report* (Washington, D.C.: The Police Foundation, 1975).

6. The Police Foundation, *The Newark Foot Patrol Experiment* (Washington, D.C.: The Police Foundation, 1981).

7. John E. Boydstun and Michael E. Sherry, *San Diego Community Profile: Final Report* (Washington, D.C.: The Police Foundation, 1975).

8. Timothy H. Hannan, "Bank Robberies and Bank Security Precautions," *Journal of Legal Studies* 11 (January 1982): 83–92. But see New York City police statistics cited by the defense in *Stalzer* v. *European–American Bank, New York Law Journal* (30 March 1982).

10.   Brian Forst: "Prosecution and Sentencing"

1. Federal Bureau of Investigation, *Uniform Crime Reports* (Washington, D.C.: 1976–1980).

2. Bureau of the Census, *Statistical Abstract of the United States* (Washington, D.C.: U. S. Govt. Printing Office, 1980), p. 200.

3. The most widely used automated record-keeping system for prosecutors in the United States, PROMIS (Prosecutor's Management Information System), was installed first in the U.S. Attorney's Office in the District of Columbia under federal funding in 1970. PROMIS is now operational in approximately one hundred jurisdictions, including several federal districts. Record-keeping in the courts is probably most advanced at the federal level, largely due to the case information collected and reported by the Administrative Office of U.S. Courts.

4. Lawrence E. Cohen, *Delinquency Dispositions: An Empirical Analysis of Processing Decisions in Three Juvenile Courts* (Albany, N.Y.: Criminal Justice Research Center, 1975); Franklin M. Zimring, "Background Paper," in *Confronting Youth Crime: Report of the Twentieth Century Fund Task Force on Sentencing Policy Toward Youth Offenders* (New York: Holmes and Meier, 1978).

5. Mary A. Toborg, *Pretrial Release: A National Evaluation of Practices and Outcomes* (Washington, D.C.: U.S. Department of Justice, 1981).

6. Brian Forst, Judith Lucianovic, and Sarah Cox, *What Happens after Arrest?* (Washington, D.C.: Institute for Law and Social Research, 1977); Kathleen Brosi, *A Cross-City Comparison of Felony Case Processing* (Washington, D.C.: Institute for Law and Social Research, 1979).

7. Vera Institute of Justice, *Felony Arrests: Their Prosecution and Disposition in New York City's Courts* (New York: Vera Institute of Justice, 1977); Forst, Lucianovic, and Cox.

8. For a more in-depth analysis of the prosecutor's witness problem, see Frank J. Cannavale, Jr., and William D. Falcon, *Witness Cooperation* (Lexington, Mass.: Heath, 1976).

9. Forst, Lucianovic, and Cox, p. 28.

10. Ibid.; Brosi.

11. This is not to suggest that the practice of aborting or retarding prosecution is an appropriate response to questionable police procedures of obtaining evidence. The 10,000 or so felony cases that are rejected annually in the United States due to such violations of rights to due process may be 10,000 too many from the victims' point of view. (See companion chapter by Steven R. Schlesinger.) We wish only to point out here that the problem is small from another perspective: for each case rejected due to an exclusionary rule violation, about twenty are rejected because the police failed to produce sufficient tangible or testimonial evidence.

12. Forst, Lucianovic, and Cox; Brian Forst, Frank Leahy, Jean Shirhall, Herbert Tyson, Eric Wish, and John Bartolomeo, *Arrest Convictability as a Measure of Police Performance* (Washington, D.C.: INSLAW, 1981).

13. Forst, Leahy, Shirhall, Tyson, Wish, and Bartolomeo.

14. Ibid.

15. Albert J. Reiss, Jr., "Discretionary Justice in the United States," *International Journal of Criminology and Penology* 2 (1974).

16. Brian Forst and Kathleen Brosi, "A Theoretical and Empirical Analysis of the Prosecutor," *Journal of Legal Studies* 6 (1977); U.S. Department of Justice, *Justice Litigation Management* (Washington, D.C.: U.S. Govt. Printing Office, 1977); Joan E. Jacoby, *Prosecutorial Decisionmaking: A National Study* (Washington, D.C.: Bureau of Social Science Research, 1981).

17. Eleanor Chelimsky and Judith Dahmann, *Career Criminal Program National Evaluation: Final Report* (Washington, D.C.: U.S. Department of Justice, 1981).

18. Arthur Gelman, *Report of a Survey of U.S. Attorneys and Federal Investigative Agents* (Washington, D.C.: INSLAW, 1981).

19. Alfred Blumstein, et al., eds., *Research on Sentencing: The Search for Reform* (Washington, D.C.: National Science Foundation, forthcoming).

20. See note 16 and accompanying text. Rhodes has found that separate career criminal units within prosecutors' offices may actually allocate excessive resources to cases involving repeat offenders. William M. Rhodes, "Investment of Prosecution Resources in Career Criminal Cases," *Journal of Criminal Law and Criminology* 71 (1980). Evidence on the effect of prior record on the sentence is reviewed in ibid.

21. Ibid. An exception was reported by William M. Rhodes, *Plea Bargaining: Who Gains? Who Loses?* (Washington, D.C.: Institute for Law and Social Research, 1978).

22. John Hogarth, *Sentencing as a Human Process* (Toronto: University of Toronto Press, 1971); Shari S. Diamond and Hans Zeisel, "Sentencing Councils: A Study of Sentence Disparity and Its Reduction," *University of Chicago Law Review* 43 (1975); Brian Forst and Charles Wellford, "Punishment and Sentencing: Developing Sentencing Guidelines Empirically from Principles of Punishment," *Rutgers Law Review* 33 (1981); Blumstein, et al.

23. Forst and Wellford.

24. Blumstein, et al.

25. Ibid.

26. William Rhodes and Catherine Conly, *Analysis of Federal Sentencing* (Washington, D.C.: INSLAW, 1981); Ilene H. Nagel and John Hagan, "Gender and Crime: Offense Patterns and Criminal Court Sanctions," in *Crime and Justice: An Annual Review of Research*, vol. 4, ed. Norval Morris and Michael Tonry (Chicago: University of Chicago Press, forthcoming); ibid.

27. Restitution and rehabilitation are often, but not always, proposed as alternatives to incarceration. Clearly, each can coexist with imprisonment, at least in principle; as practical matters, of course, restitution while in prison may be impossible for all but a few wealthy offenders, and rehabilitation has yet to demonstrate itself systematically as an achievable goal.

28. In 1972, Marvin Wolfgang and his associates at the University of Pennsylvania reported that 18 percent of a group of juvenile delinquents in Philadelphia accounted for 52 percent of all the offenses committed by the group. See Marvin E. Wolfgang, Robert M. Figlio, and Thorstein Sellin, *Delinquency in Birth Cohort* (Chicago: University of Chicago Press, 1972), p. 88. Then in 1976, Kristen Williams, analyzing PROMIS data from the District of Columbia for 1971–1975, found that 7 percent of the 46,000 different defendants arrested accounted for 24 percent of the 73,000 felony and serious misdemeanor cases handled by the prosecutor for that jurisdiction. Those findings appeared in a 1976 working paper by Williams and in a finished version in 1979, *The Scope and Prediction of Recidivism* (Washington, D.C.: Institute for Law and Social Research), pp. 5–6.

29. See note 16 and accompanying text.

30. Chelimsky and Dahmann; Rhodes.

31. Wolfgang, Figlio, and Sellin, p. 88; Williams; Brian Forst, William Rhodes, James Dimm, Arthur Gelman, and Barbara Mullin, *Targeting Federal Resources on Recidivists* (Washington, D.C.: INSLAW, 1982); Peter W. Greenwood, *Selective Incapacitation* (Santa Monica, Calif.: Rand, 1982); Jan M. Chaiken and Marcia R. Chaiken, *Varieties of Criminal Behavior* (Santa Monica, Calif.: Rand, 1982).

32. See reference to PROMIS, note 3.

33. Peter L. Szanton, *Public Policy, Public Good, and the Law* (Washington, D.C.: Rand Corporation, 1972).

34. Blumstein, et al.

35. Ibid.

36. Anthony Partridge and William Eldridge, *Second Circuit Sentencing Study: A Report to the Judges of the Second Circuit* (Washington, D.C.: Federal Judicial Center, 1974); Diamond and Zeisel.

37. Leslie Wilkins, Jack Kress, Don Gottfredson, Joseph Calpin, and Arthur Gelman, *Sentencing Guidelines: Structuring Judicial Discretion—Report on the Feasibility Study* (Washington, D.C.: U.S. Department of Justice, 1978).

38. William Rich, Paul Sutton, Todd Clear, and Michael Saks, *Sentencing Guidelines: Their Operation and Impact on the Courts* (Williamsburg, Va.: National Center for State Courts, 1981); Blumstein, et al.

39. See also Blumstein, et al.

40. Ibid.

41. Kenneth Carlson, "Mandatory Sentencing: The Experience of Two States," *NIJ Policy Briefs* (Washington, D.C.: U.S. Department of Justice, 1982); ibid.

42. Rhodes.

43. Jeffrey Roth and Paul Wice have estimated, specifically, that by incorporating factors that have been found not to be used in the bail decision, such as illegal drug involvement, and discarding factors that have been used in the bail decision but that have not been found to be related to pretrial misconduct, such as whether the defendant has a local residence, jail populations could be reduced by about 20 percent without any increase in the rate of failure to appear, or by about 40 percent without any increase in the pretrial rearrest rate. Roth and Wice, *Pretrial Release and Misconduct in the District of Columbia* (Washington, D.C.: Institute for Law and Social Research, 1980).

44. It is occasionally argued that statistical prediction should not be used as a basis for criminal justice decision-making because of the false positives problem. In truth, nonstatistical assessment of dangerousness—the method preferred in most jurisdictions—has been found repeatedly to produce false positives at a *higher* rate than statistical assessments. See, for example, John Monahan, *Predicting Violent Behavior: An Assessment of Clinical Techniques* (Beverly Hills, Calif.: Sage, 1981); Henry J. Steadman and Joseph Cocozza, "Psychiatry, Dangerousness and the Repetitively Violent Offender," *Journal of Criminal Law and Criminology* 69 (1978): 226–31; Paul E. Meehl, *Clinical vs. Statistical Prediction* (Minneapolis, Minn.: University of Minnesota Press, 1954).

The legitimacy of prediction as a basis for criminal justice decisions has been generally well established. For example, judges routinely base bail decisions on the risk of defendant misbehavior prior to trial. The exercise of discretion by prosecutors in filing charges and in "targeting" cases involving dangerous offenders for special prosecution, and by judges in making bail and sentencing decisions, has been subjected to challenge and reversal only very rarely.

45. Interviews with 180 police officers who made arrests in two metropolitan jurisdictions revealed that none of the officers (nor their immediate supervisors) routinely received information about the court outcomes of their arrests. See Forst, Leahy, Shirhall, Tyson, Wish, and Bartolomeo.

11. Steven R. Schlesinger: "Criminal Procedure in the Courtroom"

1. I would like to thank Ms. Elizabeth Malloy, a first-year student at The American University Washington College of Law, for her invaluable assistance at all stages of the preparation of this chapter.

2. Ralph A. Rossum, *The Politics of the Criminal Justice System: An Organizational Analysis* (New York: Marcel Dekker, 1978), p. 203.

3. The President's Commission on Law Enforcement and the Administration of Justice, *Task Force Report: The Courts* (Washington, D.C.: U.S. Govt. Printing Office, 1967), p. 37, finds that in New York City, 25 percent of all defendants failed to make bail at $500, 45 percent failed at $1,500, and 63 percent at $2,500.

4. According to Ralph Baker and Fred A. Meyer, Jr., *The Criminal Justice Game* (North Scituate, Mass.: Duxbury Press, 1980), p. 154, bondsmen are responsible for over 75 percent of all bail bonds in large cities.

5. *Pannell* v. *U.S.,* 320 F. 2d 698 (D.C. Cir. 1963).

6. See Caleb Foote, "Compelling Appearance in Court: Administration of Bail in Philadel-phia," *University of Pennsylvania Law Review* 102 (1954): 1031, 1053; idem, "A Study of the Administration of Bail in New York City," *University of Pennsylvania Law Review* 106 (1958): 727; Eric W. Single, "The Consequences of Pretrial Detention," paper presented at the 1972 annual meeting of the American Sociological Association, New Orleans; Pamela Koza and Anthony N. Doob, "The Relationship of Pretrial Custody to the Outcome of the Trial," *Criminal Law Quarterly* 17 (1975): 391.

7. Charles E. Ares, Anne Rankin, and Herbert Sturz, "The Manhattan Bail Project: An In-terim Report on the Use of Pre-Trial Parole," *New York University Law Review* 38 (1963): 67, 85.

8. Gerald D. Robin, *Introduction to the Criminal Justice System* (New York: Harper and Row, 1980), p. 200.

9. Foote, "A Study of the Administration of Bail in New York City," p. 726.

10. The President's Commission on Law Enforcement and the Administration of Justice, p. 38.

11. The Hearings on Bail Reform before the Subcommittee on the Constitution of the Com-mittee on the Judiciary, United States Senate, 97th Congress, 1st session, 17 September and 21 October 1981 (testimony of Jeffrey Harris, deputy associate attorney general), document the increasing number of defendants who make "extraordinarily high bond" and then flee the country.

12. Bernard Wice, *Bail and Its Reform: A National Survey* (Washington, D.C.: U.S. Depart-ment of Justice Law Enforcement Assistance Administration, National Institute of Law En-forcement and Criminal Justice, 1973).

13. The Manhattan Bail Project, conducted by the Vera Institute of Justice in New York City, was the first to test an ROR program. The success of this initial project generated na-tional interest, and similar programs quickly spread across the country; there are currently more than 120 pretrial release agencies in the nation. See Roy B. Flemming, *Punishment before Trial* (New York: Longman, 1982), p. 147. The Federal Bail Reform Act of 1966 (18 U.S.C. 3146 et seq.), the first major overhaul of the federal bail system since the Judiciary Act of 1789, emphasized nonfinancial conditions of release and encouraged the use of ROR.

14. Ronald Goldfarb, *Ransom: A Critique of the American Bail System* (New York: Harper and Row, 1965), p. 157.

15. Wayne E. Thomas, *Bail Reform in America* (Berkeley, Calif.: University of California Press, 1976), p. 103.

16. Ibid., p. 98; Paul B. Wice, "Bail Reform in American Cities," paper delivered at the 1973 annual meeting of the Midwest Political Science Association, Chicago, p. 23.

17. See Note, "The Manhattan Bail Re-Evaluation Project: A Post-Arraignment Program That Worked," *New England Journal of Prison Law* 3 (1977): 503, 535.

18. A 1978 study by the Law Enforcement Assistance Administration, *Census of Jails and Survey of Jail Inmates 1978: Preliminary Report I* (Washington, D.C.: U.S. Govt. Printing Of-fice, 1979), reports that of 158,000 persons in our nation's local jails, 40 percent were awaiting trial. In reality, however, 40 percent of the jail spaces will not be freed for convicted defen-dants, since all of those arrested will not qualify for ROR.

19. Norman Johnson, Leonard Savitz, and Marvin E. Wolfgang, eds., *The Sociology of Punishment and Correction* (New York: Wiley, 1970), p. 159.

20. Goldfarb, p. 242.

21. See Thomas, pp. 121–37.

22. See "Report of the President's Commission on Crime in the District of Columbia," Re-port 596 (Washington, D.C.: U.S. Govt. Printing Office, 1966); The Judicial Council Committee

312 *Notes*

to Study the Operation of the Bail Reform Act in the District of Columbia (The Hart Committee), 1968–69; Statement of Attorney General John Mitchell before the Committee on the Judiciary of the House of Representatives, 21 October 1969, based on a study conducted by the Attorney General's Office in the District of Columbia; Note, "Preventive Detention: An Empirical Analysis," *Harvard Civil Rights Law Review* 6 (1971): 289; Bernard Wice; Paul B. Wice, *Freedom for Sale: A National Study of Pretrial Release* (Lexington, Mass.: Heath, 1974); Wayne H. Thomas, "National Evaluation Program Phase I Summary Report" (Washington, D.C.: Law Enforcement Assistance Administration, National Institute of Law Enforcement and Criminal Justice, April 1977); *Instead of Jail: Pre and Post-Trial Alternatives to Jail Incarceration* (Washington, D.C.: Law Enforcement Assistance Administration, National Institute of Law Enforcement and Criminal Justice, 1977); D.C. Bail Agency, *How Does Pretrial Supervision Affect Pretrial Performance* (1978); Institute for Law and Social Research, *Pretrial Release and Misconduct in the District of Columbia* 41 (April 1980); *Pretrial Release: A National Evaluation of Practices and Outcomes* (Washington, D.C.: Lazar Institute, 1981).

23. *Pretrial Release: An Evaluation of Defendant Outcomes and Program Impact* (Washington, D.C.: Lazar Institute, 1981), p. 48.

24. The National Bureau of Standards, Technical Note 535, *Compilation and Use of Criminal Court Data in Relation to Pretrial Release of Defendants: Pilot Study* (August 1970), pp. 136–37.

25. The Bail Reform Act of 1981, Report of the Committee on the Judiciary, United States Senate, on S. Res. 1554, 97th Congress, 2d session, p. 38.

26. District of Columbia Code, sec. 23–1321 et seq.

27. The Bail Reform Act of 1966 adopted the concept that likelihood of appearance at trial, not dangerousness to the community, is to be the only factor considered in pretrial release decisions. However, the concept of permitting an assessment of the defendant's dangerousness in making bail decisions has the support of the American Bar Association, the National Conference of Commissioners on Uniform State Laws, The National District Attorneys Association, The National Association of Pretrial Services Agencies, Chief Justice Warren Burger, and the Attorney General's Task Force on Violent Crime. In addition, the statutes of several states (Alaska, Delaware, Hawaii, Minnesota, New Hampshire, North Carolina, South Carolina, Vermont, and Virginia) allow the court to consider a potential threat to community safety in decisions to grant bail.

28. See *Carlson* v. *Landon,* 342 U.S. 1 (1951).

29. See Note, "Preventive Detention: A Comparison of European and United States Measures," *New York University Journal of International Law and Politics* 4 (1971): 289, 306–7, for a discussion of all of the procedural safeguards in the D.C. Act.

30. See *Gernstein* v. *Pugh,* 420 U.S. 103 (1974) and *Bell* v. *Wolfish,* 441 U.S. 520 (1978).

31. *Blunt* v. *U.S.,* 322 A. 2d 579, 584 (1974). Also consider John N. Mitchell, "Bail Reform and the Constitutionality of Pretrial Detention," *Virginia Law Review* 55 (1969): 1223, 1231–32: "If such a pretrial presumption of innocence existed as a bar to detention of the dangerous before trial, it would also bar pretrial detention of those charged with capital offenses, those held on money bond, and could even be extended to prevent police from arresting persons and taking them into custody on probable cause."

32. *U.S.* v. *Edwards,* D.C. App., 430 A. 2d 1321, upheld the right to bail as a statutory tradition but not as an absolute constitutional right (sec. 1331), stated that preventive detention is regulatory, not punitive (secs. 1332–33), and concluded that the procedural safeguards of the D.C. act "satisfy the minimum demands of procedural due process before a person may be detained pending trial on the grounds of dangerousness to the community" (sec. 1333).

33. Bail Reform Act of 1981, p. 40.

34. *Pretrial Release and Misconduct in the District of Columbia,* p. 40.

35. See Note, "Preventive Detention: An Empirical Analysis," p. 325.

36. Thomas, p. 428.

37. U.S. Department of Justice, *Attorney General's Task Force on Violent Crime* (Washington, D.C.: U.S. Govt. Printing Office, 1981), p. 51, criticizes the use of high money bail to detain dangerous or violent offenders as "a phenomenon which has cast doubt on the fairness of federal release practices," and recommends consideration of dangerousness as "a more honest way of dealing with this issue."

38. M. Gary Holten and Melvin E. Jones, *The System of Criminal Justice* (Boston: Little, Brown, 1982), p. 288.

39. See Bail Reform Act of 1981, note 110.

40. Note, "Preventive Detention: An Empirical Analysis," p. 324.

41. A study in Charlotte, North Carolina, by Steven H. Clarke, Jean L. Freeman, and Gary G. Koch, *The Effectiveness of Bail Systems: An Analysis of the Failure to Appear in Court and Rearrest While on Bail* (Institute of Government, University of North Carolina at Chapel Hill, 1976), reports that the chance of avoiding rearrest drops 5 percent for every two weeks the defendant remains on pretrial release.

42. *The American Bar Association Project on Standards for Criminal Justice, Standards Relating to Pretrial Release, Draft 1968*, strongly favors the issuance of citations for minor offenses.

43. Richard D. Hongisto and Carol Levine, "Workable Alternatives to the Present Bail System," *California State Journal* (November/December 1972): 580, claim that defendants released in 10 percent cash bond programs are no more likely to fail to appear or to commit new crimes than those released on conventional bail.

44. The Fourth Amendment exclusionary rule applies to nontestimonial, physical evidence. In writing this part of the chapter, I have adapted and quoted from passages in my *Exclusionary Injustice: The Problem of Illegally Obtained Evidence* (New York: Marcel Dekker, 1975), pp. 47–49, 56–63, 71–73, 77, and 86, by courtesy of Marcel Dekker, Inc., and "It Is Time to Abolish the Exclusionary Rule," *The Wall Street Journal,* 10 September 1981, p. 24.

45. The relevant cases are *Weeks* v. *U.S.,* 232 U.S. 383 (1914) and *Mapp* v. *Ohio,* 367 U.S. 643 (1961).

46. See Steven R. Schlesinger and Bradford Wilson, "Property, Privacy and Deterrence: The Exclusionary Rule in Search of a Rationale," *Duquesne Law Review* 18 (1980): 225.

47. See, for example, *Stone* v. *Powell,* 428 U.S. 465, 486 (1976).

48. The seven studies are: Dallin Oaks, "Studying the Exclusionary Rule in Search and Seizure," *University of Chicago Law Review* 37 (1970): 665; Michael Ban, "The Impact of *Mapp* v. *Ohio* on Police Behavior," delivered at the annual meeting of the Midwest Political Science Association, Chicago, 1973; idem, "Local Courts v. The Supreme Court: The Impact of *Mapp* v. *Ohio,"* delivered at the annual meeting of the American Political Science Association, New Orleans, 1973; James Spiotto, "Search and Seizure: An Empirical Study of the Exclusionary Rule and Its Alternatives," *Journal of Legal Studies* 2 (1973): 243; Bradley Canon, "Is the Exclusionary Rule in Failing Health? Some New Data and a Plea against a Precipitous Conclusion," *Kentucky Law Journal* 62 (1973–74): 681; idem, "Testing the Effectiveness of Civil Liberties Policies at the State and Local Levels: The Case of the Exclusionary Rule," *American Politics Quarterly* 5 (1977): 57; "Effect of *Mapp* v. *Ohio* on Police Search and Seizure Practices in Narcotics Cases," *Columbia Journal of Law and Social Problems* 4 (1968): 87.

49. Canon, "Is the Exclusionary Rule in Failing Health? Some New Data and a Plea against a Precipitous Conclusion."

50. Canon, "Testing the Effectiveness of Civil Liberties Policies at the State and Local Levels," p. 75.

51. See Oaks, p. 726; Harvey Wingo, "Growing Disillusionment with the Exclusionary Rule," *Southwestern Law Journal* 25 (1971): 573, 576.

52. Oaks, p. 727.

53. See Wayne Lafave and Frank Remington, "Controlling the Police: The Judge's Role in Making and Reviewing Law Enforcement Decisions," *Michigan Law Review* 63 (1965): 987, 1005.

54. See Samuel Dash, "Cracks in the Foundation of Criminal Justice," *Illinois Law Review* 4 (1961): 385, 391–92.

55. *President's Commission on Law Enforcement and the Administration of Justice*, p. 91.

56. See *Mapp* v. *Ohio*, sec. 660.

57. For a similar argument, see Edward Barrett, "Exclusion of Evidence Obtained by Illegal Searches—A Comment on *People* v. *Cahan*," *California Law Review* 43 (1955): 565, 580–81.

58. Oaks, p. 476.

59. INSLAW, *Summary Report: Arrest, Convictability as a Measure of Police Performance*, table 1, p. 7 (1981). As Forst's chapter notes, approximately 10,000 arrests, which is less than 1 percent of felony arrests made in the United States during 1977–78, were rejected by prosecutors because of exclusionary rule violations. In addition, *Summary Report* suggests that an additional 35,000 to 45,000 serious misdemeanor arrests were rejected because of exclusionary rule violations. Serious misdemeanors include assault, petty larceny, and drug violations (the serious misdemeanors that are drug-related include a substantial number of arrests for marijuana sale or possession). The crucial point here is that, particularly from the point of view of potential crime victims, it is striking that 45,000 to 55,000 persons, many of them convictable or dangerous or both, escape prosecution entirely because of the exclusionary rule and are, therefore, free to commit crime.

60. *The Effects of the Exclusionary Rule: A Study in California* (Washington, D.C.: National Institute of Justice, December 1982).

61. Ibid., p. 1; see also pp. 10–11.

62. Ibid., p. 2; see also pp. 12–13.

63. Ibid.; see also pp. 14–16.

64. Malcolm Richard Wilkey, *Enforcing the Fourth Amendment by Alternatives to the Exclusionary Rule* (Washington, D.C.: The National Legal Center for the Public Interest, 1982), p. 13.

65. Comptroller General of the United States, *Impact of the Exclusionary Rule on Federal Criminal Prosecutions*, Rep. No. CDG–79–45 (19 April 1979), p. 1.

66. Ibid., p. 8.

67. Wilkey, pp. 15–16.

68. Ibid., pp. 17–18.

69. See Edward Barrett, "Personal Rights, Property Rights and the Fourth Amendment," *Supreme Court Review* (1960): 46, 55; Edmund Kitch, "The Supreme Court's Possessive Code of Criminal Procedure," *Supreme Court Review* (1969): 157–72.

70. As to applying the exclusionary rule only in the most serious cases, see John Kaplan, "The Limits of the Exclusionary Rule," *Stanford Law Review* 26 (1974): 1027, 1046–49.

71. See Wingo, pp. 577–78, and "Student Comment: The Tort Alternative to the Exclusionary Rule in Search and Seizure," *Journal of Criminal Law, Criminology, and Police Science* 63 (1972): 256, 258–59.

72. See Wilkey, pp. 13–14.

73. Albert Alschuler, "The Prosecutor's Role in Plea Bargaining," *University of Chicago Law Review* 36 (1968): 50, 56, 80–82.

74. For this civil tort remedy to be successful, states and localities would have to forego the protection of sovereign immunity, i.e., voluntarily assume liability for police torts related to the Fourth Amendment. Both the federal government and the states have moved in the direction of assuming liability for the misconduct of their officials. See Steven Schlesinger, *Exclusionary*

Injustice: The Problem of Illegally Obtained Evidence (New York: Dekker, 1977), pp. 78–79.

75. *Attorney General's Task Force on Violent Crime*, pp. 55–56.

76. See Monrad Paulsen, "The Exclusionary Rule and Misconduct by the Police," *Journal of Criminal Law, Criminology, and Police Science* 52 (1961): 255, 258–59; see also *Olmstead* v. *U.S.*, 277 U.S. 438, 485 (1928) (Brandeis, J., dissenting); *Weeks* v. *U.S.*, 232 U.S. 388, 394 (1914); *Burdeau* v. *McDowell*, 256 U.S. 465, 477 (1921) (Brandeis, J., dissenting); *U.S.* v. *Calandra*, 414 U.S. 338, 357 (1974) (Brennan, J., dissenting).

77. 380 U.S. 609 (1965).

78. Steven R. Schlesinger and Deborah Large, "Chilling Effects in Criminal Trial Procedure: A Balancing Approach," *Cumberland Law Review* 10 (1979): 1.

79. Collateral attack questions the legal validity of a conviction after all legal appeals have been exhausted.

80. Henry M. Friendly, "Is Innocence Irrelevant? Collateral Attack on Criminal Judgments," *University of Chicago Law Review* 38 (1970): 142, 146.

81. *Schneckloth* v. *Bustamonte*, 412 U.S. 218, 262 (1973).

82. James Duke Cameron, "Federal Review, Finality of State Court Decisions, and a Proposal for a National Court of Appeals—A State Judge's Solution to a Continuing Problem," *Brigham Young University Law Review* (1981): 545, 555.

83. Sandra Day O'Connor, "Trends in the Relationship between the Federal and the State Courts from the Perspective of a State Court Judge," *William and Mary Law Review* 22 (1981): 801, 814–15.

84. John L. Carroll, "Habeas Corpus Reform: Can Habeas Survive the Flood?" *Cumberland Law Review* 6 (1975): 363, 380.

85. Donald E. Santarelli, "Too Much Is Enough," *Trial* 9 (1973): 40.

86. Hearings Before the Subcommittee of the Judiciary on Habeas Corpus Procedures Amendments Act of 1981, United States Senate, 97th Congress, 1st session (testimony of Richard J. Wilson), p. 123.

87. Judd Bernstein, "Habeas-Corpus 'Reform' that Would Exalt Efficiency over Fairness," *Des Moines Register*, 14 April 1982, p. 12.

88. George Cochran Doub, "The Case against Modern Federal Habeas Corpus," *American Bar Association Journal* 57 (1971): 323, 327.

89. Hearings Before the Subcommittee of the Judiciary on Habeas Corpus Procedures Amendments (testimony of Jim Smith), p. 43.

90. *Brown* v. *Allen*, 344 U.S. 443, 537 (1953).

91. Santarelli.

92. *Attorney General's Task Force on Violent Crime*, p. 59.

93. Address by Chief Justice Burger, Annual Report on the State of the Judiciary to the American Bar Association, Chicago, 3 February 1980.

94. Rule 9 (a) of the Rules Governing Section 2254 Cases in the U.S. District Courts, 28 U.S.C. foll. 2254, provides that a petition for habeas corpus may be dismissed if the state has been "prejudiced" in its ability to respond to the petition by the petitioner's delay. However, if the petitioner is able to show that the delay was beyond his control, the petition will be heard regardless of prejudice to the state.

95. U.S. Department of Justice, "The Administration's Proposed Reforms in Habeas Corpus Procedures," 4 March 1982, p. 18.

96. See *Attorney General's Task Force on Violent Crime*, p. 59, and Hearings Before the Subcommittee of the Judiciary on Habeas Corpus Procedures Amendments, p. 6.

97. See *Fay* v. *Noia*, 372 U.S. 391 (1963) and *Francis* v. *Henderson*, 425 U.S. 536 (1976).

98. 433 U.S. 72 (1977).

99. See *Engle* v. *Isaac*, 102 S.Ct. 1558 (1982) and *U.S.* v. *Frady*, 102 S.Ct. 1595 (1982).

100. According to "The Administration's Proposed Reforms in Habeas Corpus Procedures," p. 8, "the practical effect of this standard, for example, in connection with attorney error would be that an attorney's failure to raise a claim properly would constitute 'cause' only if it amounted to constitutional ineffectiveness. However, attorney errors falling short of constitutional ineffectiveness would not constitute cause."

101. This proposed codification is drawn from recommendations suggested in "The Administration's Proposed Reforms on Habeas Corpus Procedures," p. 809; *Attorney General's Task Force on Violent Crime,* p. 60; and Hearings Before the Subcommittee of the Judiciary on Habeas Corpus Procedures Amendments, pp. 5–6.

102. "The Administration's Proposed Reforms on Habeas Corpus Procedures," p. 41.

103. United States Department of Justice, Proposed 28 U.S.C. Section 2254(d) in S. 2216, p. 8.

104. Ibid.

105. See "State Post Conviction Remedies and Federal Habeas Corpus," *William and Mary Law Review* 12 (1970): 149; D. E. Wilkes, Jr., "Postconviction Habeas Corpus Relief in Georgia: A Decade after the Habeas Corpus Act," *Georgia Law Review* 12 (1978): 249; Ronald W. Eades, "Appellate and Post Conviction Relief in Tennessee," *Memphis State University Law Review* 5 (1974): 1; Note, "The Need for Habeas Corpus Reform in Utah: A Challenge from the Federal Courts," *Utah Law Review* 1979 (1979): 159; J. Greenhill and M. Beirne, "Habeas Corpus Proceedings in the Supreme Court of Texas," *St. Mary's Law Journal* 1 (1969): 1.

12.   Daniel Glaser: "Supervising Offenders Outside of Prison"

1. U.S. Department of Justice, *Probation and Parole,* Bureau of Justice Statistics Bulletin (Washington, D.C.: U.S. Govt. Printing Office, August 1982).

2. Charles A. Murray and Louis A. Cox, Jr., *Beyond Probation* (Beverly Hills, Calif.: Sage, 1979).

3. For a summary of the parole-period follow-up, see Ted Palmer, "The Youth Authority's Community Treatment Project," *Federal Probation* 38 (March 1974): 3–14. The postsupervision follow-up data are in Ted Palmer, *Correctional Intervention and Research* (Lexington, Mass.: Heath, 1978), p. 44. The principal criticism, which ignores the differences in outcome between types of delinquents and was prepared before postparole follow-up data were available, is Paul Lerman, *Community Treatment and Social Control* (Chicago: University of Chicago Press, 1975).

4. Michael R. Gottfredson, Susan D. Mitchell Herzfeld, and Timothy J. Flanagan, "Another Look at the Effectiveness of Parole Supervision," *Journal of Research in Crime and Delinquency* 19 (July 1982): 277–98.

5. Deborah Star, *Summary Parole: A Six and Twelve Month Follow-Up Evaluation,* California Department of Corrections Research Report No. 60, February 1979.

6. S. Christopher Baird, Richard C. Heinz, and Brian J. Bemus, *A Two-Year Followup Report,* Wisconsin Case Classification/Staff Deployment Project, Report No. 14 (Madison, Wis.: Wisconsin Department of Health and Social Services, Division of Corrections, July 1979).

7. Howard R. Sacks and Charles H. Logan, *Does Parole Make a Difference?* (Storrs, Conn.: University of Connecticut School of Law Press, 1979); idem, *Parole: Crime Prevention or Crime Postponement?* (Storrs, Conn.: University of Connecticut School of Law Press, 1980).

8. Gottfredson, Herzfeld, and Flanagan, pp. 277–98.

9. William H. McGlothlin, M. Douglas Anglin, and Bruce D. Wilson, *An Evaluation of the California Civil Addict Program,* U.S. Department of Health, Education and Welfare, Publication No. (ADM) 78–558, 1977.

10. Baird, Heinz, and Bemus.

11. Douglas Lipton, Robert Martinson, and Judith Wilks, *The Effectiveness of Correctional*

Treatment (New York: Praeger, 1975), pp. 115–42.

12. Albert Wahl and Daniel Glaser, "Pilot Time Study of the Federal Probation Officer's Job," *Federal Probation* 27 (September 1963): 20–25; Daniel Glaser, *The Effectiveness of a Prison and Parole System* (Indianapolis, Ind.: Bobbs-Merrill, 1964), pp. 442–48, and the abridged edition (1969), pp. 299–303.

13. Lipton, Martinson, and Wilks, pp. 212–14, 225–26, 228–29; Paul Gendreau and Bob Ross, "Effective Correctional Treatment," *Crime and Delinquency* 25 (October 1979): 463–89, 476–77; D. A. Andrews, "Some Experimental Investigations of the Principles of Differential Association through Deliberate Manipulations of the Structure of Service Systems," *American Sociological Review* 45 (June 1980): 448–62.

14. Joseph E. Scott, *Ex-Offenders as Parole Officers* (Lexington, Mass.: Heath, 1975).

15. Jack Cocks, "From 'WHISP' to 'RODEO'," *California Youth Authority Quarterly* 21 (Winter 1968): 7–11; E. Farley Hunter, *RODEO: Reduction of Delinquency by Expansion of Opportunity,* Los Angeles County Probation Department, Research Report No. 33, 1968; Ruth L. Rushen and E. Farley Hunter, *The RODEO Model,* Los Angeles County Probation Department, 1970. A more recent experiment emphasizing total family involvement, academic studies, work, nutrition, and youth aiding other youth in their group, all to build an anti-crime subculture, is reported in LaMar T. Empey, *The Monrovia Project* (Chino, Calif.: Boys Republic, 1982).

16. Robert B. Coates, Alden D. Miller, and Lloyd E. Ohlin, *Diversity in a Youth Correctional System* (Cambridge, Mass.: Ballinger, 1978). See also *Crime and Delinquency,* vol. 27, no. 4 (October 1981), which is devoted to updating this and other research on juvenile correctional systems.

17. James W. Thompson, Michelle Sviriodoff, and Jerome E. McElroy, with Richard McGahey and Orlando Rodriguez, *Employment and Crime,* U.S. Department of Justice (Washington, D.C.: U.S. Govt. Printing Office, 1981), ch. 4; Philip J. Cook, "The Correctional Carrot: Better Jobs for Parolees," *Policy Sciences* 1 (Winter 1975): 11–53; Mark R. Wiederanders, "Some Myths about the Employment Problems of Young Offenders," *Federal Probation* 45 (December 1981): 9–12.

18. James L. Beck, "Employment, Community Treatment Center Placement, and Recidivism," *Federal Probation* 45 (December 1981): 3–8.

19. Glaser, ch. 14, and the abridged edition, ch. 13; Craig Reinarman and Donald Miller, *Direct Financial Assistance to Parolees,* California Department of Corrections, Research Report No. 55, 1975; Peter H. Rossi, Richard Berk, and Kenneth J. Lenihan, *Money, Work and Crime* (New York: Academic Press, 1980), ch. 2.

20. Rossi, Berk, and Lenihan, ch. 2.

21. Richard A. Berk and David Rauma, "Capitalizing on Nonrandom Assignment to Treatments: A Regression Discontinuity Evaluation of a Crime Control Program," *Journal of the American Statistical Association* (March 1983).

22. C. E. Susmilch, *Impact of the Mutual Agreement Program on the Amount of Time Served in Wisconsin Correctional Institutions* (Madison, Wis.: Wisconsin Council on Criminal Justice, 1977); Leon Leiberg and William Parker, "Mutual Agreement Programs with Vouchers: An Alternative for Institutionalized Female Offenders," *American Journal of Corrections* 37 (January–February 1975): 10–13; Steve Gettinger, "Parole Contracts: A Way Out," *Corrections Magazine* 2 (September/October 1975): 3–8, 45–50.

23. Marvin Bohnstedt and Saul Geiser, *Classification Instruments for Criminal Justice Decisions,* U.S. Department of Justice, National Institute of Corrections (Washington, D.C.: U.S. Govt. Printing Office, 1979); Peter B. Hoffman and Sheldon Adelberg, "The Salient Factor Score: A Nontechnical Review," *Federal Probation* 44 (March 1980): 44–52; Don M. Gottfredson, Leslie T. Wilkins, and Peter B. Hoffman, *Guidelines for Parole and Sentencing* (Lexington,

Mass.: Heath, 1978); William D. Rich, L. Paul Sutton, Todd R. Clear, and Michael J. Saks, *Sentencing by Mathematics: Sentencing Guidelines in Three Courts* (Williamsburg, Va.: National Center for State Courts, 1982).

13.   Alfred Blumstein: "Prisons: Population, Capacity, and Alternatives"

1. Age-specific arrest rates peak in the 16–18 age range for all index crimes. The rates then drop quickly to half the peak rate by age 21 for property crimes, 23 for robbery, and 35 for person crimes (which primarily reflect aggravated assault).

2. Alfred Blumstein, Jacqueline Cohen, and Harold D. Miller, "Demographically Disaggregated Projections of Prison Populations," *Journal of Criminal Justice,* vol. 8, no. 1 (1980): 1–26.

3. Of course, other factors such as changing economic conditions or sanction policies could influence the crime rate and make it higher or lower than that projected on demographic considerations alone.

4. Pennsylvania State Police, Bureau of Research and Development, *Uniform Crime Report: Commonwealth of Pennsylvania Annual Report 1981* (Harrisburg, Penn.: Pennsylvania State Police, 1982).

5. U.S. Department of Justice, Federal Bureau of Investigation, *Uniform Crime Reports in the United States: 1981* (Washington, D.C.: U.S. Govt. Printing Office, 1982).

6. Since the age of those who commit crimes is largely unknown, the "crime ages" discussed here are based on the age of those arrested for various crimes.

7. Blumstein, Cohen, and Miller.

8. U.S. Department of Commerce, Bureau of the Census, *Statistical Abstract of the United States: 1979,* 100th ed. (Washington, D.C.: U.S. Govt. Printing Office, 1979).

9. A decrease in the crime rate (crimes per capita) was noted for each of the index crime types except robbery, which showed an increase of 2.9 percent.

10. U.S. Department of Justice, Bureau of Justice Statistics, "Prisoners in 1981," *Bulletin* NCJ–82262 (May 1982).

11. U.S. Department of Justice, Federal Bureau of Investigation, *Uniform Crime Reports for the United States: 1981.*

12. The most influential synthesis of these studies was Robert Martinson, "What Works?— Questions and Answers about Prison Reform," *The Public Interest,* no. 35 (1974): 22–54. This study was based on D. Lipton, R. Martinson, and J. Wilks, *The Effectiveness of Correctional Treatment: A Survey of Treatment Evaluation Studies* (New York: Praeger, 1975). The results were reexamined in a study by the Panel on Research on Rehabilitative Techniques, National Research Council, *The Rehabilitation of Criminal Offenders: Problems and Prospects,* ed. Lee B. Sechrest, Susan O. White, and Elizabeth Brown (Washington, D.C.: National Academy of Sciences, 1979); this review confirmed the previous findings of no net rehabilitative effect.

13. See, for example, Andrew Von Hirsch, *Doing Justice: The Choice of Punishments* (New York: Hill and Wang, 1976).

14. Alfred Blumstein, "On the Racial Disproportionality of U.S. Prison Populations," *Journal of Criminal Law and Criminology,* vol. 73, no. 3 (1982), pp. 1259–81.

15. *Criminal Justice Newsletter,* vol. 13, no. 5 (15 March 1982): 2–5.

16. Kenneth Carlson, et al., *American Prisons and Jails: Volume II, Population Trends and Projections,* Abt Associates, Inc. (Washington, D.C.: National Institute of Justice, 1980).

17. Alfred Blumstein, Jacqueline Cohen, and William Gooding, "The Influence of Capacity on Prison Population: A Critical Review of Some Recent Evidence," *Crime and Delinquency,* vol. 29, no. 1 (January 1983).

18. There are some preliminary indications that race is *not* a good predictor. The large

differences in crime involvement between the races are associated more with differences in *prevalence* or rates of participation than with differences in propensity to commit further crimes among those who have already become involved. It is the propensity for recidivism—and not prevalence—that is relevant to selective incapacitation. See Alfred Blumstein and Elizabeth Graddy, "Prevalence and Recidivism in Index Arrests: A Feedback Model," *Law and Society Review,* vol. 16, no. 2 (1982).

19. See, for example, Peter Greenwood, with Allan Abrahamse, *Selective Incapacitation,* R–2815–NIJ (Santa Monica, Calif.: Rand Corporation, 1982); Jan and Marcia Chaiken, *Varieties of Criminal Behavior,* R–2814–NIJ (Santa Monica, Calif.: Rand Corporation, 1982).

20. See James Austin and Barry Krisberg, "The Unmet Promise of Alternatives," *Crime and Delinquency* 28 (July 1982): 374–409.

21. For example, Laura Winterfield, *Community Corrections: A Realized Alternative to Corrections,* working paper (Pittsburgh, Penn.: Urban Systems Institute, Carnegie-Mellon University, 1982).

22. For a review of the literature, see Daniel Nagin, "General Deterrence: A Review of the Empirical Evidence," in *Deterrence and Incapacitation: Estimating the Effects of Crime Rates,* ed. Alfred Blumstein, Jacqueline Cohen, and Daniel Nagin (Washington, D.C.: National Academy of Sciences, 1978).

23. See Alfred Blumstein, Jacqueline Cohen, and Paul Hsieh, "The Duration of Adult Criminal Careers," Final Report to the National Institute of Justice (Pittsburgh, Penn.: Urban Systems Institute, Carnegie-Mellon University, 1982).

24. Such a method was developed in Minnesota by Kay Knapp and her colleagues; see Kay A. Knapp, "Estimating the Impact of Sentencing Policies on Prison Populations," paper presented at 32nd Annual Meeting of the American Society of Criminology, San Francisco, Calif., 5–8 November 1980.

25. John R. Manson, *The Prison Overcrowding Dilemma: A New Approach,* unpublished manuscript, Connecticut Department of Corrections, Hartford, Conn., 1981.

26. Alfred Blumstein and Jacqueline Cohen, "A Theory of the Stability of Punishment," *Journal of Criminal Law and Criminology,* vol. 64, no. 2 (1973): 198–206; Alfred Blumstein, Jacqueline Cohen, and Daniel Nagin, "The Dynamics of a Homeostatic Punishment Process," *Journal of Criminal Law and Criminology,* vol. 67, no. 3 (1977): 317–34; Alfred Blumstein and Soumyo Moitra, "An Analysis of the Time Series of the Imprisonment Rate in the States of the United States: A Further Test of the Stability of Punishment Hypothesis," *Journal of Criminal Law and Criminology,* vol. 70, no. 3 (1979): 376–90.

14.   Peter W. Greenwood: "Controlling the Crime Rate through Imprisonment"

1. Lee Sechrest, Susan O. White, and Elizabeth D. Brown, eds., *The Rehabilitation of Criminal Offenders: Problems and Prospects* (Washington, D.C.: National Academy of Sciences, 1979).

2. Daniel Glaser, "Disillusion with Rehabilitation: Theoretical and Empirical Questions," in *The Future of Childhood and Juvenile Justice,* ed. LeMar Empey (Charlottesville, Va.: University Press of Virginia, 1979).

3. Franklin Zimring and G. Hawkins, *Deterrence: The Legal Threat in Crime Control* (Chicago: University of Chicago Press, 1973).

4. Alfred Blumstein, Jacqueline Cohen, and Daniel Nagin, eds., *Deterrence and Incapacitation: Estimating the Effects of Criminal Sanctions on Crime Rates* (Washington, D.C.: National Academy of Sciences, 1978).

5. C. R. Shaw and H. D. McKay, *Juvenile Delinquency and Urban Areas* (Chicago: University of Chicago Press, 1942); Sheldon Glueck and Eleanor Glueck, *Unraveling Juvenile Delinquency* (New York: The Commonwealth Fund, 1950).

6. E. H. Sutherland, *The Professional Thief* (Chicago: University of Chicago Press, 1937).

7. M. Wolfgang, R. M. Figlio, and T. Sellin, *Delinquency in a Birth Cohort* (Chicago: University of Chicago Press, 1972).

8. Lyle W. Shannon, "A Longitudinal Study of Delinquency and Crime," in *Quantitative Studies in Criminology,* ed. Charles Wellford (Beverly Hills, Calif.: Sage, 1978); David P. Farrington, "Longitudinal Research on Crime and Delinquency," in *Crime and Justice: An Annual Review of Research,* vol. 1, ed. Norval Morris and Michael Tonry (Chicago: University of Chicago Press, 1979).

9. Joan Petersilia and Peter W. Greenwood with Marvin Lavin, *Criminal Careers of Habitual Felons,* The Rand Corporation, R–2144–DOJ, August 1977.

10. Mark A. Peterson and Harriet B. Braiker, with Suzanne M. Polich, *Who Commits Crimes: A Survey of Prison Inmates* (Cambridge, Mass.: Oelgeschlager, Gunn, and Hain, 1981).

11. Mark A. Peterson, et al., *Survey of Prison and Jail Inmates: Background and Method,* The Rand Corporation, N–1635–NIJ, August 1982.

12. Michael Hindelang, Travis Hirschi, and Joseph G. Weis, *Measuring Delinquency,* vol. 23, Sage Library of Social Research (Beverly Hills, Calif.: Sage, 1981).

13. Stevens Clarke, "Getting 'Em Out of Circulation: Does Incarceration of Juvenile Offenders Reduce Crime?" *Journal of Criminal Law and Criminology,* vol. 65, no. 4 (1974): 528–35; J. Marsh and M. Singer, *Soft Statistics and Hard Questions,* Discussion Paper HI–1712–DP (Croton-on-Hudson, N.Y.: Hudson Institute, 1972); M. A. Greene, "The Incapacitation Effect of Imprisonment Policy on Crime" (Ph.D. diss., Carnegie-Mellon University, 1977); David Greenberg, "The Incapacitation Effect of Imprisonment: Some Estimates," *Law and Society Review,* vol. 9, no. 4 (1975): 541–80; B. Avi-Itzhak and R. Shinnar, "Quantitative Models in Crime Control," *Journal of Criminal Justice,* vol. 1, no. 3 (1973); S. Shinnar and R. Shinnar, "The Effects of the Criminal Justice System on the Control of Crime: A Quantitative Approach," *Law and Society Review* 9 (1975).

14. Jacqueline Cohen, "The Incapacitative Effect of Imprisonment: A Critical Review of the Literature," in *Deterrence and Incapacitation: Estimating the Effects of Criminal Sanctions on Crime Rates,* Assembly of Behavioral and Social Sciences (Washington, D.C.: National Academy of Sciences, 1978).

15. Shinnar and Shinnar.

16. Clarke; Greenberg.

17. Shinnar and Shinnar.

18. Cohen.

19. Peterson and Braiker.

20. Alfred Blumstein and Jacqueline Cohen, "Estimation of Individual Crime Rates from Arrest Records," *Journal of Criminal Law and Criminology,* vol. 70, no. 4 (1979): 561.

21. John Monahan, Stanley L. Brodsky, and Saleem A. Shah, *Predicting Violent Behavior: An Assessment of Clinical Techniques* (Beverly Hills, Calif.: Sage, 1982).

22. Peter B. Hoffman and Sheldon Adelberg, "The Salient Factor Score: A Nontechnical Overview," *Federal Probation* 44 (March 1980): 44–52; Michael Gottfredson and Don Gottfredson, *Decisionmaking in Criminal Justice: Toward the Rational Exercise of Discretion* (New York: Ballinger, 1980).

23. Peterson, et al.

24. Peter W. Greenwood with Allan Abrahamse, *Selective Incapacitation,* The Rand Corporation, R–2815–NIJ, August 1982.

25. Ibid.

26. Andrew von Hirsch, *Doing Justice* (New York: Hill and Wang, 1976).

27. Michael Sherman and Gordon Hawkins, *Imprisonment in America* (Chicago: University of Chicago Press, 1981).

28. Longitudinal arrest histories can give the rate at which offenders are arrested for any specific crime (u). Their offense rate is then just

$$\lambda = \frac{u}{\text{probability of arrest}}$$

(Blumstein and Cohen).

29. Of course, to be used as predictor variables, the arrest histories would have to be combined with another file containing the individual characteristics.

15. James Q. Wilson: "Crime and Public Policy"

1. James Q. Wilson, *Thinking about Crime,* rev. ed. (New York: Basic Books, 1983), ch. 10.

2. James Q. Wilson and George L. Kelling, "Broken Windows: The Police and Neighborhood Safety," *Atlantic Monthly,* March 1982, pp. 29–38.

CONTRIBUTORS

ALFRED BLUMSTEIN is the J. Erik Jonsson Professor of Urban Systems and Operations Research, and director of the Urban Systems Institute, for the School of Urban and Public Affairs of Carnegie-Mellon University. He has had extensive experience in research on the criminal justice system, first as director of the Task Force on Science and Technology of the President's Commission on Law Enforcement and Administration of Justice, and currently as chairman of the National Academy of Sciences Committee on Research on Law Enforcement and Administration of Justice. For the Academy, he has chaired panels on deterrence and incapacitation and on sentencing, leading to the reports "Deterrence and Incapacitation" and "Sentencing Research." He also serves as chairman of the Pennsylvania Commission on Crime and Delinquency.

JAN M. CHAIKEN, a senior mathematician at the Rand Corporation, is the designer of a police patrol car allocation model and an analyst of the effects of fiscal contraction on the criminal justice system. His recent criminal science activity includes developing methods for estimating crime commission rates of individuals from survey data, and analyzing the reliability and predictability of crime rate data. He is coauthor of *The Criminal Investigation Process* (1977) and, with Marcia R. Chaiken, of *Varieties of Criminal Behavior* (1982).

MARCIA R. CHAIKEN is a member of the UCLA faculty, Department of Sociology, and a consultant to Narcotic and Drug Research, Inc., New York. Formerly a resident consultant at the Rand Corporation, she is coauthor, with Jan M. Chaiken, of *Varieties of Criminal Behavior* (1982).

BRIAN FORST is director of research and vice-president of INSLAW, Inc. (formerly the Institute for Law and Social Research). He was previously a faculty member at George Washington University (1967–70), a research fellow at MIT (1970–71), and a member of the research staff of the Public Research Institute in Arlington, Virginia, until 1974, at which time he joined INSLAW. He has written a number of articles on the police, the prosecutor, sentencing, crime deterrence, and the measurement of crime.

RICHARD B. FREEMAN, the Sherman Fairchild Distinguished Scholar at the California Institute of Technology, is on leave from the faculty of the Economics Department at Harvard University. He is also program director for labor studies at the National Bureau of Economic Research. A prolific writer on the topics of supply and demand, economic development, trade unionism, the labor market, and economic discrimination, his latest books include *Labor Economics* (1979), *The Youth Employment Problem* (edited with D. Wise, 1982), and a volume in progress entitled *What Do Unions Do?* (with James Medoff).

DANIEL GLASER has been a professor of sociology at the University of Southern California since 1970, prior to which he served for fourteen years on the faculty of the University of Illinois at Urbana. Formerly president of the American Society of Criminology, he spent a number of years working in prison and parole agencies in Illinois and in the U.S. Military Government of Germany. He has authored or edited nine books, including *Handbook of Criminology* (1974) and *Crime in Our Changing Society* (1978).

PETER W. GREENWOOD, a senior researcher for the Rand Corporation, also serves on the faculty advisory committee of the Rand Graduate Institute and is president of the Association for Criminal Justice Research (California). He is currently directing studies of California's juvenile justice system for the California Assembly, and of the relationship between juvenile records and adult sentencing practices for the National Institute of Justice. Dr. Greenwood has served on the faculties of the California Institute of Technology, the Air Force Institute of Technology, and the Rand Graduate Institute, and has written extensively on criminal careers, prosecution, law enforcement, and sentencing practices. His works include *Prosecution of Adult Felony Defendants* (1973), *The Criminal Investigation Process* (coauthor, 1977), and *Selective Incapacitation* (1982).

RICHARD J. HERRNSTEIN is the Edgar Pierce Professor of Psychology at Harvard University and a member of the American Academy of Arts and Sciences and the American Association for the Advancement of Science. Formerly editor of *Psychological Bulletin,* his latest book is *Quantitative Analyses of Behavior, Volume II, Matching and Maximizing Accounts,* which he has edited along with M. Commons and H. Rachlin (1982).

TRAVIS HIRSCHI, professor of sociology at the University of Arizona, has also served on the faculties of the University of Washington, the University of California at Berkeley and at Davis, and the State University of New York at Albany. His affiliations include the Crime and Delinquency Review Committee of the National Institute for Mental Health, the American Sociological Association, and the American Society of Criminology, where he now serves as president. He is the author of numerous books and articles, including *Causes of Delinquency* (1969) and *Measuring Delinquency* (with Michael Hindelang and Joseph Weis, 1981).

MARK H. MOORE is the.Guggenheim Professor of Criminal Justice Policy and Management, Kennedy School of Government, Harvard University. Formerly special assistant to the administrator and chief planning officer of the Drug Enforcement Administration, U.S. Department of Justice, he has also served as chairman of the Panel on Alcohol Control Policies for the National Academy of Sciences and consultant to the National Institute of Drug Abuse. His latest book is *Alcohol and Public Policy: Beyond the Shadow of Prohibition* (edited, with Dean Gerstein, 1981).

CHARLES A. MURRAY was for ten years a senior researcher with the American Institutes for Research. His publications include *Studies of Delinquency* (1979), *Beyond Probation: Juvenile Corrections and the Chronic Delinquent* (1979), *Integration of Social Services for the Disadvantaged* (1980), *Community Crime Control* (1980), and *Inner-City Education* (1982). A research fellow associated with the Manhattan Institute, he is currently writing a history of postwar U.S. social policy.

STEVEN R. SCHLESINGER, director designate of the Bureau of Justice Statistics in the U.S. Department of Justice, is currently on leave from his position as associate chairman and associate professor in the Department of Politics at The Catholic University of America, Washington, D.C. Formerly adjunct scholar at the National Legal Center for the Public Interest and a consultant to the Subcommittee on the Constitution of the United States Senate Committee on the Judiciary, he has written more than twenty articles on subjects of legal interest. He is also the author of *Federalism and Criminal Justice: The Case of the Exclusionary Rule* (1975), *Exclusionary Injustice: The Problem of Illegally Obtained Evidence* (1977), and *The United States Supreme Court: Fact, Evidence, and Law* (forthcoming), and editor of *Venue at the Crossroads* (1982).

LAWRENCE W. SHERMAN has been director of research of the Police Foundation in Washington, D.C., since 1979. Formerly project director at the Criminal Justice Research Center and executive director of the National Advisory Commission on Higher Education for Police Officers, he also teaches criminology at the University of Maryland. His latest books include *Scandal and Reform: Controlling Police Corruption* (1978) and *Ethics in Criminal Justice Education* (1982).

JACKSON TOBY is professor of sociology and director of the Institute for Criminological Research at Rutgers University. One of his interests, viewing crime and its control in cross-national perspective, developed while he served as regular consultant to the Youth Development Program of the Ford Foundation from 1959 to 1963 and traveled on site visits in the United States and abroad. For the past four years he has been studying the causes of crime and disorder in public secondary

schools; his article "Crime in American Public Schools" appeared recently in *The Public Interest,* and others are in press. He also wrote
"Where Are the Streakers Now?" for Hubert M. Blalock's *Sociological
Theory and Research* (1980), on the subject of the cultural basis for deviant behavior.

JAMES Q. WILSON, Henry Lee Shattuck Professor of Government at
Harvard University, has served as chairman of the White House Task
Force on Crime in 1967 and of the National Advisory Council for Drug
Abuse Prevention in 1972–73, and as a member of the Attorney
General's Task Force on Violent Crime in 1981. He is currently the vice-
chairman of the Police Foundation. Dr. Wilson's most recent publications
include *The Investigators* (1978), *American Government* (second edition,
1983), and *Thinking About Crime* (revised edition, 1983).

INDEX